A Woman's Guide to Jobs in Film and Television

Anne Ross Muir is a freelance director and producer. Between 1972 and 1982 she lived in the United States where she worked in educational television production and on television commercials as an assistant director and director. Since her return to Britain, Anne Ross Muir has worked on news, current affairs, documentary and drama programmes for the BBC and as a freelance director for ITV companies.

» 'There have been certain times in my career when I've wished I could work with female technicians and if enough women read this book, perhaps one day that dream can come true . . . . Only if young women read this book and then go on to work in film and television is there any hope of having freedom of expression in our media.'

Julie Walters

» 'I welcome this book on careers for women in the broadcasting industry.

'Girls and women often do not consider careers in this fascinating industry because most of the literature on the industry is written for men and by men and women are lucky to be mentioned as a footnote. Often even the traditional job titles seem to preclude women, e.g. cameraman.

'ACTT, as one of the trade unions in the industry, is fighting to improve opportunities for women. I am sure that this book will help in that fight by providing much more information both on the women who are already working and for those who would wish to do so.'

Sandra Horne, ITV Organiser, ACTT

A Woman's Guide
to Jobs in Film and Television

Anne Ross Muir

First published in 1987 by
Pandora Press (Routledge & Kegan Paul Ltd)
11 New Fetter Lane, London EC4P 4EE

Set in 11 on 12pt Sabon
by Columns, Reading
and printed in Great Britain
by The Guernsey Press Co. Ltd,
Guernsey, Channel Islands.

British Library Cataloguing in Publication Data

A Woman's guide to jobs in film and television.
1. Women in the motion picture industry—
Vocational guidance—Great Britain
2. Women in the television industry—
Vocational guidance—Great Britain
I. Muir, Anne Ross
384.8'0941   PN1998

ISBN 0-86358-061-0 (c)
     0-86358-238-9 (p)

Contents

Illustrations

In memory of Sarah Noble

Acknowledgments

This book might never have been written without the help and support of Sandra Horne, the Equality Officer of ACTT and I cannot say how grateful I am for her valuable criticism and guidance. My thanks are also due to the members of ACTT's Equality Committee who gave me their unstinting support for this project. Others whose assistance made this book possible include Joyce Reid, Lena Mitchell and Isobel Muir. I am also warmly appreciative of the constructive criticism offered by my editors, Jane Hawksley and Candida Lacey. But perhaps most of all I owe my thanks to the many women and some men who gave their time to answer my questions and share their experiences to help the next generation of women enter the industry. It is they who will shape the way we perceive not just women, but the whole of our society.

1 Women in film and television

One has only to watch the credits roll by at the end of a film or television programme to realise that women are sadly under-represented in the worlds of cinema and broadcasting. One major reason for this state of affairs is that women have been discriminated against and have been barred from many jobs in the film and television industry. It is a depressing picture. Over the years, a large number of very talented women have tried to break down those barriers – and failed. Pessimists point out that such discrimination is so entrenched and long-standing, that it could taken generations to wipe out. It is not surprising, therefore, that many women don't even try to enter the industry. They are defeated before they begin.

Yet it is because of this attitude that we are in danger of losing an unprecedented opportunity for women to sweep aside the barriers which have kept them out of key jobs in film and television. The conditions for change are right. For example, many of the major broadcasting organisations have now agreed, in principle, that women should have an equal opportunity for careers alongside men.

It is, however, a fragile opportunity. If past experience is anything to go by, such policies may make little difference, unless women take them at their word and make things happen. It's up to us – and that's what this book is all about. It taps into the experience of those women who have made it into the industry, passing on what they have learned and demonstrating that, with a little courage and a lot of hard work, it can be done. It is an attempt by one generation of women to foster the next, to open up opportunities for others, so that, hopefully, they can alter the way our society perceives not only women, but the world around us.

There is no doubt that the present situation is desperately in need of improvement. In 1975, the results of an inquiry into the state of women in the film and television industry which was conducted for ACTT (The Association of Cinematograph, Television and Allied Technicians) showed that the position of women had not improved since the Second World War, but had, in fact, deteriorated. In the 1950s women worked in a wide variety of grades and represented 18 per cent of the labour force within the industry. By 1975, they represented only 15 per cent and had been buried in ghetto jobs, that is, in jobs which are held almost exclusively by women, which are often lower paid and which are given little status.

By 1986, the situation was hardly better. The figures for employment provided by the ITCA (The Independent Television Companies Association) showed that, of 306 camera operators, only 12 were women; there were only 8 female sound technicians compared to 269 male ones, while of 1395 engineers, 19 were women. On the other hand, none of the production assistants or secretaries were male.

A survey of the situation of women within the BBC, conducted by Monica Simms and released in 1985, reached similar conclusions. In the BBC's top grade of personnel, there were 159 men and only 6 women, while only 8 per cent of staff in the category which includes Heads of Department, senior producers and correspondents were female. When I interviewed Michael Grade, then Controller of BBC 1, he admitted that, at his level of decision-making, there were no women involved.

It is also apparent that women from ethnic minorities encounter even greater discrimination in almost all parts of the industry. There is very little concrete data available – perhaps an indication that those in power hope that if they ignore black and Asian women long enough, they'll just disappear! A preliminary survey conducted by ACTT and released in 1987, however, indicated that less than 2 per cent of their members employed in ITV companies – and an even smaller percentage of those working in the BBC – belong to ethnic minorities. And it is probably safe to assume, based on general employment patterns outlined earlier, that very few of those are women.

The film industry is, if anything, worse. It's true that the National Film School has now increased its intake of female students from 1 out of 25 when it opened in 1971, to around 30 per cent in the last few years. Yet, although qualifications from the NFTS have been a passport to success for a number of male graduates, one has only to watch the credits roll by to realise that it has not helped very many women to break into mainstream film-making. Sir Richard Attenborough can be moved to tears at the racial discrimination suffered by Gandhi, while women are more likely to be scrubbing studio floors than directing movies and that doesn't seem to worry anybody.

In fact, it is very easy to get the impression that women have simply *never* figured in the film and television industry at all, except as performers, production assistants and secretaries. Yet, recent research by film critics and historians has shown that women helped to lay the foundations of modern cinema.

The movie business started up around the beginning of the century and Hollywood was soon established as one of the main centres for film-making. In most histories of those early days, women are allocated a place on screen, portraying girlish innocence or vampish sexuality. But this had little to do with reality. Mary Pickford might embody the masculine ideal of demure femininity in her films, but in real life she was a hard-headed business-woman, setting up United Artists (which until recently was still a major film company in America) with her husband, Douglas Fairbanks, and with Charlie Chaplin.

Women, in fact, worked in every part of the industry. The critic, Molly Haskell, has counted at least 26 female directors in the period 1913-23.[5] Another film historian, Antony Slide, refers to Dorothy Dunn, Grace Davison and Margery Ordway who were among many successful camerawomen in those early days. John C. Mahoney points out that the majority of important screen writers between 1914 and 1930 were female, including June Mathis, Anita Loos and Frances Marion, who won an Oscar for *The Big House* and *The Champ*.[7]

Many of these women were outstandingly successful. Lois Weber was one of the best paid directors in Holly-wood during the period 1916-34.[5] Dorothy Arzner's 1932 movie, *Merrily We Go To Hell*, was one of the highest grossing films in a period of forty years, according to *Motion Picture Daily*.[7] Leontine Sagan directed *Mädchen in Uniform*, which was voted one of the ten best pictures of 1933 by *Film Daily*. Women were particularly successful as editors. Barbara Rose Maclean was Darryl Zanuck's editor and received several Academy nominations, before finally winning an Oscar for *Wilson* in 1944. Margaret Booth worked for Louis D. Mayer at MGM and has been described by the noted film historian, Kevin Brownlow, as 'one of the great motion picture editors'.[2]

Even in those early days, however, there were signs of unease about allowing women a creative identity and power. Molly Haskell argues that one reason that women were allowed to direct films at all during those formative years was because it was not yet considered a glamorous job. Nevertheless, the critic Nancy Ellen Dowd has discovered that some of the work of Alice Guy Blaché (who directed almost every kind of movie in Hollywood during the early years of this century) was wrongly attributed to Emile Cohl and Victorin Jasset.[3] The same researcher also states that in 1922, the work of Alla Nazimova was released under the name of her husband, Charles Bryant.

It is clear from such examples, that the process of discrimination had begun, even in those early days of the cinema. As the film industry became less of a maverick operation and more a part of the establishment, that process gained momentum. When cinema's potential for profit-making, public influence and power was realised, the social conventions and prejudice against women of that era began to have a greater impact. During the 1920s and 1930s, women were gradually elbowed out of the way and were discouraged or actively barred from creative and decision-making jobs in the industry.

The process was reversed during the Second World War, however, when women had to take on jobs previously done only by men. By that time, there was a thriving British film industry and women like Dorothy Thomson, Roseanne Hunter and Yvonne Fletcher were given the opportunity to direct. At the BBC, women were offered the chance to move up the career ladder on the understanding that they would give up their jobs when the menfolk returned from fighting. Some women did lose their promotions when that happened, but others were able to hang on. After the war, television broadcasting began to expand, attracting many of the bright young men and leaving the way clear for women to establish themselves quite successfully in radio, where several rose to the rank of Controller.

Generally, however, once the war was over, the pattern of discrimination was re-established. A study conducted by the Policy Studies Institute in 1968 concluded that most of the really senior women in the BBC had taken advantage of unprecedented opportunities during the war and had no obvious successors. The results of a follow-up study by the same group which was begun in 1979 confirmed those findings and even indicated that the position of women at the top in the BBC had deteriorated.[6]

Within the film industry, the experience of Kay Mander was typical. She started out as a 'continuity girl' (see chapter 20 for an explanation of this). When the war broke out, she was given the opportunity to direct and write scripts 'because there weren't any men around so it was much easier to get work'. When peace was declared, she went to Java where she continued directing films with her husband. A few years later, when she returned to Britain, she co-scripted and directed *The Kid from Canada* which won a special award at the Venice Film Festival. In spite of this success, she found that 'from 1957 onwards, I failed to get any satisfactory work as a director, so I went back to feature continuity.' Michael Balcon, one of the most influential figures in British cinema at that time, told her 'quite flatly, that women couldn't handle film crews and anyway there weren't any suitable films for women to direct'.[6]

Given such attitudes, it is not surprising that the role of women in the film industry declined. Some were able to find work in the less lucrative and less prestigious areas of documentaries or educational and training films. As in the pre-war days, any creative power which women did have in feature film-making was often either not recognised at all, or else it was disguised. Thus, Nancy Ellen Dowd's research revealed that Ida Lupino's first film, *Not Wanted* (1949) was credited to Elmer Clifton.[3] Two years later in 1951, Muriel Box had a similar experience in Britain, when, having already won an Oscar for co-scripting *The Seventh Veil*, she decided to try her hand at directing. She records in her autobiography (1975) *Odd Woman Out*, that 'the hardest part initially was to persuade artists to accept an unknown director and a woman into the bargain. To avoid difficulties . . . agents were told it would be a joint directorial effort between my husband and myself.' Even though she then went on to direct over a dozen international features, Muriel Box is listed in Roy Armes's *A Critical History of British Cinema*, published in 1978, as the 'script-writer wife' of Sidney Box. Since she retired from the cinema, there have been almost no female directors in feature film-making in this country and Zelda Barron can testify to the fact that the prejudices against women have changed little since the 1950s. (See the interview with Zelda Barron in chapter 7.)

A few women continued to be successful as editors in the post-war period, among them Adrienne Fazin, who won an Oscar for *Gigi* and who also cut classics like *Singin' in the Rain* and *An American in Paris*. Margaret Booth went on to become one of MGM's top executives and editor-in-chief. Yet her promotion was exceptional. As John C. Mahoney points out, very few female editors made the step up to directing, unlike many of their male colleagues.[7]

The impact of such historical research is to demonstrate, beyond any doubt, that women have not been excluded from key positions in the film and television industry because they couldn't do the work. Whenever women have been given the opportunity, they have proved themselves as competent as their male counterparts and, in many cases, far outshone them. Their exclusion is not only unfair to women, but represents a great loss of talent to the film and television industry.

The lack of female representation in the media also has wider implications, however. It affects us all, not just those women who would like careers in film and television. The EEC has targeted the media as being instrumental in any campaign against sex discrimination, recognising that television, which is viewed heavily by children and is the main source of news for adults, can shape our attitudes. If a film or television company is a mini sexist society, with women congregated in the lower-paid, service and support jobs, how can we expect the image of women that they produce to be anything but sexist?

For example, most sportscasters are male, as is the majority of those who produce, film and record our news programmes. Thus, women's sports are rarely treated seriously or at length and women and the issues that affect them are often ignored on the news. Reports on redundancies will refer to '500 men' who have been laid off, when there are a number of female workers amongst them. Betty Heathfield, the wife of Peter Heathfield, a senior NUM official, has described a rally held in London by 10,000 miners' wives in 1984 to support their husbands' strike. Yet that was ignored by the media. The lack of weight given to women's interests is made even more obvious in the way that they are relegated to day-time television rather than peak viewing time or are considered to be minority programming, more suitable for Channel Four.

If there are no true records of women and their lives, then the way is clear for a false picture to emerge which can then be misused. Researchers exploring the US National Archives found that news film of women in the pre-war era referred to them as 'girls' and portrayed them at events supporting this image, such as beauty contests or Easter parades. Yet, during the war, women were no longer shown in such a frivolous light. They were shown working for the war effort. Thus, the image of women which was presented was not a documentary record, but was tailored to social and political expediency.

In more modern times, we are presented with situation comedies, dramas and commercials which show women in roles which bear no relation to the reality of most of our lives. Various entrepreneurs make large sums of money from broadcasting beauty contests which treat women's bodies as objects to be rated. We are bombarded by commercials which use images of women to sell everything from cars and washing machines to alcoholic drinks and record albums.

It is a pattern of distortion and misuse which is repeated in the cinema. As Ann Kaplan has pointed out in her excellent book *Women and Film* (1983) the 'gaze' or viewpoint in most films is masculine. Women become objects to be looked at, not only by the camera and the audience, but also by the men in the film. Women are often stalked like prey. Their bodies come to represent, not whole human beings with individual personalities, but sex. On screen, they are rarely allowed to be powerful in their own right. If they are strong and forceful, they are usually shown to be evil or aberrant in some way, secretly wishing to be dominated, or they are penalised by being lonely, unloved, frigid or desperate.

To sum up, the exclusion of women from many of the key jobs in film and television means that we are denied opportunities for work which is not only challenging, creative and lucrative, but which can influence the ways in which women are perceived and view themselves in our society. We are also being shut off from an important means of self-expression and a form of communication which could link women across this and other countries, by presenting common experiences. As it is, children are being shown a one-sided (basically male) view of the part that women play in our society, while women themselves are presented with role models which are very far from reality, which make individuals feel isolated and aberrant when they do not conform to those stereotypes and which tend to inhibit, rather than stimulate women's belief in their own strength and capability.

But I did say that conditions are right for change. For example, we are now at a stage where almost every ITV company advertises itself as an equal opportunities employer. This may not be the case in practice, but it does mean that they are recognising their responsibility in this respect and are receptive to the idea of women working in television. They can now be challenged to live up to their assertions in a way that they couldn't before.

The same is true of the BBC. Their Board of Governors now includes three women and, according to Monica Simms, it was at their suggestion that her survey on the status of women within the BBC was commissioned.[8] As a result, she has come up with nineteen recommendations including the two-year appointment of a Women's Employment Officer, job sharing and flexible working hours – all heady stuff for the BBC. In 1985, too, the Controller of BBC 1, Michael Grade, reached a landmark decision – made purely on principle, he insists – not to broadcast the Miss Great Britain Contest, because it was out of step with the modern role of women in our society. According to Grade, 'The important thing was to have made the public statement as to why we were dropping it.' Nothing is more likely to end the degrading spectacle of beauty contests than the withdrawal of the funding and publicity generated by television sponsorship.

More than any other company, however, Channel Four has forged a way through prejudice to give women a chance. They have shown a willingness to hire women for key positions and to broadcast programmes giving serious consideration to issues affecting women. In addition, their policy of commissioning material from outside producers has created enough work to allow many women to leave dead-end jobs with BBC and ITV and set up their own production companies. Channel Four has also provided the backing for a number of workshops (see p.28 for an explanation of this) which in turn have given many women access to film and television facilities.

Within the film industry, there has been less dramatic progress, largely because it has a freelance, constantly moving workforce, which makes it more difficult to organise campaigns for reform from within the ranks. On the consumer side of the industry, however, there has been a growing interest in films made by women about women's lives. A number of movies – mostly from the USA or Europe – which have been written and directed by women and in which the central character is female, have been highly acclaimed in this country. Money talks and the box-office success of a film like *Desperately Seeking Susan* established that films made by women about women are worth backing, thus paving the way for other female directors, writers and technicians.

The argument in favour of more productions like that has been given weight in recent years by a new wave of academic scholarship. When Ann Kaplan began lecturing about women and films in 1972, she found that she was working in a vacuum and that there was very little research done on that topic. Now there is a body of feminist film criticism which has been able to identify some of the ways in which the cinema discriminates against women and perpetuates images which are harmful to all of us.

There has also been a remarkable groundswell of support for equal opportunities from the trade unions associated with the entertainment industries – largely because of the tireless campaigning of some very brave and committed women within their midst. Many unions have now appointed a member of staff who has specific responsibility for women's issues and have set up committees on equality to lobby for improved working conditions and opportunities for women. One outstanding example of how successful women can be when they organise is evident within ACCT. Since the appointment of a full-time Equality Officer in 1981, women (who represent only 20 per cent of the membership) now participate at every level of union management. As a result of their efforts to change attitudes amongst their male colleagues, they have gathered enough support to pass motions condemning pornography and endorsing equal opportunities, maternity and paternity benefit packages, workplace nurseries and the appointment of a full-time Training Officer.

It all adds up to one thing. The idea of women being given equal opportunities for jobs in the television and film industry has been given support in principle by employers, trade unions and critics alike – but unless women make it happen in practice, it may well go no further than that.

The BBC is under financial and political pressure. They may find it easier to make some token concessions to Monica Simm's recommendations and quietly drop the rest. Certainly, the BBC has ignored some damning evidence of discrimination against women in the past, following the reports made by the Policy Studies Institute. Michael Grade admitted, 'I personally point out whenever I see the worst examples of sexism and will pull the producer or head of department aside and make them think a bit harder. That's about the best I can do. You can't make edicts about a subject matter like this.' Apparently, we can deduce from this statement that the BBC feels no active commitment to the fair representation of women on its programmes. Within the ITV companies, the current economic recession has cut advertising revenue and could lead to a period of retrenchment and an unwillingness to promote change. There are also many men who see the advancement of women as a threat to their jobs. Others resist change because it would disrupt the pattern of their lives. Some men base their identity on an image of themselves as superior to women and are unwilling to give that up.

In addition, the direction that the film and television industry seems to be taking could make it far more difficult for women to press for equal opportunities in the future. One trend to emerge is the move towards cutting permanent staff jobs in television and production companies and casualising the workforce. This does not bode well for women. Freelancers are notoriously difficult to keep track of. Contracts can be very short and hiring and firing done on the spur of the moment, making it very difficult to implement or monitor equal opportunities policies. Short-term staff are also less likely to join forces and campaign for their rights for fear they won't be re-hired. There is also the danger, already prevalent, that permanent jobs will be given to men, while women are employed on short-term contracts and become a dispensable workforce. Thus, whenever there are any cutbacks, female workers will be the first to go.

Another development with serious repercussions for women is the move towards ever more sophisticated technology. Many jobs which previously required little or no knowledge of electronics, now require considerable technical expertise. For example, editing has traditionally been thought of as a creative, artistic job in which women have been very successful. But, with the advent of video, many companies are now recruiting their editors from amongst the engineering staff which means that, since there are so few women working in technical areas, there may be almost no female editors in the future. If women do not get a toehold and grow with the new technology, then we may be left hopelessly behind.

In other words, women must act *now*, if we are to take advantage of opportunities for equality in film and television. What is needed is a greater number of female workers in the industry, preferably in key positions. All the evidence suggests that the more female candidates there are for jobs in film and television, the more women are successful in getting in. According to Christina Driver of BETA (The British Entertainment Trades Alliance), the same percentage of female applicants as male ones are successful in getting jobs in the BBC. It's just that fewer women apply in the first place, so fewer end up being employed.

It is important also that those who do apply are well

qualified for the work. Otherwise, if employers do hire a woman, they may do so for the wrong reasons, because she has nice legs or seems biddable. It is only too easy for employers to sabotage equal opportunities policies by appointing a woman who is not qualified and who can't do the job. That's the best excuse they could want for not hiring more women.

So the situation is in the balance. The potential for overcoming discrimination against women in the film and television industry is there. Whether the opportunity is taken up and succeeds or not depends on the efforts of women both inside and outside the industry.

References

1 Sarah Benton, 'Patterns of Discrimination Against Women in the Film and Television Industries', *Film and Television Technician*, March 1975.
2 Kevin Brownlow, *The Parade's Gone By*, New York, Bonanza Books.
3 Nancy Ellen Dowd, 'The Woman Director Through the Years', *Action*, vol.8, no.4, July-August 1973.
4 M.P. Fogarty (ed.) Isobel Allen, A.J. Allen and Patricia Walters, *Women in Top Jobs*, London, George Allen & Unwin, p.152.
5 Molly Haskell, 'Women Directors: On Toppling the Male Mystique', *American Film*, vol. 1, no.8, June 1976.
6 Sheila MacLeod, 'A Woman's Place', *Action*, The Association of Cinematograph, Television and Allied Technicians.
7 John C. Mahoney, 'Cinema's Women at the Top', *American Cinemeditor*, vol.25, no.4, Winter 1975-6.
8 Monica Sims, 'Women in BBC Management', London, BBC, 1985.

Further Reading

Helen Baehr, 'Women's Employment in British Television', *Media, Culture and Society*, 3;125-34, 1981.
Margaret Gallagher, 'Myth and Reality in Women's Employment in Broadcasting', *MedieKultur 4*, Aalborg, Denmark, 1986.
Margaret Gallagher, *The Portrayal and Participation of Women in the Media*, Paris, UNESCO, 1979.

Gillian Skirrow, 'Representation of women in the Association of Cinematograph, Television and Allied Technicians', *Screen*, vol.22, no.3, 1981.

US Commission on Civil Rights, *Window Dressing and the Set – Women and Minorities in Television*, 1977.

2 Using this book

One of the reasons that not enough women apply for jobs in the film and television industry is, simply, that there are so few role models. It may never occur to a young woman to consider certain careers because she has never heard of, for example, a female television engineer, or lighting electrician. Even if she does overcome that barrier, she may still encounter opposition and it is hard to argue against statements that a certain job can't be done by a woman, when you can't think of a single example of a woman who *does* do that job.

Having once decided on a career in the media, a woman is still likely to be at a disadvantage compared to a man in the same situation, because she is less likely to have access to the 'old boy's network' that men do. Most people, whether male or female, are more helpful to those with whom they can themselves identify. Thus, an older man is more likely to see himself in a likely young lad than in a young woman and fathers are more likely to encourage sons to follow in their footsteps than daughters. In this way, information about job vacancies and the benefits of years of experience tend to be passed from one generation of men to the next, by-passing women completely. Yet, without such inside knowledge, it is extremely difficult to gain entry to many of the most competitive and rewarding jobs in the industry. Many women discover too late that they have studied the wrong subjects to qualify for the work they would like to do. Young girls are not motivated at an early enough age to gain valuable experience operating school computers and video equipment or editing the student newspaper. Women turn up for gruelling interviews totally unprepared.

Clearly, there is a need for an 'old girls' network' which would provide role models for young women and which would tap into the experience of those already working in the industry. That is what this book has set out to do. Questionnaires were sent out to several hundred women employed in a range of film and television jobs covering most of the technical and production areas. A further fifty women were then interviewed in depth about their experience of working in the industry. The result is a guide to some twenty-three careers, presenting negative as well as positive aspects of the work and emphasising the wide variety of work situations that can be found within the industry.

Each chapter begins with a job description followed by basic information about the hours and working conditions as well as the qualifications and experience required, plus advice on books to read and things to do in preparation for applying for such a job. After that, women who are already working successfully in that area give their personal account of the advantages and disadvantages of the job. They talk about how they cope with any problems they encounter because they are women and how they reconcile the demands of their work with their domestic responsibilities and social life.

These interviews do not shirk the fact that some apparently glamorous jobs can be boring or that women do encounter hostile and discriminatory behaviour in some areas. Yet the overall tone is encouraging and positive. Women present reasonable, courageous and often humorous responses to harassment or discrimination. They break their isolation as lone pioneers working in male-dominated areas by sharing their feelings of hurt and anger with those who may find themselves in similar situations in the future. They defy the rules in many cases by succeeding in their chosen career without formal qualifications or when they have embarked on that course later in life than is usual. Such is the range of backgrounds and personalities represented, that any woman reading this book, no matter what her race or personal circumstances, should be encouraged to find a job in film and television.

Even if you have already decided on the career you would like, however, it is important that you read not only the chapter relevant to that profession. Many jobs in film and television are interrelated and require at least a working knowledge of other aspects of production. You may find, also, that as you read through this book, you become interested in careers which you had not previously considered. In addition, much of the advice and some of the information given for one job is applicable also to others.

Having decided which career you do wish to aim for, it is worth considering the type of work situation you would prefer, because the exact conditions may vary from one sector of the industry to another. The average person who is unfamiliar with the media is often unaware of the alternatives to working either in broadcasting or feature films. Different sectors of the industry offer different rewards. Some are better paid, some are less pressured. Others offer greater artistic or political freedom. Some are more 'people-oriented' and less concerned with profit. It is important, therefore, to consider where you would be happiest working and which environments would best suit your lifestyle. It is also worth considering that some sectors may be more accessible than others. For example, you may find it difficult to gain entry to a job in independent television if you don't already have ACTT membership, or to get work in feature films unless you have good contacts in that area already. It could be easier, therefore, to get your first job with the audio-visual department of your local college than to persuade Steven Spielberg to take you on for his next blockbuster. So, bear that in mind as you consider the following sectors and decide which is right for you.

1 Feature film

Generally speaking, a feature film is the main film you see when you go to the cinema. Some examples are *Gandhi*, *Chariots of Fire* and *Police Academy*. In this country, feature films are usually made at one of the big studios in the London area, such as Elstree, Pinewood or Shepperton. They have huge buildings, like aircraft hangars, which are large enough to accommodate the sets (the background scenery) for each film. Sometimes part, or all of a movie will be shot 'on location', that is, in a real setting. For example, if a scene took place against the background of the Cornish cliffs, it would probably be much easier and cheaper actually to film in Cornwall than to try and build a replica of the cliffs in a studio.

Feature films can take weeks and even months to make and can cost many millions of pounds. Working conditions can be difficult. The crew can find themselves living in a remote area, perhaps in difficult terrain and extreme weather conditions. They may be expected to work long hours or even all through the night to complete a production on schedule.

There is also very little job security. In the past, many film technicians were permanently employed by one of the big production companies. Nowadays, most films are made by independent producers who find investors willing to put up the money to make the movie. They then hire a freelance crew. The implications of this system for those who work in this sector are considerable. Because there is so much money at stake, producers are unwilling to take risks by hiring people whom they don't know and who don't already have a track record. It can be extremely difficult for newcomers to break into working in this sector. Another barrier is that ACTT, in effect, operates a closed shop in feature films (see p.30 for an explanation), which means that it can be very difficult to obtain employment unless you already have union membership. Those who are successful can earn fees resembling telephone numbers but it can take years of hard work to reach this level.

Many of the jobs in the feature film industry are similar to those in television production, except, perhaps, in the scope of the work and the size of the budget – that is, until you get to the producer/director level. Often a first, second or even third assistant director will be employed on a film to take over the more routine aspects of the director's job, such as supervising crowd scenes. The role of the producer can vary from being simply a dealer in finance and a behind-the-scenes fixer, to making creative decisions about the choice of scriptwriter, director, actors, and crew as well as having the final cut, that is, the final say on how the film is edited.

It is very difficult to break into feature film work, unless you happen to be related to someone already in the business who can help you get a job. There is a great deal of nepotism in this sector. If you really do want to work in the movies, however, your best bet is to try and get into one of the film schools or on to a training scheme which is recognised by ACTT. Then, when you graduate, you will immediately be eligible for unrestricted union membership as soon as you get an ACCT-graded job. (See p.31 for further details.) Alternatively, you can begin your career in another sector of the industry, such as television. Then, once you have completed your training, got some experience and made contacts, you may be able to move into feature film production. You could also try making a film of your own with the help of friends. Then, if your film is good enough to impress the people with clout in the industry, you may be able to get a job or backing for another film. That's how Bill Forsyth started out. He made *That Sinking Feeling* with a group of friends and it received such critical acclaim when it was shown at The Edinburgh Film Festival, that he was able to go on to make *Gregory's Girl*. Only a very few people succeed in this way, however, and it might be better to have an alternative plan in mind.

2 Commercials production

This is the sector of the industry which makes television commercials for broadcast on independent television channels and Channel Four. Much of the work is done by independent production companies who often work with a largely freelance crew, but a number of ITV companies also produce commercials in-house for local clients. Like the feature film industry, it can be a lucrative area in which to work, since large sums of money may be spent on commercials which will last only 30 seconds.

Usually, a storyboard (a sort of strip cartoon of the action) for each commercial will be drawn up by the advertising agency handling the campaign. The production company and crew then have the job of turning those drawings into moving pictures and real-life action. They must use all their talent and expertise to create an atmosphere and 'image' that will sell the product. Because the stakes are so high, every second must count and the technical and creative standards are usually excellent. As a result, this is often the first sector in the industry to experiment with the latest technology.

Most of those working in this area of production are freelance and highly skilled. The best of them earn high fees for their efforts, but they may have to work very long hours. They may also have to be away from home to work on commercials which are shot 'on location', that is, not in a studio, but in some real setting which could be anything from the Sahara Desert to the Antarctic.

Jobs are not usually widely advertised in this sector of the industry and you must have excellent contacts as well as a good track record to break in. Many women complain that they are discriminated against when trying to find work in commercials production. Another potential barrier to finding a job is that ACTT effectively operates a closed shop in this sector (see p.30 for explanation of this), which means that it can be difficult to obtain work unless you belong to that union.

Since getting a job in commercials production often depends on who you know, it is probably easier to start your career in another part of the industry. Then, when you have established your professional reputation and made the necessary contacts, you can go freelance and work on commercials. Alternatively, you could contact the production companies directly and try to get work as a trainee or general dogsbody in the hopes that you can progress up the career ladder from there. Such companies will be listed in trade directories such as *Kemps Film and Television Yearbook*, *Contacts*, or *Film Bang* (refers to Scotland only). You can also try to get a job with a television company and become involved in their commercials production.

3   Broadcast television

In Britain, there are currently four broadcast television channels. BBC 1 and BBC 2 are part of a public corporation and are supported by television licence fees. Their activities are monitored by a Board of Governors appointed by the government to ensure that the BBC is serving the public interest and remains politically independent. The main base of operations is in London, although the BBC has a number of regional television centres which contribute programmes. The Independent

Television (ITV) companies together form a national network of separate, regional broadcast stations. Most of their income derives from the sale of broadcasting time to show commercials during their programmes. The Independent Broadcast Authority (IBA) monitors their activities to ensure that they maintain their technical standards, remain within the law, observe standards of good taste and serve the public interest. Each company produces and makes its own programmes, some of which will only be broadcast locally and some of which will be broadcast nationally *via* the link-up with the other companies in the network.

Channel Four is supported by levies from all the ITV companies and also shows television commercials to raise revenue. It produces very few programmes in-house and commissions most of its material from independent producers.

ACTT effectively operates a closed shop within the independent television companies, which means that it can be difficult to get a job in this sector unless you have union membership (see p.30 for further details). At the BBC, there is no closed shop, although many employees belong to BETA (see p.32 for an explanation of this). What does happen, however, is that the BBC advertises most jobs internally and gives priority to staff over outsiders applying for jobs. It is often said that you should get into the BBC any way that you can (even as the tea lady), and then apply for jobs from within the organisation. In practice, this system may not work as well for women, however. There are a number of female university graduates who have found that being a secretary at the BBC led nowhere except to being a secretary at the BBC. Rates of pay at the BBC are frequently lower than for comparable jobs in ITV, but this may be off-set by the opportunities for advancement through training schemes which the BBC offers to employees.

4 Cable television

BBC and ITV channels reach our homes by broadcasting signals which are then picked up by aerials which feed into our television sets. Cable television sends its signals *via* cables which must be physically connected up to each television set from the immediate source of the signal, whether that is the cable television station itself or a satellite station. Each company has access to multiple channels for programming by this means.

The government is in the process of granting cable television franchises in different parts of the country and there is likely to be a station near you already or else planned for the future. The companies get their income from the fees paid by subscribers for their services and also from advertising revenue. The advantage which cable television offers to customers is that there is a different programming policy from that of BBC or ITV. For example, a cable television company may offer a twenty-four hour rock music channel, or an all-news channel, or a channel which shows nothing but movies. Most companies also produce some locally-based programmes, but much of the material which is shown is bought from independent producers. Many companies also offer access to equipment and facilities to community groups so that they can produce their own programmes for screening on one of the cable television channels.

Since it is relatively new in Britain, it is difficult to predict how cable television will develop in this country. Some companies have experienced difficulties in setting up and there have already been some redundancies in this sector of the industry. On the other hand, since they are just starting out, many cable companies might be looking for programme ideas and be willing to recruit staff locally. If you are interested in working in this area, then you should approach the companies directly. You should be able to obtain an up-to-date list by writing to The

Cable Authority, Gillingham House, 38-44 Gillingham St, London SW1V 1HV.

5 Non-broadcast film and video production

This is a growing field which caters to industrial training and public relations needs. For example, a non-broadcast production company might be hired by a manufacturing firm to make a film about safety in the workplace which would be used to educate workers at a factory, or they might make a video tape for the local tourist board about beauty spots in the area which can then be shown at conventions, trade fairs and travel agencies. In other words, these are not productions which would be shown on television or exhibited in a commercial cinema. They are not, therefore, required to meet broadcast or cinema exhibition standards and would probably be shot on either $\frac{3}{4}$ inch video tape or on 16 mm film.

It is possible to work in this sector without having union membership, which can make it easier for a beginner to find work – but take care. Since virtually anyone can set themselves up for this type of work by renting or leasing basic equipment, some of these companies are very unreliable. In addition, since budgets and profit margins for such productions can be quite small, wages in this sector can be low and there may be little job security.

If this is the type of work that interests you, however, then you should try contacting companies directly. You may find them listed in the Yellow Pages under headings such as 'film and video production' or you could also contact your local Chamber of Commerce for a list of those operating in your area. Video or photographic supplies stores can also be helpful because they are likely to keep track of such potential customers in their area. Some of the bigger production companies are listed in trade directories such as *Film Bang* (refers to Scotland only), or *Kemps Film and Television Yearbook*, or the *BFI Film and Television Yearbook*.

6   Educational technology

Most educational technology facilities are attached to some sort of college, university or school. Generally speaking, the material produced is not intended for broadcast, but for use in classrooms and lecture halls or audio-visual laboratories and libraries. The current economic climate has meant that some ed. tech. departments now also do productions for outside companies and organisations in order to help finance their operations.

The equipment in ed. tech. facilities ranges from the most rudimentary to the most sophisticated. Some departments will have little more than some portable video equipment, while others have fully-equipped colour studios and outside broadcast vehicles.

Some people prefer to work in this part of the industry because it is often less pressured than, for example, broadcast television. It is also less concerned with making a profit and meeting deadlines than with accomplishing teaching objectives. Usually crews are small and there is the opportunity to develop a rapport with colleagues and to have a greater flexibility in working practices than is normally possible in broadcast television or large production companies. Ed. tech. staff are sometimes recruited for their knowledge of the teaching content rather than for their familiarity with the technology and sometimes former educators can move into programme-making. Union membership is usually optional in this sector of the industry. If you did decide to join ACTT, there would probably be a two year restriction on your membership. (See p.31 for an explanation of this.)

If you think that you would prefer to work in this sector, you should contact local education authorities as well as colleges and universities to find out about employment opportunities. Jobs may also be advertised in the *Guardian*'s Creative and Media Section on Mondays, in the local press or in the *Times Educational Supplement* and other academic trade publications.

7 The laboratories

The laboratories were originally set up to provide services such as film processing, editing and printing for the movie industry. Now that video tape has replaced film in many areas and there are fewer feature films being made, a number of labs have extended their operations to include video services as well. They may make mass copies of popular films for the home video market, or provide editing and various electronic effects for video producers. In addition, a company like VISNEWS offers an international video news gathering and distribution service.

Most of the major labs are located in the London area, although smaller facilities may also be found in regional centres. The work that they do is vital and producers, camera operators and directors often go out of their way to establish a close working relationship with a particular lab or even with individual staff members at the lab, in order to ensure that their wishes are communicated and carried out exactly.

Most employees at the labs work a shift system, although women at some facilities complain that they are kept off the night shift because that work pays higher wages. There also appears to be sex discrimination at some labs in which women are restricted to working in the lower grades.

Many companies promote from within and it is often easier to enter at a low grade and work your way up. Some labs have been under financial pressure leading to redundancies over the last few years and there has been a tendency to fill vacancies by re-deploying staff from those areas rather than take on new people. If you would like to work in this sector, however, a list of major laboratories is included in *Kemps Film and Television Yearbook* which should be available through most libraries.

8 Workshops

There are two broad categories of film and video workshops – franchised and non-franchised. A workshop can become franchised under the Workshop Declaration, established in 1982 by ACTT in consultation with the English Regional Arts Associations, the Welsh Arts Council, the British Film Institute and Channel Four, which allocated half a million pounds to fund workshops. If a workshop does become franchised, then Channel Four will accept up to one hour's worth of programmes from that workshop per year for broadcast, provided that the topics are ones in which they are interested.

To give an example of how one workshop became franchised, the Edinburgh Film Trust was set up in 1977 when David Halliday got a small grant from Kodak. Subsequently, the workshop obtained funding from the local district council and the local regional council, as well as a few one-off grants from organisations like the Gulbenkian Foundation. It then got support from Channel Four, which prefers to give only matching funds (that is, it gives an amount equivalent to that raised from other sources of funding). Once the workshop had become established and their work was acceptable to Channel Four, then it became franchised.

Usually workshops are set up to serve the local community in some way, either by providing access to equipment and technical training, or by producing films or videos which reflect the life and values of a particular sector of society. Often, a workshop will have a specific social or political emphasis – perhaps presenting a feminist viewpoint, or a Marxist perspective.

Non-franchised workshops may function under a variety of arrangements, and it is impossible to draw general conclusions about their organisation. Franchised workshops, however, are usually cooperatives, with each member earning the same amount, currently about £10,000. Under the Workshop Declaration, any one staff member can do several jobs. For example, the same person may function as a sound technician, camera operator and editor if that is required, which is not allowed under normal union agreements.

Many people are attracted to working in this sector because of the non-traditional structure and the political and creative freedom. It can be a precarious existence, however, since a number of workshops are funded only from one year to the next. Even if you don't want to make your career in this area, workshops offer facilities and training and it is useful to make contact with any that exist in your area. The Scottish Association of Workshops may be contacted through the Edinburgh Film Trust, 17 Great King Street, Edinburgh EH3 6QW. Otherwise, there seems to be no organised central source of information about workshops, although ACTT should be able to provide a list of those which are franchised under the Workshop Declaration. Many groups take their name from their location (i.e. the Leeds Animation Workshop, the Birmingham Film and Video Workshop etc.) and it is worth looking up in the phone book under the name of your town or city to find any operating near you.

As you read the following chapters and consider pursuing a career in some sector of the film and television industry, you should bear in mind that there may be certain trade union requirements to be considered. It is sometimes said that if you want to work in the media, the easy part is finding a job. The hard part is getting your union 'ticket' so you will be allowed to do the job. The main unions which organise in film and television are the Association of Cinematograph, Television and Allied Technicians (ACTT), the British Entertainment Trades Alliance (BETA), the Electrical, Electronic Telecommunications and Plumbing Union (EETPU), Equity and the National Union of Journalists (NUJ).

It is possible to belong to more than one union, if you do two jobs or if the job you do combines elements of two professions. For example, a news producer may be a member of the NUJ because her job has a strong journalistic slant, but she may also belong to BETA, if she is a BBC employee, or to ACTT if she works for an ITV company.

Membership of a union is not only a virtual necessity if you want to work in certain sectors of the industry, but it can be a great asset. Most of the media-related trade unions support equality for women, at least in principle, and are willing to use their clout to negotiate for improved working conditions for women as well as to support individuals in cases of sex discrimination or harassment. Even if union membership is not strictly necessary for the career you have chosen, therefore, it is still advisable that you learn what you must do to join and about the potential difficulties involved; – make sure it works to your advantage, rather than becoming a barrier to employment.

ACTT

The Association of Cinematograph, Television and Allied Technicians has about 25,000 members, about 5,000 of whom are female. They are employed in independent television companies, independent local radio stations, the BBC, film and video laboratories, workshops, educational technology facilities and many small production companies.

ACTT officials state that the union does not operate a closed shop (that is, it does not prevent non-union members from being employed in ACTT-graded jobs) although many of its members are under the impression that it does apply such restrictions in the ITV, feature film, television commercials and film laboratory sectors of the industry. The official line is that ACTT-graded job vacancies are advertised through the union and anyone may apply. If a non-member gets the job, he or she is then asked to join ACTT. In practice, however, the local branch may object if a non-member is hired in preference to a qualified union member and may threaten industrial action in support of their fellow trade unionist. ACTT has little impact on employment practices at the BBC, however, since it is not recognised there and cannot enter into negotiations with the management as a result. Nevertheless, many BBC staff belong to ACTT, partly because they wish to support the union's activities and policies in regard to the media and partly to facilitate any future moves to jobs in ITV or other ACTT-graded work.

The conditions of membership of ACTT are that one should have a job in an area in which that union organises and be sponsored by four current ACTT members. A weekly list of job vacancies in ACTT grades is published by the union and is usually on display in companies where there is an ACTT shop (branch). When a new member joins, she will often be restricted to that particular job or sector for two years – that is, she cannot apply for a different ACTT-graded job in another company for that period. For example, a woman employed in a university television service might join ACTT in the educational technology division and be given a two-year restriction which would prevent her applying for a job in ITV until that period of time had elapsed. Certain training courses are recognised by ACTT, which means that graduates from those classes will be given union membership with no restrictions as soon as they get an ACTT-graded job. (See p.311 for a full list of these courses.)

ACTT has an equal opportunities policy and has drawn up a Code of Practice on Sexism and one on Race. There is also a full-time Equality Officer, a Committee on Equality which meets regularly and an Equality Representative in each shop. In addition, there is a full-time Training Officer to help establish opportunities for women to gain the skills they need for employment in the industry. For further information, write to ACTT, 11 Wardour Street, London W1V 4AY.

BETA

The British Entertainment Trades Alliance has been formed by the merging of two previously existing unions – The Association of Broadcasting Staff (ABS) and The National Association of Television, Theatrical and Kine Employees (NATTKE). There are now approximately 37,000 members of whom about 15,000 are women. They are employed in the BBC, the Independent Broadcasting Authority, independent local radio, and in educational television at the Inner London Educational Authority. They are also found in ITV and film production in the craft, skilled, manual and ancillary categories and amongst non-performing theatre staff, cinema and Bingo hall employees. A significant number of members, particularly in the theatre, cinema and Bingo halls, are part-timers. This union does not operate a closed shop and membership is open to all those earning their living in the areas mentioned above.

BETA actively opposes discrimination and has a positive action policy for promoting women's employment and union participation. The practical work of developing that policy is done through an Equality Committee and a paid union official who has responsibility for equality issues. Further information can be obtained by writing to Christina Driver, BETA, Thorndike House, 70-6 Bell Street, London NW1 6SP.

EETPU

The Electrical Electronic Telecommunication and Plumbing Union has a membership of about 400,000, of whom approximately 36,000 are women. This trade union represents electrical, electronic and lighting operatives in television, film and all other areas of the entertainment industry. It is in the process of adopting equal opportunities policies and setting up an equal opportunities committee. In order to qualify for full membership, workers have to have served an appropriate apprenticeship and be receiving the rate for a skilled worker, or else must have been offered a job at the skilled rate. Further information can be obtained from Liz Allen, Women's Officer, EETPU, Hayes Court, West Common Road, Bromley BR2 7AU.

EQUITY

This is the actors' union, but it also covers many professional broadcasters, presenters and continuity announcers as well as some television floor managers who previously worked in the theatre. It is possible, however, to work as a professional broadcaster without being a member of EQUITY. Membership of this union can be quite difficult to obtain, as you must furnish proof of a current EQUITY contract before being admitted. Of course, many aspiring actors complain that they cannot get an EQUITY contract unless they are already members. One way around this problem is to work in a theatre job for which union membership is not required. Then you can apply for jobs which carry an EQUITY contract with a reasonable chance of being successful because of the experience you have acquired. Further information can be obtained from The British Actors' Equity Association, 8 Harley Street, London W1N 2AB.

NUJ

The National Union of Journalists has a membership of approximately 33,000, of whom just over 9,000 are female. Their members work on newspapers, journals and magazines and in publishing, write investigative books, prepare and present news and current affairs programmes on radio and television and represent various companies and agencies as press and public relations officers. The majority of journalists working as reporters, sub-editors and producers in television news and current affairs departments belong to the NUJ.

In order to become a member, you must be a full-time working journalist. If you have a part-time job as a journalist, you can still be eligible to join the union provided that that is your primary occupation. If journalism is just something you do aside from your main job, then you can't become a member. For example, a teacher who makes occasional contributions to a local television station's sportscasts would not be eligible for membership because her primary occupation, by which she earned her living, would still be teaching. If you wish to join this union as a freelance member, then 60 per cent of your earned income must come from your journalism.

The NUJ has a full-time Equality Officer, as well as an Equality Council. There are also Equality Representatives appointed in each chapel (branch). Anyone wishing further information should contact The NUJ, Acorn House, 314-20 Gray's Inn Road, London WC1X 8DP.

3 The animator

1 Job description

An animator makes the drawings for the cartoons and animated films or commercials that we see on our screens. The action which is to be animated is broken down into very slight movements. These are then drawn on to individual sheets of paper so that, if one of the characters scratched his head, that might be represented by a series of drawings, each showing his hand raised up a little further, then reaching his head and, finally, scratching. The drawings are then traced on to sheets of transparent material, known as cells, which are then photographed, one frame at a time, so that when the film is projected at normal speed, it seems as if the characters are moving. Sometimes, all the different parts of a scene that might move are each put on a different 'level', that is, the arms will be drawn on one cell, the legs on another and so on. These sheets, when laid on top of one another, make up one complete drawing. This technique is used to save time because if, for example, one character waves her hand, then the only cell which has to be re-drawn, is the one on which her arms appear. All the other sheets would be the same. Sometimes, however, the entire drawing will be put on one cell, which means that every time there is a movement, the entire drawing has to be re-done.

There are usually several people involved in making an

animated sequence. The key animator will do most of the creative work, designing the scene, deciding how the action will happen and dreaming up the characters, their expressions and their appearance. An assistant animator might then tidy up those initial drawings and perhaps fill in minor characters, such as birds or butterflies flitting about in the background. She may also prepare the instructions for the camera operator (sometimes known as dope sheets), saying how the sequence should be shot and how many frames of each drawing are required. There may also be assistants known as 'in-betweeners', who will do the drawings which fill in between the important action. There may also be a 'paint and trace' department which takes the completed drawings and copies them on to cells to be photographed.

2 Hours and conditions of work

It should be possible to work regular hours in these jobs, although overtime may be necessary whenever there are tight deadlines to be met. Since the work is all done in the animation studio, there should be little or no travel involved and no nights away from home, unless, of course, you were freelance and got a job in another city. There are some stresses involved in trying to complete creative work according to a schedule. Some people might also find it a strain to sit and draw for hours on end, so it is important that you enjoy this kind of work. Depending on your expectations, you could find some of the work boring — for example, if you were employed in the 'paint and trace' department, much of what you would be asked to do would be very routine and would give little scope for creativity.

In the past, there has been discrimination against women which has prevented them from being promoted above assistant level to become key animators. That has proved to be frustrating for many talented women. Those prejudices are beginning to disappear now, however.

3 Qualifications and characteristics required

If your goal is to work in a 'paint and trace' department, then you should get a good general education with at least O-level, or preferably A-level Art or equivalent qualifications. If, however, your aim is to become an animator, then you should attend art school – ideally one which offers a course in animation.

If you are attracted to this kind of work, you are probably the type of person who has been drawing all your life and, obviously, you must have artistic talent. It is just as important, however, to have an instinct for being able to visualise characters, so that the audience can instantly identify personalities and moods from a simple drawing. You also need to develop a sixth sense for drama and how it can be created in a few scenes.

It takes a lot of patience to be able to sit for hours working on a drawing and it may be many years before you are allowed to have much creative input, so you must be prepared to be an assistant and work on someone else's ideas to begin with. A good animator is someone who has a great deal of talent and initiative. You must be able to combine the creativity to come up with ideas along with the practicality to make those ideas work. For those who do have those skills, however, this can be an absorbing and thoroughly rewarding profession.

4 How to become an animator

While still at school, you should aim for enough qualifications to enter art college. In the meantime, practise your drawing skills, trying to create strong characterisations with a few strokes of your pen. You can begin to understand how animation works by making 'flicker books', that is, a series of drawings set out in a small book so that when you flick the pages they merge into one animated sequence. If you are very lucky, you may have access to video or film equipment through your school and can experiment with making your own little cartoons and animated stories. There are a number of textbooks around which you may find helpful, including Zoran Perisic's *The Animation Stand* (1980), which describes the camera techiques; *Timing for Animation* (1981) by Harold Whitaker and John Halas; Stan Hayward's *Computers for Animation* (1984); or Tony White's *The Animator's Workbook* (1986). You should also watch as many animated films and cartoons as possible to study the techniques used.

After school, you may decide to apply for a job in a 'paint and trace' department. Jobs may be advertised in the *Guardian*'s Creative and Media section which is published on Mondays, or you can contact companies directly. A list of names and addresses can be obtained from trade directories such as *Kemps Film and Television Yearbook* or the *BFI Film and Television Yearbook*. If you can, however, you should try to get in to art school — preferably into one which offers a course in animation techniques, such as West Surrey College of Art and Design. After that, you can start applying for jobs as an assistant. You may wish to write to animation companies, enclosing a copy of your *curriculum vitae* and asking for work, or you can also approach freelance animators in the hopes that they might either know of any vacancies, or be looking for an assistant themselves. The names of individuals can be found either in the directories mentioned above, or by contacting ACTT.

Joanne Gooding

☐ Animator
☐ Freelance

Joanne Gooding is a freelance animator who works on films, commercials and television programmes and who is based in the London area. She is thirty-five, single and has no children.

» 'I first decided I wanted to draw for a living when I was about thirteen and towards that end, I did O- and A-level Art and went to art college without any clear idea of what I wanted to do. I did a Diploma in Art and Design and Graphics at the local art school and during that time, because I hated the course, I made a cartoon film on my own. On the strength of that, I got into a training course for animation, run by Halas and Batchelor, which was a company owned by Tyne Tees Television at that time. They were doing a lot of sub-contract work for Hanna-Barbera in the States and didn't really have enough trained people so they'd set up the training school. There was a guaranteed job at the end of it and, as far as I know, that was the only time there's ever been a course like it. In fact, we were over-trained for series work, which is a very limited style of animation. It takes a particular sort of discipline, using split levels and cycles,* so it requires a minimal amount of drawing. Classic animation, on the other hand, is very full animation which rarely repeats cycles and which has everything on the same level so each drawing is re-done, even if the movement is only slight.

'Mostly I work on paper. Very, very rarely do I work on cells. All my drawings are produced on paper then given to somebody else to trace and paint. The key animator will do the main drawings and the assistant will do the in-between drawings which involve only minor changes. They may have an "in-betweener" to do the really simple in-betweens so that the assistant will do only the main ones. Then, as the relationship between the animator and the assistant gets better, the assistant will move on to doing "clean-ups". She will make the animator's rough drawings beautiful, putting all the buttons on the characters' jackets etc. and she may start doing minor animation with the characters that aren't really important (e.g. birds flying along or something). She may also do "doping" – that is, she will prepare all the instruction sheets for the camera operator – and work out all the plans and do all the technical stuff. Once the assistant is doing that much work for a key animator, then she should be rated an animator herself – which is a kind of trainee key animator.

'So, to get back to my story, I worked for Halas-Batchelor for a while until the whole thing collapsed because Hanna-Barbera decided not to send work to Britain anymore and I got made redundant. So then I had to try and get work in the freelance field, which was initially very difficult. During that time, I probably had about two months' work over a nine month period. Then I got some work with Dragon Productions. I think I got taken on for two days. That turned into four and a half weeks. Then I went back again a couple of weeks later for another two weeks' work and that turned into about six years. The company at that time had a high reputation and I was working with someone who, I think, is probably the leading animator in Europe. Having worked with him for that long meant that when I tried again to break into the freelance market, I had no trouble finding work.

'In the past year or so, which has been fairly typical, I've worked on two promo videos and at the moment I'm working on some very limited stuff for a live action animatic.* I've also worked on a medical film for a drugs company and done a TV series as well. It's not a highly paid profession compared with being a crew member on a live action film. After thirteen years experience and having done some direction as well as animation, my pay is less than a film editor's. Very rarely do I get above book rate (that is, the established rate for the job). It's either famine or feast and it's very unpredictable. If there's a feature in town then there's going to be a lot of work around. Promo videos is a new area which is just beginning to provide quite a bit of work.

'It's very difficult to say whether I've encountered much harassment in this job. What would be harassment to one person, would not be to another. At one company where I was the shop steward, whenever I went to talk to the managing director about something new that had come up with the union, he would say, "Oh, it's that union lady again. Take your T-shirt off before you speak to me." That could be conceived as sexual harassment, but what I was dealing with was someone who had to find some way to negotiate with a woman in that sort of role. He had to try and keep above it all and I think his own sexual insecurity was much more involved than anything else. I always had some stock reply such as, "I never take off my T-shirt on Wednesdays." I never found that difficult to deal with at all. But there was one time when somebody in the studio was sort of slimily physical – not in an openly harassing way, however. If he came and borrowed a pencil, he'd put his hand on my shoulder and lean over me. I remember one day getting tired of it and turning round and saying, "Please don't do that, Ray, it makes me sick", in a very loud voice so that everyone in the studio just laughed. He gave a little laugh because I smiled at him and he didn't know if it was a joke or not, but he never did it again. I think that the direct approach is always the best. I think if you're outrageous enough, it's less likely to offend the other party.

'For a long time, the person that I lived with was also in the animation business so my work was never a problem between us. Very often you get panic jobs where you're literally working fourteen hours solidly. That's a problem now with the person I live with because he has no idea what it's like to work in this industry and can't understand why I can't take an hour off to go down to the shops. He says I work like an animal because I just sit there and work solidly until I've finished. If I have to do thirty drawings in a day, then there isn't time to sit back and have a fag and a cup of tea.

'Traditionally, in animation, women have tended to be ghettoised. They tend to be in the paint and trace department. Even if they can get out of that and get to be an assistant animator, they tend to be stuck at that for far longer than men do. I don't think this is direct discrimination against women. What has happened in the past is that most animators are men and when they see a young man coming from art school, they see themselves in that person and give them a lot more encouragement. Women have traditionally become assistants – albeit high level assistants.

'So, I would advise a young woman starting out in this field to go to art college and take a course in animation. It's not, I don't think, a good idea at eighteen to try and get into a 'paint and trace ' department and work your way up because the industry is not really set up to train people via that route. It's much better to go to art school.'

Glossary

split-level   see p.35 for an explanation of this.
cycle   a repetition of one animated sequence, for example, when a character is running and only one step is drawn and then repeated over and over.
animatic   when a live commercial is done first as animation to see how it works out.

4 The camera operator

1 Job description

A camera operator may decide to concentrate on either film or video work. Although there are skills, such as the ability to frame and compose shots and the mastery of camera moves, which are required for both types of work, the technology for each is different. Some people would argue that film is being phased out – certainly in television production – while others would argue that we still need film because it is aesthetically more pleasing, with more subtle colour and greater resolution (image sharpness). It is difficult to predict future developments with either medium, but it is possible for a camera operator either to specialise or to work in both film and video.

Different circumstances can also affect the job of a camera operator. For example, you may work on a studio production, where you will be one of several camera operators, and will be connected via a headset to the gallery, where the director and others will be situated. The camera you operate will be fairly large and is likely to be mounted on a big portable stand. Despite its size and weight, it is relatively easy to move around, however, since there are wheels or castors and sometimes a steering mechanism and the pedestal can often be hydraulically raised or lowered. Studio productions are often rehearsed, which means that you will have practised the camera movements in advance and you may even be provided with a list of the shots that the director wants. You will, moreover, receive a stream of instructions and cues from the gallery throughout the production. Many studios are too small to allow for very complicated camera moves and most programmes don't require very sophisticated shots. Thus some camera operators find this kind of work frustrating.

You could also be sent to work on outside broadcasts (OBs), for which the studio situation is often duplicated. A truck containing a mobile gallery may be used, the cameras may be similar to those in the studio, or may be lighter and portable, and you will probably be linked to the gallery *via* a headset. You may be expected to operate a camera mounted on scaffolding, or on a crane, or on a mobile platform known as a dolly. (This equipment may also be used in the studio, although that is less likely.)

As a camera operator, you might also work on location, shooting 'film-style'. The director would be present on the set, rather than sitting in a gallery, and there would be pauses between each shot, while lights and the camera are repositioned. Different scenes might be shot out of sequence and then edited together in their proper order later. You might also be assigned to work on a documentary, in which case you would probably use a lightweight camera and have to be prepared to move fast and shoot scenes with very little preparation.

Alternatively, you could be part of a news crew, in which case, the camera will probably be lightweight because you have to be able to move quickly. There may not be a director assigned to the crew, so the camera operator in this situation often has to decide for herself which pictures to shoot and ensure that the various shots can be edited together into a coherent whole. Usually, there is only one camera operator assigned to each news crew.

The senior camera operator may be known as the lighting cameraman or camerawoman, because they will make decisions about the amount of illumination required and will work with the lighting director (if there is one) to plan where the lights should go. In feature films, the senior member of the camera crew is the Director of Photography. She, or he, may not actually operate a camera but will decide on exposure settings, filters, lighting and how camera moves should be executed to achieve the look that the director wants. There may be several camera operators working on the same film, or there may be a second crew employed to shoot less critical scenes in order to save time. It is the Director of Photography's job to ensure, that no matter who is operating the camera, all the film is shot the same way and has a uniform appearance and style.

No matter what kind of work situation the camera operator finds herself in, however, it is her responsibility to ensure that her camera is set to the correct exposure, that she is using the appropriate filters if necessary, and that, if she is using film, she has the right kind properly loaded in the camera. It is also important that she understand about lenses so that she selects the one that is appropriate for that shot. If she is working with video, there are also a number of critical procedures that must be carried out before shooting begins to make sure that the equipment is properly adjusted for colour and light and meets the electronic requirements.

Once those preliminaries are taken care of, she must then position her camera and frame up her shot. Composing the elements of a picture so that they are pleasing to the eye and create the effect that the director wants, is an important part of the job. Some people are of the opinion that this artistic sensibility cannot be taught, while others feel that it is something that can be developed with practice. There are also a number of camera moves that the operator must master, so that they occur so smoothly that the audience is not aware of the camera technique. These include being able physically to move the camera in any direction on a tripod or pedestal fitted with wheels, being able to tilt the camera up or down quite smoothly, or pan (swivel) it to left or right. With special lenses, it is also possible to zoom in or out on a picture, something which it takes a great deal of skill to do without jolting the camera, either at the beginning or the end of the move.

In the film industry, there are also a number of camera assistant jobs. A focus puller is someone who operates the focus ring on the lens if the camera operator alters the shot while filming is going on so that the focus has to be changed. An example of this occurs when the foreground is fuzzy as we watch the action in the background, then the focus shifts and the foreground becomes crystal clear, while everything beyond is misty. There are also assistants, known as loaders, who put the film in the camera or in the magazine (a film container which is loaded then attached to the main body of the camera, which allows for a quick change of reels of film, because it is only a matter of detaching one magazine and attaching another).

2 Hours and working conditions

These vary enormously. You might be a studio camera operator with a small television company which makes very few programmes. In that situation, your hours might be regular and you might be expected to work very few nights. Most television companies require camera operators to work shifts, however.

The amount of travel you would be expected to do would also vary. If you were a studio camera operator, you might never leave home base. You might, however, be assigned to do outside broadcasts, which could mean being gone overnight, while camera operators who are sent out on location or who work on feature films, may spend long periods away from home.

It can be an extremely stressful job, because the camera work is critical to the success of a production. You may be responsible for getting a number of details correct, such as the exposure, the colour balance, the filters, the choice of lens and film, the camera angle and so on. Juggling all these facts and remembering them all can be a strain. You could find yourself under stress because of the amount of work you have to do. For example, a news camera operator could spend every day rushing around the countryside, covering stories and then racing back to make the lunchtime or evening news. Alternatively, the stress might come from boredom. Some studio camera operators working for small companies may find their duties very light. The skills required may be very simple and monotonous and there may be periods of inactivity between programmes.

As a woman, you are also likely to encounter discrimination in this area. ITCA figures for 1986, show that only 12 out of 306 camera operators working for ITV companies were female. If more women apply for such jobs, however, then more women might be employed as camera operators and find themselves working along-side female colleagues who can give them support.

3 Qualifications and characteristics required

It is important that you study Physics, and preferably Mathematics also, to at least O-level. It may also be helpful to have taken a course in photography, electronics or film and television production. A number of film schools also offer training for camera operators. Some of these like applicants to have a background in Art, because they feel that that helps to develop a sensitivity to colour, shape and composition. Some art colleges also offer photography and film and video production as options for students.

As far as physical requirements are concerned, you should be reasonably fit and agile as well as having a lot of stamina. It is not necessary to have superwoman strength. Many camerawomen are quite small and slightly built. Most heavy equipment can be moved on trolleys or is already mounted on portable stands and no one, whether male or female, would be expected to lift excessive weights. You should have good eyesight with or without glasses, and good colour vision (i.e. you are not colour blind). Since you may be expected to wear headphones to receive instructions from the director in the gallery, you should also have good hearing.

Some jobs are more creative than others and demand different degrees of artistry. There are those in the industry who feel that such talent is in-born, but there are many others who feel that it can be developed. In either case, you should end up with some appreciation of how colours and shapes and movement can create various effects.

You should also be the sort of person who remains calm under pressure – or who can, at least, appear to be in control. Even if you do feel nervous, your hands mustn't shake or your knees tremble because that might affect your camerawork. It is important that you are able to concentrate because there are a great many people at work during any production and there may be instructions flying in all directions. Many camera jobs require a lot of initiative but, at the same time, you may be expected to work as part of a team. Other jobs can be routine and boring, which means that you must also be very patient at times.

4 How to become a camera operator

There are several routes you can take to become a camera operator. If you wish to work in television, then (apart from working towards the educational requirements mentioned above), you should learn about still photography and put together a portfolio of your work which you feel demonstrates your 'eye' for composition, a flair for colour and your creativity. Find out as much as you can about film, as well as television production, because many companies still use both film and video tape. Write to the head of the camera section at your local television station and ask if you can come along for a visit and observe them at work. Some of the larger companies require audiences for their shows and you can write to their public relations office asking if you can have some tickets. Even sitting in the audience, you can gain valuable information about how a programme is made and how the camera operators work. You may be able to take some courses in electronics at your school or college or else at evening classes nearby. Books such as Gerald Millerson's *The Technique of Television Production* (1985) or Peter Jones's *The Technique of the Television Cameraman* (1972) should also provide useful information. Other texts which you might find relevant include *Video Camera Techniques* (1983) by Gerald Millerson and Ken Daley's *Basic Film Technique* (1980). You should also try to get as much practical experience as possible. Many schools and colleges have film or video tape recording equipment which is available to students. Perhaps you could offer to record a school drama production or a football match and so demonstrate your ability with a camera. Then you should write to television companies expressing your interest. If you are eighteen, you will be eligible to apply for a position as a trainee camera operator. Such jobs will probably be advertised in the local and national press (such as in the Creative and Media section of the *Guardian* on Mondays) and also in the trade press.

If you want to specialise in film making, then there are a number of art colleges, film schools and universities which offer courses on cinematography and which may offer you the opportunity to shoot your own film. In the meantime, you should learn all that you can about film production. If there is a film company nearby, then you could contact them and ask if you can observe their crew at work. Watch as many films and television programmes as you can and take note of the camera techniques which are used. You will find it helpful to read books such as David Samuelson's *Motion Picture Camera Techniques* (1984), Steven Bernstein's *The Technique of Film Production* (1987), or H. Mario Raimondo Souto's *The Technique of the Motion Picture Camera* (1982). When you feel you are ready, contact film production companies and established camera operators and ask for a job as an assistant. Lists of companies can be found in production directories such as *Kemps Film and Television Yearbook* or in the Yellow Pages under the headings 'Film Production' or 'Audio-Visual Production' etc. The names of established freelance camera operators can be obtained from the directories published by ACTT. Alternatively, if you are already a proficient camera operator and have some examples of your work to prove it, you may be able to persuade a producer or director to let you shoot their film. This is most likely to happen in the independent sector and with small productions, such as corporate films.

Zoe Hardy

□ Camerawoman
□ ITV

Zoe Hardy was formerly a camera operator at London Weekend Television. She started out as a production assistant before training to do camera work. She did not find that being a camera operator was a very happy experience and she has now moved into other areas of production which she hopes will be more fulfilling. She is in her mid-twenties, is unmarried and lives in the London area.

» 'I would say that the main problem for me wasn't the weight of the camera or anything, it was that I was the only woman in the camera section. If there had just been another woman there, it would have made all the difference. If you're a young lad and a new recruit and they're teasing you and making you unhappy, there'll be some man to come along and say "Oh, let's go to the pub. They did that to me when I was a new recruit." If you're a woman, however, they may come along and say that to you but it's less likely because they're quite uneasy with you anyway. There's no one therefore, that you can turn to and say, "Am I mad?" If there had just been another woman there, I could have said that to her and she could have said, "You're exaggerating" or she might have said, "You're right, they're a load of bastards." It's so difficult to deal with on your own. The men used to make comments about my clothes. Every single day, there would be some joke about my appearance and it was very difficult to turn around and say, "Let's discuss this." In conversations like that they just wouldn't take you seriously at all. It's much more difficult to deal with than somebody coming up and pinching your bottom. If I found myself in a situation like that again, I think it would be better to take a firm line from the beginning.

'They did ask for Physics O-level at LWT, which I didn't have. But they will overlook that if they feel you're passionately concerned with pictures. They're a bit frightened if they think you're brainy and you've got A-levels. I think it's because they want somebody who's quite young and will just fit in and do what they want them to do. This is a bit biased, but I was twenty or twenty-one when I started and boys are more *gauche* than girls at that age, so I felt older. If they've been to a boy's school, they find it's just the same hierarchy and they fit right in. You're expected to idolise the older cameramen and one day, if you look right and they've played jokes on you and you've laughed, then they'll give you a camera to try. With me, no matter how much I tried, I could never fit into that sort of hierarchy so it took them much longer before they trusted me. Even when my training finished, I never got the sort of breaks to operate a camera as the others did. I made the mistake of becoming sort of snappy. I wouldn't recommend that anybody take a job where they are the only woman. You feel terribly isolated.

'The essential thing, if you want to be a camerawoman, is to have some feeling of how pictures are composed. You've also got to be interested in editing films. I took some photos to my interview. I'd suggest that you take not very many photographs with you – say, about four – but each one in a different style. When I went for my interview, I'd also been working at LWT already in another department as a production assistant and I'd been going on an attachment one day a week, just standing around watching so they had got used to me. In most companies, if you're interested in being a camera operator and you said that to the head of camera, they'll usually give you a little tour and let you watch so that when you go up for an interview, you have already met the people.'

Belinda Parsons

☐ Lighting camera operator
☐ Freelance

Belinda Parsons is a freelance lighting camerawoman who works on documentaries and filmed dramas. She is in her late twenties, is unmarried with no children and is based in Hertfordshire.

» 'I left school and went straight into Art school which was the most obvious thing for me to do since I wanted to pursue some sort of career in illustration. Once there, I started doing photography and by the end of my first year, I decided that I wanted to do moving pictures so I started making films on Super 8mm film. Working in film brought all my potential talents together in terms of working with a team, my photographic abilities, my eye for things, my imagination and my not liking to sit down at a desk job. So I decided that I should go straight on to film college, at the National Film School. I am of the opinion, in retrospect, that art school is a superb preparation for becoming a camerawoman. I didn't think it was wonderful at the time because there was very little direction given, but it's given me a centre from which I am able to make my own decisions about the images. I feel that someone who's trained in the industry hasn't got that opportunity. Also, if you come up through the ranks, as you're supposed to do, according to the industry, you start by being a runner, then a loader, then a focus puller and by that time ten or fifteen years have gone by and you still haven't had a chance to get your own eye to the camera and take your own decisions. If you do it *via* the industry, then the only way to get in is by personal contacts – that's in the freelance sector anyway. My own inclination is to stay clear of the institutions such as television companies because I think it would kill my creativity and kill my ambition or my ability to change direction or to expand.

'All the time I was at film school, I followed the principle that I wasn't going to work on just anything that came along, but only on things I felt I could morally work on. Since leaving the film school, I've continued to follow that policy. Because of this bias and because I'm one of the few female lighting camera operators around, there's a certain type of person who's going to ask me to work for them. There's also very obvious areas in which I'm not going to get asked to work, such as on commercials. I think there is a general bias throughout the industry against women camera operators or technicians except amongst women film producers or directors who actually have a positive interest in employing women. Then, of course, there are quite a lot of fairly liberal male producers who aren't against employing women, but you've got to put those women in front of them before they'll think of it.

'People always mention the weight of the equipment. You don't have to be a musclewoman, you just have to practise. Where equipment is heavy, you shouldn't be lifting it on your own anyway and when it comes to the modern 16mm camera, there's no problem at all. The 35mm camera is heavier, but it's a very different kind of situation – you will have more crew to help and if you are the lighting camera person, you have got the choice as to whether you carry the equipment or not. You don't actually have to do all the work yourself if you're in charge. I'm not talking from a woman's point of view now, I'm talking from any camera operator's point of view.

'You have to be totally mobile, otherwise there's no point even trying to go freelance. You've got to be ready to, say, go to Africa tomorrow morning. The way that the freelance area works is that you have to be in contact continually and you have to be available. It means that there is no such thing as a routine life and I don't think I want to do it for the rest of my life. If you look at people who've worked in the industry, the mass do not stay in films for life, or they certainly don't stay in the same area. I think it's to do with the pressures of being freelance. I think I would have to assume that if I had children, that I would risk losing my career.'

Diane Tammes

☐ Lighting camera operator
☐ Freelance

Diane Tammes is a lighting camerawoman who started out as a stills photographer and studied at a photography college in Ealing. After seven years taking pictures, she applied to the National Film School and became a student there. Since graduating, she has worked on numerous television programmes and feature films, including the BBC's *Police* series, segments of *Disappearing World* for Granada Television and the recent film, *Sacred Hearts*. She has two children and is based in the London area.

» 'It doesn't get through that working on the technical side is a career for women. I think it's really a matter of understanding the equipment and being confident enough to use it as a tool. Film school was good for me because I'd already worked as a photographer and I didn't have to learn the discipline of working. Even when I finished film school, I still worked as an assistant and a focus puller as well as shooting for myself. It is a tremendous responsibility to have the visual side of a film in your hands and it's a good idea to see how other people do it. I wanted to do film because my background was in film. Tape and film are completely different. From the electronics side of it, tape is more complicated although it is possible to be simply the camera operator and to take a technician with you. I think that in the future, people will have to make a choice because they'll feel there won't be as many opportunities of shooting film as tape.

'You have to be quite determined because in any area where there are few women, you are always going to be in the spotlight so everything you do is going to be seen by everyone else. Therefore, you have to be very sure of what you're doing and be quite confident. When you're shooting with a camera, you're actually thinking of four or five things at once so it's quite good if you can split your mind into five different areas . . . . Is this the right shot? Is it in focus? I also think you have to be aware of people. You're going into people's lives and filming them when you make documentaries, so you have to respond to them and make them feel comfortable and you've got to like meeting people. In drama productions, you've also got to get on with an enormous crew.

'I'm not sure that anyone can teach you to be creative and I wouldn't actually like to say what creativity is. Most people have their own style and that comes out of them and who they are. The best thing is to discover what you enjoy doing and to develop that within yourself. That can be done by looking at other people's work or by looking at things around you, such as the way the light falls on things and so on.

'There's more competition to get into film schools now so they like people to have made a film already. That's very difficult for women because very often in school the boys are more likely to do the technical things. Girls don't wake up to the realisation that they can do it till too late. You have to be determined and don't ever allow anyone to say to you that you can't do it because people have been saying that to me always.

'I encounter a lot of surprise when I turn up on a job. I don't know how much discrimination goes on when my name is put up for a job and they say, "No, we don't want a woman." I'm sure that does happen but I'm not aware of it. I'm always conscious that it's up to me to create my own work because if I sit and wait for that phone to ring, it isn't going to happen. If you feel you weren't chosen because of your sex, there's no point getting upset about it – that's the way it is. You can do what you can to change it, but you can't say to someone who would rather work with a man, "You've got to work with a woman", because the relationship isn't going to work anyway.

'It isn't a nine to five job. Once you're in the middle of a film, it takes over. I'm freelance so I can control how many films I want to make a year. As far as my children are concerned I have to believe that as long as I am there enough and as long as I have time to listen, it's okay. If I didn't believe that, I wouldn't be able to do it. If I'm away out of the country, I write back or telephone and keep in contact. My partner and I try never to be away at the same time. When the children were wee, I had someone to live in and look after them when I was away. I don't have somebody permanent. If I'm not working, I have to stay home because I can't afford to have someone come in.'

5 The casting director

1 Job description

Casting directors are usually employed on drama productions, both for television and the cinema, or on any production which uses artistes, including commercials, variety programmes and quiz shows. This job does not formally exist at the BBC, but many of the larger ITV companies as well as a number of independent production companies, employ casting directors. Often, however, the work is done on a freelance basis and casting directors are employed only for the duration of a particular film or production.

The casting director begins by reading the script and discusses with the director and producer what type of actor is required for each part. Some roles may call for a specific physical type (say, tall and blonde), others may simply require an actor capable of tackling that sort of part. A good casting director may be able to make suggestions that go beyond the director's immediate concept. For example, the lead role in *The Graduate* could have been typecast as an all-American boy, tall, muscular, blonde and good-looking. Instead, the part was cast against type and Dustin Hoffman, who is small, dark and Jewish, was launched in his film career. Sometimes the casting director will have to use great ingenuity to come up with suitable actors. Susie Figgis, casting

Comfort and Joy, was asked to find Italian-Glaswegian actors, even though there isn't even a very big population in Glasgow with Italian origins. According to the director, Bill Forsyth, she cast the roles within a few days, by stopping people in the streets of Glasgow and asking if they knew any Italians in the city. In this way, she was able to get in touch with the Italian community there and find suitable candidates for the parts – some of whom had no previous acting experience and so could not have been located through conventional sources.

Normally, however, once the casting director has some idea of what's required, she will scout around for possibilities in a number of ways. She will probably interview actors, watch performances in theatres around the country, view films and search through casting directories, until she has drawn up a shortlist of likely candidates to be interviewed by the director. The function of a casting director is, therefore, to save time and draw on wider resources in casting than would be possible for the director or producer.

Once an actor has been selected for a part, then it is also the casting director's job to negotiate the terms of the contract and the schedule of work.

2 Hours and conditions of work

It is obvious, from the description above, that this could become a twenty-four hour a day job. It is almost inevitable that a casting director works some evenings, at least, in order to see theatrical performances and films, although she may have some flexibility in her working hours at other times. For those who love the theatre and show business, it can be an absorbing and rewarding profession, but it can also be hectic and draining. Juggling timetables, dealing with personalities, arranging contracts, keeping to schedules and coping with the anxieties of producers and directors when the success of a film may depend on getting the right actor for the part, can be harrowing. It is, however, one area in which women are not discriminated against, since most of the casting directors in this country are female.

3 Qualifications and characteristics required

Many casting directors have had some connection with the acting profession before going into casting. Either they had studied drama – perhaps to become teachers – or they had been actresses or actors' agents themselves. Since there is some typing and administrative work involved, many casting directors started by taking a secretarial course. There are, however, no formal qualifications necessary for the job – simply an interest in all it entails. Since every casting director is dependent on contacts within the industry, newcomers must persuade someone who is already established to take them on as an assistant. After four years or so in this capacity, or two years with previous experience, they are then ready to launch out on their own.

In order to do this job well, a casting director will constantly be on the lookout for new faces, making a note of actors' strengths and weaknesses, keeping up to date with who is available and who is on the other side of the world filming for the next six months. She needs to understand actors' fears, be able to identify their strong and weak points and have an imaginative instinct for what reserves an individual actor might have which are as yet untapped. (Who would have guessed that Sally Fields, who played the part of a flying nun in a long-running comedy series, could turn in an Oscar-winning performance as Norma Rae, a labour organiser and strike leader? It takes a good casting director to have that kind of insight.)

It is also a job that requires tact and sensitivity to deal with the members of a profession which is often insecure and who consequently can be very emotional and vulnerable. You also need a great deal of strength to cope calmly with directors and producers who may throw tantrums and put pressure on you if the right actor has not been found quickly. Millions may be at stake and it takes a cool nerve to juggle schedules, hoping that the actor whom the producer and director want, will be free in time to start shooting when planned.

4 How to become a casting director

You should become involved in the theatre in some way. Even if you don't study drama or become an actress, you should watch television and go to the theatre and cinema as often as you can. Practise being a casting director by taking note of actors and the types of roles they play well. It is probably helpful to acquire some secretarial training. You can then apply to a television or production company which employs casting directors. You may have to start out as a secretary, moving on to become a bookings clerk or an assistant casting director when an opening becomes available. Alternatively, you can approach freelance casting directors in the hope that one of them will take you on as an assistant. You can find the addresses of casting directors in a very useful book called *Contacts*, published every two years by French's. You may also be able to obtain names and addresses through ACTT. You should then write to each one, asking if you can go and talk to her and offering your help as an assistant. It won't be easy, but it is possible.

Rebecca Howard

☐ Casting director
☐ Freelance

Rebecca Howard is a freelance casting director and has recently worked on the films *1984* and *Lady Jane*. She is forty-one, has two children and lives in the London area.

» 'I went to Bristol University where I read English and Drama. At that time I wanted to be an actress. When I left Bristol, I decided I didn't want to be an actress and that I wanted to work on the other side of the business. My boyfriend at the time was an actor and he was leaving Bristol Old Vic Drama School. Three agents wrote to him, offering to represent him and I wrote to them asking for work. One of them gave me a job. It was terribly easy because it was the 1960s and there was lots of work around. I worked for her for six months and then applied for a casting assistant's job which I got. I stayed with that for a year, then I got a job with another casting director and worked there for three years. We did, *If*, *Oh What a Lovely War* and *Isadora*. It was a time when there were a lot of really good British films being made. After that she said it was time I did something on my own so I did various on-and-off sorts of jobs because it's terribly difficult to establish yourself freelance. It was also terribly difficult to get into the union. In those days, the assistant's position wasn't recognised. Even now it's difficult because you have to do a four year apprenticeship and you have to get a casting director to guarantee you that kind of work, which is probably difficult because they don't know where the work is coming from themselves. I worked for the Royal Shakespeare for six months as their casting director and then worked on the film *Triple Echo*. After that, I had my first baby and I didn't work for about eighteen months. When he was about eight months old, I decided that I didn't really like sitting at home and wanted to go back to work. It was just after *Triple Echo* had come out and I was offered a couple of freelance jobs plus a regular job at Thames Television, which I took. I worked there from 1973 to 1979. Then I worked for ATV which became Central Television. I left there at the end of June 1983 to become freelance. The two big films I've done since then are *1984* and *Lady Jane*.

'If you work for a big company, you have to do whatever programmes they're making. You can't pick and choose really. You have to do all sorts of things, including situation comedies and game shows as well as dramas. It's just a matter of choice whether you work in a big company with a pension and a car and all that sort of thing or whether you want to do it on your own.

'Obviously, to do this job, you have to be able to judge talent. You must have a very good memory and be able to get on with all sorts of people. You have to have a good head for figures too, because you have to do all the contracts and a lot of that means working out complicated percentages.

'It's also an anti-social job in one way because you have to work in the evenings. I had to have help with the children. One of the reasons I took the job with Thames was because I knew how much money I would be getting so I was able to pay a nanny. I couldn't and wouldn't take a job away from home, however, because of the family.

There are so few casting directors to work for that it's very difficult to get in. It's really like looking for a needle in a haystack that you just find somebody at that moment who's looking for a secretary. Certainly typing is essential because you have to type contracts. One encouraging thing, however, is that in this country I think it's an area that's predominantly female.'

Pam O'Connor

☐ Casting director
☐ ITV

Pam O'Connor is a casting director with Central Television. She is forty-three and lives in the London area with her two teenage sons.

» 'I joined Central Television twenty-five years ago as a receptionist. I had my children and left a couple of times and went back again. I became a secretary to one of the casting directors about eleven years ago. After a couple of years, however, I decided to leave and try something else; but I couldn't stay away and I got back into the business again as another casting director's secretary, until I became a booking assistant three years ago. I was actually made a temporary casting director in February last year. I started on *Crossroads* which I'm still working on. I went through a board and got the job officially in September. Most casting directors started as secretaries to somebody.

'I didn't have any trouble getting a union ticket. I was a member of NATTKE first when I was a secretary and then became a booking assistant which is the lowest grade recognised by ACTT in this area.

'Usually you work on two or three programmes at once. We all do the work differently. Each casting director has – I wouldn't say favourites – but different slants. It's all a matter of judgment, really, about an artiste's skills. It's got to be a fairly objective judgment though, in order to cast the programme so that other people are going to enjoy it. It's a case of what you judge to be *good*, whether you like it or not, in some cases. You also need the ability to get on with people and have a tremendous amount of energy. We have to see a lot of things. We go to the theatre, we watch television, we go to films and visit drama schools. You need to have done that for some time in order to give yourself a working repertory of actors, really, because it has to be very large. How much choice you have in casting depends very much on the project and what sort of budget there is. You're limited when you take on a project that doesn't have a great budget and you have to cast accordingly.

'The demands of the job would be very difficult were

it not for the fact that my sons are very supportive and can operate without me. Between Monday and Friday, I do my research, you might say, and go to the theatre and films etc. Since I work on *Crossroads*, I have to be in Birmingham a lot and may have to stay overnight. Also, I visit a lot of repertory companies and they can be quite far away, so I have to be gone overnight then as well.

'I start by reading the script and do a breakdown of that script to see the kind of characters that are required. The producer and director will have had the script first and quite often they will have some ideas about the kind of person they want for the starring parts. They may even have specific people in mind. Very often, writers have ideas of their own about casting, too. So you have a fairly extensive discussion to start with – really to get to grips with the characters. Different people will have very different ideas, depending on their own experiences. So you've got to get together on age, nationality, personality etc. So, again, that's a matter of opinion. Then I'll pull in a selection of artistes and the director would interview them. You may invite artistes to write in and then audition as many as you can and get it down to a short list for the director and producer. It's hard work, but it's what I enjoy.'

6 The costume designer

1 Job description

The costume designer is responsible for clothing the actors and performers in a manner appropriate to the style and mood of a production. She begins by reading the script to identify the period in which the action takes place, the social class and personalities of the characters, the kind of events in which they participate, the climate and terrain of the setting and the general style and atmosphere of the film or programme. For example, the type of clothing she would choose would depend on whether she was working on a drama set in the seventeenth century, or on a futuristic science fiction piece. An upper-class character might wear a different style and quality of clothes from, say, a workman and would require evening dress if there was a scene at the County Ball, or tweeds and waterproofs for a shooting expedition, and so on. If a production was set in a hot climate, then that would not only affect the style of the clothes but also the kinds of fabric used in their construction, and the same would be true if a film was shot in a cold climate. The designer might also have to bear in mind the changes in the seasons because in some countries, the time of year can have a dramatic effect on the clothes worn there. Over and above all these objective details, however, she must take account of the personality of the character, since a flamboyant type of person might wear much more exotic clothes than someone else in the same situation who had a more sombre personality. She would also examine the script carefully to determine if duplicate sets of clothing would be needed. For example, perhaps one scene requires the leading lady to get soaked to the skin and if the action had to be re-shot (as usually happens) then it would be impossible to dry her clothes quickly enough and another set would have to be ready. Perhaps, too, the main character might have to perform some dangerous feats and a set of identical clothes, perhaps in a different size, would have to be prepared for the stunt artist who would actually undertake any risky operations.

Once she had taken note of such preliminary details, the costume designer would consult with the director, the production designer and possibly other members of the crew, such as the lighting director, the director of photography and the sound supervisor. The director would discuss the personality and emotional state of the main characters and the mood she wanted to convey. Close cooperation is required between the costume designer and the production designer to obtain the desired 'look' and to ensure that the clothing and the sets complement each other. The kind of lighting which is decided upon can affect the choice of colours because, for example, if very bright lights are to be used, then the costume designer may decide to avoid pastel colours which would fade to insignificance in a strong glare. Her choice of style and fabric might also be affected by the requirements of the sound crew (if, say, they wished to hide a microphone in a singer's clothing), and because artificial fibres usually rustle more than natural ones when an actor moves.

Once the general style of the costumes had been agreed upon with the director and other crew members, the designer would set about assembling the wardrobe within the budget allowed. If the film or programme is set in modern times, many of the clothes may simply be purchased from ordinary shops. If something more exotic is required, then she may decide to design the outfits herself. This may involve a great deal of research in libraries, museums and antique shops to duplicate authentic historical styles. Once the actors have been cast, she may then have to modify her choice of designs to suit the tastes and shapes of the artistes.

Although she will probably not actually make the garments herself, the costume designer will supervise their construction, as well as the purchasing of accessories such as shoes, belts, hats, tights and handbags. Some costumes may be hired, in which case she will select the outfits she wants and supervise the fittings.

During the production, she will be assisted by a number of staff who will help the extras and the main actors to get dressed for each scene, and wash, clean and iron all the costumes and accessories when needed. One of the major problems which the costume designer may have to deal with is finding adequate washing and drying facilities at a location which is miles from anywhere.

Yet, despite all these headaches, this is a fascinating job for those who are interested in design, fashion and fabrics and who appreciate how costumes can contribute to characterisation and the atmosphere of a production.

2 Hours and working conditions

The length of a costume designer's working day depends on the programme or film she is involved in as well as the production schedule. Some jobs may be less demanding than others. For example, a half-hour television play set in modern times requiring only one set of clothing for each of two actors, would not be as taxing as a feature film or drama series set in another time period at a distant location. If she has to design everything from scratch, then the pre-production phase could be hectic as the designer struggles to complete the costumes on schedule. If there are complicated special effects requiring changes of clothing, or if there are complex scenes involving hundreds of extras who must be dressed in authentic period fashion, then the actual shooting of the film or programme can be arduous for the designer. She may still be working long after the rest of the crew have finished for the day, making sure that all the costumes are ready for the next scenes to be shot.

If a costume designer is working on a drama or other programme which will be shot entirely in the studio, then there may be little or no travel involved in the job, provided she lives within commuting distance of the studio. If, however, she is assigned to a film or show which is shot on location, then she may have to spend days, weeks or even months far away from home.

The stresses of the job vary from one situation to another. There may be the pressures of keeping to a tight schedule and remaining within the budget. There may be tension generated by her involvement with other members of the crew, because she must try to interpret the director's concepts and be creative while adjusting her designs to fit in with the work of the production designer, the director of photography and so on. She may have to endure the frustration of dealing with suppliers and sub-contractors who don't meet deadlines so that she is left without the fabrics or accessories she needs or with garments that are not completed on time.

3 Qualifications and characteristics needed

Obviously, you must have an interest in fashion, design and fabrics as well as being sensitive to the ways in which details of clothing can contribute to characterisation, mood and style. It is not absolutely essential that you be able to make clothes yourself, but you should be thoroughly familiar with tailoring and construction techniques. Since much of your skill will involve keeping track of your department's budget and organising staff and schedules, it helps to be a good administrator and to have some business acumen. Most companies require a degree in theatre or fashion design, including the history of costume. In addition, it is helpful if you have had prior experience working in the theatre or with a firm of costumiers. You should have good eyesight and colour vision.

It is helpful, also, if you are intuitive and perceptive about people, partly because you must be able to interpret personality in the garments that a character wears, but also because you will be working closely with the artistes. Sometimes an actor may dislike a particular style or may have an inferiority complex about some aspect of his or her physique and the costume designer should be able to realise what the problem is and then deal with it tactfully. An actor's clothing can either boost her morale or undermine her confidence in her ability to play a particular part.

4 How to become a costume designer

While still at school, you should learn all you can about dressmaking and tailoring and the history of costume. Watch films and plays and note how the designer has chosen to interpret the mood of the play and demonstrate the personalities of the characters in the costumes. Get as much practical experience as you can by helping to design and make clothes for school productions or for amateur theatrical groups. You might also be able to help out as a wardrobe assistant or dresser, helping to clean and press the costumes and get the actors ready to go on stage.

Ideally, when you leave school, you should take a degree in Theatre or Fashion Design at a drama or art college. If possible, try to get some professional experience working in a theatre wardrobe department or for a costumier which makes and hires costumes for film and television or stage production. Write to companies and freelance designers expressing your interest, asking to be informed of job opportunities and suggesting that you would like to observe a costume designer at work. You can find the addresses of companies in directories such as *Contacts* or *Kemps Film and Television Yearbook*. Some costume designers will also be listed in such reference books or may be contacted through ACTT or BETA. Advertisements for jobs as an assistant costume designer will appear in the local and national press, such as the *Guardian* and the *Stage*.

Mary-Jane Reyner

□ Costume designer
□ Freelance

Mary-Jane Reyner is a freelance costume designer who now works mainly on feature films. She is thirty, married with one child and lives in Orkney.

» 'I did three years of Speech and Drama at Queen Margaret College in Edinburgh where I specialised in costume. My first job was with a pantomime in Motherwell as wardrobe mistress, which means you do the sewing before the production starts and then, while it's on, you do the wardrobe maintenance, which is washing and ironing and all that kind of stuff. I went from there to Scottish Opera for three years as assistant wardrobe mistress to start with, then as wardrobe mistress. That was really good. I don't think there's anything better for costume than opera. That was a NATTKE job. Funnily enough, it's not difficult getting union membership in theatre and opera. It's only when you come to independent television and film that it becomes complicated. Then it's an ACTT grade.

'I did some more theatre, then went to BBC for two

years as a costume designer. Then I came up to Orkney to do a film for Bill Forsyth with the BBC and decided to pack in the BBC and go freelance. It's been really good ever since. I've done *Comfort and Joy*, *Restless Natives* and *The Girl in the Picture*.

'I've worked mostly on films where the director has also been the writer. Normally, you would discuss with the director what his or her interpretation of the characters was. If he or she is also the writer, that makes it a lot easier because you don't have two sources of information. You have a general outline of what the director wants and what the art director wants and then you work closely with the actors themselves. On modern stuff it demands a lot of observation of people and types. You can tell so much about people from what they wear, down to the kind of wristwatch somebody has and how particular people are about their general appearance, how well-groomed they are, quite apart from what colours they wear or what kind of style they have. When I've decided what should be done, I supervise that being carried out. That means buying fabrics and any clothes we buy off the peg, arranging fittings, having dressmakers lined up and having everything ready at the right time.

'An awful lot of the job in film nowadays is administration and paperwork. The best training I had was with Scottish Opera. I had a boss who taught me how to organise something on paper. In any design job, you're lucky I think, if you spend 25 per cent of the time on actual design. The rest of the time is organisation. You have to know exactly what everybody's wearing at any given moment. You have to know sizes. You also have to understand the character and the actor really well and that everyone agrees with you on the image. That's very important because if you suddenly present an artiste with a costume that they think is completely wrong, then it's never going to work. You have to coordinate everything with the make-up people and know what the sets are like. Another worry is the budget because you have deadlines to make and you have to find out what everybody's going to charge for the work before you start. You must also make sure that you won't be under-staffed and have three hundred extras turn up one day when you've only got two people to dress them. If it pours with rain, then you have to be ready to cope. In that situation, you'd need an awful lot of people and probably washing and drying facilities and duplicates of clothing. The actors may have special effects or stunts to do that demand duplicates of costumes also, so you've got to have those ready.

'You don't need to know how to sew clothes but it really helps if you do. What makes a good designer is that, when you design a garment on paper, you know exactly what it's going to look like. So I think you do tend to know about construction.

'Working for television is very different from working for film. I think probably it's because the BBC does tend to make you a bit complacent. In the freelance market, you're only as good as your last job. There's so much competition and the schedules are so demanding, but then the results are much better. If you're working in 35mm, you know that every detail is going to show up. It's going to be absolutely enormous on screen. Also in film, I would concentrate on getting the look right. At the BBC, realism is all, which I find quite difficult. For example, *The Borgias* was very accurate to period, but it was very ugly. Now, if I was working in film or theatre, I wouldn't necessarily conform to period. I wouldn't sacrifice the look just to get the period accurate, because if it looks all right, people aren't going to pick up on that detail.

'When I first started at the BBC, you still had to design with black and white in mind and choose strong contrasts. That doesn't exist any more. But in film, you still have to think about what will happen to your colour. In feature films, you would have to know what film stock you were using, because some film stocks are very yellow, some are very red etc. You also have to know what the lighting designer is doing. That's not so important in television, because they go so much for realism and so it's generally quite brightly lit. But somebody like Chris Menges (a lighting cameraman) lights everything very dark, so you can't afford to use very dark colours for the costumes.

'There is still an attitude in some areas that costume and make-up are just ladies' hair and beauty departments. That's really the old school. You get people saying, "Excuse me ladies, could you remove yourselves from the set?", which is very odd. That's the only thing I've found to be irritating. In films, they don't mind what you do as long as you come up with the goods. If you do well, then you work for one company and they pass you on because they know you're a good bet. A lot of it is who you know.

'It's very demanding because you have to work so many hours. You have to have a very strong relationship and so many break down because you're apart so much. One year, I spent only five months of the year with my husband. It really does create a big gap, because you don't know what the other person is doing all the time. I think that it's only with experience that you learn how to handle that. In fact, we try now not to be apart and the intention now is that my husband and the baby and I will all base ourselves in the same place. He worked offshore for a while but now he's actually packed it in. We found the demands of my job and his job too much. I'm very, very lucky that he's open-minded enough to cope with it.'

7 The director

1 Job description

The director is responsible for supervising the work of the cast and crew on a production, making sure that they all cooperate to create the sound and images which will produce the desired effect. Other people, like the producer or the production manager, will worry about raising the money, overseeing the budget, paying the crew, arranging catering and organising equipment, but the director's primary concern is with the actual creation of the sound and image. Sometimes the same person will be both producer and director, in which case their responsibilities will be correspondingly broader. Even if that is not the situation, however, the director will often confer with the producer over major decisions.

If the production is pre-planned (and isn't something which is ad-libbed, like a documentary), then she begins with a script. From this, she develops a clear impression of the mood and look which should be created for each scene and how any transitions to a different mood and look will be effected. Usually she will try to create sound and images which fit with the dramatic action or the events portrayed. For example, if she is planning a variety show, she might envisage a glittery set with colourful costumes, lit by coloured spotlights and using fast-moving camera shots and snappy editing techniques. Once she has a general idea of the effect to be created, she will collaborate with the different technical departments to come up with specific ideas for set design, make-up, lighting and camerawork etc. which will achieve that effect. On big productions, there may be a storyboard, which is a sort of strip cartoon of the various shots to give some idea of how they are composed and how they match with what has gone before and what comes after. This may be used as a point of reference by the director and crew. During the pre-production phase and while shooting is going on, however, the crew will usually turn to the director to make sure that their particular creative contribution fits into the whole scheme of things. It's no use if the designers create sets and costumes which are soft and dream-like but the lighting director has chosen to create a hard, cold glare.

The director's relationship with the cast, on the other hand, can vary widely from situation to situation and from one individual to the next. A very experienced actor may require little direction because she or he knows instinctively how to shape their performance to reach an audience and yet fit in with the overall effect. For less experienced actors, however, the director is there to be a sort of sounding board, letting them know how an audience would respond to their performance, helping them to pitch it just right and giving them the feedback they require to make their acting complement the performances of the rest of the cast. For example, a drama could be ruined if one actress camped it up when the others were portraying their characters in a very serious fashion. The director should be the touchstone for what is appropriate and ensure continuity in the perform-ances so that they create whatever effect is required.

It is particularly important that the director has communicated what she wants in a situation where the film or programme has not been rehearsed, for example, for documentaries, live television programmes and some news broadcasts. The action in these is unpredictable, to a certain extent, and the director can only try to anticipate what might happen and plan for that. For the rest, she must rely on the crew to use their initiative in situations that need an instantaneous response and, if she has communicated her overall aim well, then the end product should still appear completely professional.

In a television production, the director may not have any control over the choice of theme or content or script for the programme. That may have been decided by the producer. It is the director who sees that those ideas are implemented effectively, however, and during a studio production, she sits in the gallery where she can monitor everything that is happening on the set, see all the camera pictures at once, choose the shots as they happen, send last minute instructions to the crew and monitor that everything happens as planned while the programme is actually being made. The situation may be very similar on an outside broadcast, also, because often there is a mobile gallery set up inside a truck which will have been brought to the site, so the director can proceed as if she was working in a studio set-up.

The situation is very different on location, however, particularly for feature film production. In those circumstances, there is no gallery, not even for television productions. The director is present on the set while shooting goes on. Television studio productions are often shot as one continuous whole, but films and some television drama series etc. which are shot on location, will be filmed or recorded one scene at a time with breaks in between while the camera is moved to another angle and so on. The director gives the cue for the camera(s) to roll and for the actors or performers to start. When the shot is completed, she indicates that the camera should stop rolling and the action should cease. On large productions the director may have one or more assistants, who actually give the cues and organise the extras and crowd scenes etc.

When shooting has been completed, the director will usually be involved in the editing, unless, of course, it was a live production and no editing is required. In some cases, the director may have the final say about how the scenes will be cut together. In other situations, it may be the producers, backers, or even the star performer who has the most clout and has the final cut, as it is called.

2 Hours and working conditions

The hours that a director works depend on the job she is doing. She may work for a small company where she is only required to work intermittently as projects become available, or she may be directing a relatively simple programme so that her duties are quite light. In such situations, her hours might be regular and won't exceed eight hours per day. If the studio is heavily booked, however, it might mean working late in the evening, or perhaps all night because that's the only time it is available. On some jobs, however, the director could have very long hours, because she may have to keep to a punishing production schedule and her presence is required most of the time – certainly while the shooting or recording is going on. For example, if she was working on a feature film, it would probably mean an early start to get organised for the day and to take as much advantage of the natural light as possible if the film is shot outdoors. Even if filming ends early in the evening, there will probably be 'rushes' to look at (i.e. film from previous days' shooting which has been rushed to the labs for processing and rushed back for viewing so that the director and others can see how it turned out and spot mistakes as quickly as possible). Then there may be meetings with various members of the crew and preparations to be made for the next day's shooting. The director can be lucky to get even a few hours rest and, if the production lasts a period of months, she can become exhausted.

It can be an extremely stressful job, because the work of so many people depends on the decisions made by the director and often the responsibility for the success of the whole venture rests with her. She must cope with artistic egos, reconcile various technical departments which are in conflict and get the most out of their creativity and originality, while persuading everyone to work as a team towards the effect she wants to achieve.

The job may, or may not require you to be away from home. A studio director with a local television station or production company may always work locally; but a feature film director could be gone to the other side of the world for months on end. It all depends on the work situation that you choose or can find for yourself.

Many women feel they have been discriminated against when they have applied for jobs as directors. One still encounters employers who cannot believe that a woman could cope with a largely male crew, despite the evidence that there are a number of women around who are doing just that very successfully. Women who wish to work in this job have to be determined.

3 Qualifications and characteristics required

There are no specific educational requirements for this job, although, since competition is fierce, it is wise to get the best academic qualifications that you can. The most important requirement, however, is that you know about all aspects of production. For this reason, many directors previously had experience working in another grade within the industry. There are cases of floor managers, production assistants, script supervisors, camera operators and researchers who have gone on to become directors. It depends on being able to convince the management or the backers that you can do the job.

As well as having a sound knowledge of technical aspects of production, you should be able to demonstrate that you are creative in terms of sound and images, and that you have ideas for programmes which would grab an audience's attention. You must be good at handling people, not only to get the most out of your crew, but also to maintain an harmonious atmosphere. It is the director's job to coordinate the talents and creativity of a great many people and that sometimes requires great tact and diplomacy when two artistic temperaments are in conflict. If there are bad feelings amongst the crew, it will very quickly show up in the production.

Part of the ability to maintain a good working atmosphere lies in being able to cope with stress. If the director goes to pieces or becomes very irritable and bad-tempered, then the production can fall apart. All of that requires great resilience and stamina, to cope with the strain for long periods of time, sometimes even for months.

If a director wishes to specialise in one particular type of programme, then it may be helpful to have had previous experience in that area. For example, a number of drama directors are recruited from the theatre. If you want to concentrate on sports or music programmes, then you should be able to demonstrate a lifelong interest in that subject, even if you don't actually have professional experience in that area.

In the feature film industry, the trick to becoming a director is to persuade someone to back you in a film. But most investors would want to ensure some return on their money by choosing a director who had a track record. So, in this area, too, you will probably need to have had extensive prior production experience. It is likely that that will include working as an assistant director which may include duties such as acting as a 'call boy' for the cast, organising crowd scenes and making sure that everything and everyone that's needed on set shows up.

4 How to become a director

Although there are no specific academic requirements for this job, you should get the best education you can, paying particular attention to subjects that might interest you in the future. For instance, if you wished to specialise in music programmes, or concentrate on drama, then you would study music, on the one hand, and English literature or Drama, on the other.

At the same time, you should learn everything you can about film and/or television production. Try to get permission to visit studios and location sets to observe the director at work. Read relevant books about film and programme making, such as Gerald Millerson's *The Technique of Television Production* (1985) or Steven Bernstein's *The Technique of Film Production* (1987). Watch as many film, television and theatre productions as you can. In particular, it is helpful to see the same play or film in different versions which have been directed by different directors. That, more than anything, can make you realise how, working with the same words and action, each director can produce a completely different production. Lastly, get as much experience of directing as you can, even if it's only working on the local amateur drama group's pantomime. If possible, borrow equipment from your school, college or community centre and make your own film or programme, so that when it comes to applying for a director's job, you have something to show what you can do.

You may decide to take a course in film or television production at a college which might qualify you to apply directly for a trainee or assistant director's job. For example, the National Film and Television School and the London Film School offer degree courses and graduates are eligible for ACTT membership when they find a job. Otherwise, obtaining a union ticket, as it's called, can be very difficult. The best route for many people, is to find any job within the industry, learn all they can about production, make contacts and then start applying for jobs and badgering companies to give them their big break.

Zelda Barron

☐ Feature film director
☐ Freelance

Zelda Barron's fascination with the cinema has led her to spend most of her working life in the film industry. It is only recently, however, that she was finally given the opportunity to direct her first feature, the critically acclaimed *Secret Places*. The success of that has launched her on a career as a director quite late in life, although she has found that offers of work come from abroad and not from her native Britain. She is divorced, with two grown-up children and several grandchildren.

» 'I wanted to go to RADA. I wanted to do all sorts of artistic things but the only thing my father was willing to do by way of further education was to send me to shorthand and typing school. My sisters and I loathed and despised the thought of office work and wanted to do different things, but, in fact, it turned out to be very useful for all of us, even though I played hookey and went to see films constantly. My very first job was in the typing pool of a film company. Then, when I was eighteen, I had a tremendous yearning to go to the US and landed a job as a secretary to the vice president of Universal Pictures. But eighteen was very young in those days and I got a bit homesick. When I came back to the film business in England, I eventually moved over to the technical side and became a production assistant. I worked on films like *Our Mother's House*, *If . . .*, *Morgan, A Suitable Case for Treatment* and *Isadora*. I worked with the bright directors of the

1950s and early 1960s. Then I moved into continuity and discovered I liked that enormously, It's a tremendously demanding job. It entails being ultimately responsible for everybody's mistakes and not letting them get past you. If you have an eye for film and an ear for scripts, you can also have a big input, as I found over the years. I did that for a long time, culminating in doing *Reds* for Warren Beatty – a wonderful thing for me as he virtually demanded that *I* direct *him*, because he was in almost every shot. He is probably the only director I've ever worked with who was generous enough publicly to praise the input that key technicians (including me) made to his film. That is not often acknowledged by directors who tend to give the impression that they alone are the creators of their films. I worked in the same way with Barbra Streisand in *Yentl*. Those were the beginnings of people saying, 'You should be directing', something which I hadn't even thought about as a possibility.

'There were three things against it happening to me. I'm a woman, I'm getting on a bit and I'm a technician. As a technician, you stand on the studio floor and work with directors, some of whom are absolutely brilliant and some of whom are absolutely useless. What better university could you have for learning the rights and wrongs of film making? Yet it's very rare that anyone would risk putting up money for a technician to direct a film. They'd rather risk a huge budget on a young chap who's done one pet food commercial. It's a funny old business and its very unfair in many ways.

My colleague, Ann Skinner, who was also a former continuity girl, approached me about forming a company to make our own films – not an original idea, of course. We roped in Simon Relph to give us a masculine edge (and to provide the extraordinary qualities he possesses as a producer) because, at that time, it was less easy for women to be taken seriously in the macho film world. We made *Return of the Soldier*. It became apparent around about this time, that I probably wasn't producer material. Ann used to say that whenever she talked to me about money, my eyes went out of focus. But I had a kind of reputation for being a bit of a script doctor and I'd done lots of instant re-writes on the set, so Ann said I should write something and our company, SKREBA, would produce it. We acquired an option on *Secret Places* but couldn't get anyone interested in financing it in book form. So I decided to write the script on spec. When I presented it to Ann and Simon, they liked it enough to say, "You're going to direct it." I said, "Okay" happily enough, but thought to myself, "They're crazy. There's no way anyone's going to finance me as a director." I had no track record – not even *one* pet food commercial. During my latter years in film, I would never have been fazed by somebody saying, "You direct this", if it was a subject that I was incredibly involved in and loved a lot. So, when the day came that nobody had replaced me as the director of *Secret Places* (as I thought was bound to happen), I wasn't frightened in any way at all. Virgin Films had raised the finance – their first feature – and no one seemed to object to the director being me.

'I think there are very basic skills you need as a director that I acquired by being a continuity girl – a cinematic eye, reading a script and being able to visualise it, having a really good ear for dialogue and a very good rapport with technical crews and actors. I've always loved actors and I have a lot of time for talent.

'I've never encountered real discrimination as a woman in films. My main ambition was always to enjoy what I was doing and as they were "women's jobs", I didn't come across anything like discrimination. As a director, I hand-picked my talented crew and knew of no resentment amongst them. When *Secret*

Places opened in America, it opened very nicely and I had wonderful reviews. The Americans love you to be successful and want to share in it and want you to have more successes. In England, it doesn't apply in the same way. This is just an observation, but I have not been offered a single project here, whereas other directors (male) who have had thumping failures (both critically and at the box office) have continued to direct film after film. American interviewers would say, "I suppose as it's British Film Year, you're the token woman director at all the events." And I just laughed. There's no way I'm even the token anything. I am preparing two feature films, but they're both to be made in America. Frankly, I would prefer to work in England, but I feel that producers I have worked with as a continuity girl find something rather unpleasant about someone stepping out of their "box", especially women. I just put it down to an inherent British characteristic. We women are loved dearly in the film business as long as we're doing our womanly job, in addition, of course, to making the coffee, handing out aspirins and pats on the head. I think it is changing, but it will take a long time. It's a slow process.

'My directing-writing future looks wonderful, but this business is full of vagaries and who knows, one day I might be back doing continuity again and I won't be desolate. I do like the job.'

Sally Potter

☐ Film director
☐ Freelance

Sally Potter is one of the few women in Britain who has managed to raise the funding for a feature-length film, *Gold Diggers*, which was made with an all-female crew. Her previous short film, *Thriller*, attracted a great deal of critical attention not only here, but abroad. Now thirty-five, she is based in London.

» 'I left school when I was fifteen and a couple of years later I went to St Martin's Art School for one year. But what I really wanted to do was make films and at that time there didn't appear to be any film course that I could go to. So I started out basically with an 8mm camera doing any old job and making very short things and I became a member of the London Filmmakers Coop. But I was also involved with a theatre group at the time called Group Events and did a fair amount of dance and choreography with them. I did a course at the London School of Contemporary Dance and worked as a professional dancer for a short period in a company called "Striders" and then had my own company with another woman. During that time, I was still connected somewhat to the Filmmakers Coop, and was gradually making larger films. Then I made a come-back film with *Thriller*, in 1978-9.

'I started out to do *Thriller* with a very small Arts Council grant – £1500 or something – and then overshot that and borrowed money from my bank and got completion grants afterwards. But the final budget was tiny – less than £5,000. There were no labour costs. I was the crew and the performers worked for free. Somebody at the BFI saw and liked *Thriller* and suggested that I put in a proposal. I got together with Rose English and Lindsay Cooper and we drafted an idea and put it in and it sort of grew from there.

'If someone wanted to become a film director, my advice would be to be extremely flexible at all times, seize every opportunity that arose and turn everything to good fortune, including disasters. In *Thriller*, one could say that the budget was disastrously low, but I saw it as a challenge to see what one could do with one light instead of five lights and so on. As I understand it from a lot of women that I've spoken to who have gone into the mainstream or worked at the BBC or something, even that route has its pitfalls. There's the trap then of ending up as a production assistant or taking years and years before one gets to the place where one has some artistic control. On the positive side, however, a job like that would mean more financial security, which gives some peace of mind and also that when you do get some artistic control, there's going to be a sizeable audience. The route that you decide upon must bear some relation to your deepest longings of what you want to do. If your deepest longing is to take control of the medium very quickly and experiment and do what you want to do, then you've got to do it in the independent sector, probably. It would be much better, I think, if one could be much more flexible and move in and out of the mainstream and the independent sector.

'As a director, you need an ability to hold a vision of what the final product might be in your head through a mass of apparently contradictory detail, and also enormous stamina to hold to that. You also need to enjoy the variety of working situations that being a director takes you through – from planning and building dreams up to the actual shoot – and be able to stand the very long hours and the hectic and exciting atmosphere on the set as well as the more private intensity of the cutting room and then having to face the public afterwards. You've got to have a great love for it, and probably a great love for other people's ability, because a lot of the time when you're directing, you haven't got your own hand on the medium so you're bringing out other people's genius.

'On my second film, *Gold Diggers*, everyone on the crew got paid the same rate. I think that was a good, bold statement and it was actually BFI policy at the time as well. Unfortunately, I don't think that equal pay across the board like that, especially when it's so low, really works out fairly, because different people put in different amounts of time and energy. But it's a step in the right direction, away from the idea that some jobs are trivial and some jobs are superbly important. As far as artistic decision-making was concerned, it was very conventional. It wasn't a collectively made film. Everyone had very clear cut ideas of what their job was.

'It's been a very hand-to-mouth existence and still is. Even Peter Greenaway, who made *The Draughtsman's Contract*, had difficulty raising the money for his next feature and I think the employment situation for all independent film-makers is so bad because it's basically not about making a quick buck. But it's true that I haven't yet gone on to make my next feature. There has been some cautious interest expressed but, depending on what the idea is, I think that what tends to happen is that you get pigeon-holed. It's the syndrome of having to prove yourself every time as if for the first time and that's what I'm facing now. In a way, I envy the days when there were film studios and a director could get a sense of continuity of work. It all depends on the capitalist economy, whether it's going to be a money making topic or not, nowadays.'

Mary Williams

☐ Director
☐ Freelance

Mary Williams is a freelance television director who, in the past, has worked for the BBC and for Granada Television, where she directed *Union World*. She is thirty-seven, single and resident in Scotland.

» 'From school, I went to university to read Drama and

American Studies at Hull and I chose a degree that had a television course in the third year because I knew that was what I wanted to do. There were only seven men out of about twenty-five people in my year and what happened was that the women got the chance to do a lot of the technical stuff. I got involved with the film unit and made my first film there. Then I went on to film school at Guildford – the one that's now called the West Surrey College of Art and Design. The most important thing about film school is not that you go in and are deeply creative. The most important thing is that you can have a go at everything, including the technical side which is quite significant later on because you know what you are asking people to do. But the most crucial thing is that you learn how to fight a project through because nobody helps you. I did that for two years, then I got offered a third year (at the college) because I became interested in working with kids on probation and the college wanted to extend its teaching content in that direction. But after two terms of that, I left. It was completely wrong for me.

'I started applying for various things. I interviewed for the Granada Television trainee director scheme and Derek Grainger, who did *Country Matters*, was on the interview board. He said that on no account should I get in on the secretarial side because I'd never move. He asked me, "Whose work do you most admire?" and I said, "Tony Garnett". I didn't get it (the traineeship), but a fortnight after the interview, I got a letter from Tony Garnett saying, "Derek Grainger has written to me about you. Can we have a chat?" For two years, Derek Grainger sent me to see various people he thought could help. [In the meantime, she began applying for jobs as a researcher, but found that most of them required journalistic training and that her drama background was not helping very much.] Derek Grainger sent me to Granada where they were setting up a script unit and I got myself some work reading scripts. I got similar work with Thames. All this reading was done at home and I got very cheesed off with my own company. Someone suggested that there was a route into the BBC where you could go in as a floor assistant, so I applied for that. It turned out that a drama degree was actually a good thing to have for that. But one of the problems I had was that I wasn't sure whether I wanted to do drama or documentary. I had a chat with someone at the BBC and he said that the best thing to do was to take this six-month attachment as a floor assistant and see what I liked best. (An attachment is a temporary appointment.) He said that it's very easy in the BBC to get into the wrong area because once you've applied to one, it's very difficult to apply for another.

'What you do as a floor assistant, basically, is work on lots of different productions. You're doing the lowest of the low, like calling people to the studio (telling the actors when they're wanted on the set). It was obviously much easier for the women who were doing the job than for the men, because nobody had any problems at all about asking women to do things that were menial. But you could see then that the men didn't quite fit with them because they didn't expect men to do something so menial.

'The next progression after that is to become an assistant floor manager. A staff job at that grade came up in Cardiff and because I spoke Welsh, I got that. Then you're in charge of props, rather than people. I'd been in Cardiff as an assistant floor manager for a year before I got my first attachment as a director. I then did various jobs as an acting floor manager in Cardiff while I applied for permanent floor manager and director jobs. I think I must have had about twelve boards (interviews) in about eighteen months. Nothing. Since I'm five foot one and blonde and softly spoken, you can imagine me sitting in front of a BBC board and them saying, "Oh Miss Williams, how do you manage to control the studio floor?" There was a time when I seriously considered that I ought to have my hair razored and dye it black, but I didn't. Then I applied for another attachment as a director in Manchester on children's programmes and got it. I did six months of that, then another six months there working on *The Oxford Road Show*. Then I decided I didn't want to go back to Cardiff, so I resigned, which shocked them rigid, because nobody ever resigned. People in Manchester had said they'd like me to do another six months, but there weren't any staff jobs coming up. So, just because I felt I had to do this, I just sold up in Wales and came up to Manchester and bought a house without having any firm contract at all. I'd been asked to put in an idea for a half-hour programme and was led to believe that I'd be directing it. I learned that summer the hard lesson that there's never any point putting an idea to anybody without typing up the constituent parts. Also, you should hold back part of the research. You never give anybody anything on a plate because what happened was that they used the presenter I suggested, they ended up in Wales like I said, but somebody else was going to be directing it and they'd even hired a different researcher. All I was offered was a few weeks' work doing a lot of fixing for them for the filming in Wales, using the subject matter and presenter I had suggested.

'I then worked on contract for the BBC in Manchester as an assistant producer. Sometimes I had a three-month contract, sometimes six months, but it was altogether for about three years. The BBC will use you twenty-four hours a day. It expects that and it's very easy to get into the way of doing that and very easy to have no other life at all. I decided then that I had to stop working in this way because I had no other life. Without thinking about it, I turned down the next contract and thought, "What am I going to do now?" I then had a year off and looked at the possibility of doing pop promos independently, which I decided against because I'd have had to be in London. I also investigated setting up my own production company. A lot of people are very frustrated by the fact that the BBC has at least a two-year turn around. That is, you put in an idea and then, if it is accepted, it's two years before you ever get anywhere near it (because of the time it takes to go through all the procedures necessary to get an idea into production). Even then, there are no guarantees that you'll be the one who gets to do it. So, it appealed to me to be involved in selling and setting up my own ideas. I spent a long time looking at the business side. I found out that the one area in which women are completely and utterly ignored, is business. I had to buy myself business suits. It all just stuck in my craw. Nobody was interested in the quality of the work, just the price. I got my show reel [a reel of film or video tape showing samples of her work] passed round Granada and went in to see the head of local programmes. He offered a month's contract. So I did a month and then was offered *Union World* and worked on short contracts there for eighteen months or more. The one thing that surprised me about Granada was the number of women who came up and said, "We heard there was a woman director. It's so nice to meet you."

'There are some crews you work with and you don't know them so they start going through the jokes about women directors. The way I always dealt with them was that they could have two hours to do that after which it's obvious to me whether they're actually interested in doing the work or they're more interested in pissing around. My attitude is basically, "All right, you don't want to give your input to this work, so you're going to do what I want." I must say that I've had fewer problems than other female colleagues probably because of the floor manager experience. There is a certain age of man who only knows how to treat women as daughters. You might call it patronising, but there is a certain type of man who, with the best will in the world, does want to help you, but it comes out as, "Let me do that for you." If that is not obstructive, I am quite happy to accept that. I don't think that when you are dealing with a group of people, you go in at a particular level and say, "I'm going to deal with everybody the same way." People are not the same and people have different backgrounds and I think it would be foolish to treat everybody as if they all know what feminism is about. Basically, as a director, I've got to get people to do what I want them to do.'

8 The editor

1 Job description

It is possible to specialise in either film or video editing, but many editors – particularly in broadcasting – work on both because a number of companies are in the process of changing from one medium to the other or to a mixture of film and video tape production. In both, the editor works to arrange the shots in a sequence and relationship to each other to achieve the desired effect. In film editing, the various shots will be physically glued or taped together, but in video editing, the scenes which are selected will be re-recorded on to another video tape so that they link up exactly as required. For both systems, a method of identifying the shots has to be used. In film, there are usually numbers which appear every so often along the edges; in video, there is often an on-going time code measured in hours, minutes, seconds and number of frames, all of which is electronically recorded on to the tape and can be seen with the use of special de-coding equipment.

In film editing, a degree of manual dexterity and meticulousness are required because the editor actually handles the film. Even though she usually works with a copy of the film (known as a workprint) at first, great care has to be taken not to tear or damage it, or to get dirt on the surface. Often thin white cotton gloves are worn to keep the film as clean as possible. Editors may be required to work with different gauges of film, such as 16mm, 35mm, or 70mm, which refers to the width of the film. In order to edit the film, you must be able to see what you are cutting. You may do this working at a manual bench, cranking reels of film by hand so that it passes over a small viewer in front of you. Alternatively, you may use a motorised editing bench, such as a Moviola or a Steinbeck, which runs the film at a consistent speed and projects the image on to a screen about the dimensions of a medium-sized television set.

Although the sound track can be recorded directly on to the film (this method is known as single system), it is more often recorded onto $\frac{1}{4}$ inch audio tape and is later transferred on to magnetic tape. This must then be synchronised with the film. If you've ever seen a film being made, you may have noticed a small contraption like a small blackboard on which is written details of the scene to be shot and which has a clapper attached to the top or bottom. This is used at the beginning of each shot to identify it and to make a loud noise. Thus, when the editor has to match the sound and pictures, she matches the point on the film at which she sees the clapper make contact, with the loud noise on the sound track. When these are synchronised, all the sound and pictures that follow should also match for the length of that shot. Frequently, however, there will be several sound tracks which have to be mixed together. For example, the dialogue may be on one track, the music on another and the sound effects (such as thunder, or the wind howling) on another. Evntually, these will all be mixed on to one track. Then, when the editing has been completed, the sound and picture will be combined on to the same piece of film, by translating the magnetic sound track into an optical one, i.e. a visible system of lines which runs alongside the picture at the edge of the film, which the film projector will translate into sound.

Video editing is usually carried out on some sort of console from which all the relevant video tape machines may be controlled. Some consoles are mini-computers with a keyboard rather like a typewriter. The sound may have been recorded directly on to the video tape along with the pictures, although in some productions, the sound may have been recorded on audio tape as for film and later transferred to the video tape.

One of the advantages of video over film is that it is immediate. You can view scenes as soon as they have been shot and the sound tracks can be mixed and synchronised with the pictures during the editing process. It is also possible to add many sophisticated special effects at this stage which could only be accomplished on film by using complex and expensive techniques at the lab.

Regardless of which medium is used, however, the editor must make the same aesthetic decisions. The degree of autonomy which she is allowed varies from one job to the next, even when she is a fully-fledged editor. In some instances, she may be left to make all the creative decisions herself. In other cases, the director, producer or presenter – and sometimes even the star actor – may call the shots, leaving the editor with very little scope. In an ideal situation, however, she will be able to collaborate with whoever else is involved. The director will know what effect she wishes to achieve and roughly in which order the shots should appear. Hopefully, the editor can then suggest ways to create the right effect and will have a sense of the timing and rhythm which work best. She might, for example, recommend using the close-up of a scene, rather than the long shot which was filmed from a distance. The end product may be a result of compromise, but the audience should never be conscious of the editing techniques being used. They should be seamless and contribute to, rather than distract from the action.

2 Hours and working conditions

These vary considerably. If you worked in broadcasting, you might have regular eight-hour days, or you could be expected to work shifts if the editing rooms were only available in the evening. You might also be required to put in overtime, in order to complete a programme according to schedule. If you worked in the feature film industry, then your hours might be more flexible, but you might still find yourself working late at night to finish the editing on time.

One disadvantage of this job, according to some people, is that you work in a darkened, windowless room for most of the time. Looking at flickering images all day can be a strain, also. The amount of travel involved with this job varies from assignment to assignment. The average television editor always works in the same place and is rarely called upon to be away overnight. If you work on feature films, however, you may be expected to travel extensively if the film is shot on location and the director wants you there so she can see how the shots cut together as the film is being made.

This is an area in which women have long been accepted as assistants but have found it difficult to gain promotion as editors. That situation is gradually changing in broadcasting. Discrimination still lingers on in the film industry, however, despite the fact that there have been many outstanding female editors in the past, as well as at the present. The challenge is there for any young woman with the ambition and perseverance to want to be a successful feature film editor.

3 Qualifications and characteristics required

There are obviously some basic physical requirements that must be met, such as having good eyesight (with or without glasses) and accurate colour vision (i.e. you're not colour blind). You must also be able to hear well and have excellent eye-hand coordination, because you will be handling narrow strips of film, and operating complex keyboards for video editing.

As far as personality goes, you should be someone who is fairly organised. It can be a nightmare if you can't keep track of all the individual scenes that you will need, and the job is certainly made more difficult if you don't work methodically. You must be able to concentrate intently on the sound and images for extended periods of time – and sit working in a darkened room for hours without becoming restless.

You should also be imaginative and capable of appreciating how different effects can be achieved by altering a sequence of shots, or changing the pace of the edits, using longer or shorter scenes. It is important to have a sense of rhythm, both visual and auditory, although this is something you could probably develop if you worked at it. That should enable you to know instinctively when to cut from one shot to another, when to slow the action down, or when to speed it up with a succession of quick changes of scene. It also helps if you are sensitive to the mood and emotional temperature of the scene, so that you know when to cut to maximise the dramatic impact.

You may have to work under pressure at times, either to meet deadlines or because the director or producer is being very demanding. It helps if you get along easily with people and can work as part of a team, because much of the art of editing involves being able to interpret the director's ideas so that they work, as well as persuading her to accept what is possible. Obviously, this can require a great deal of tact, at times.

There is less emphasis placed on having formal educational qualifications in this job than in some others. It is more important to have the necessary talent and skill. But it is advisable to get as good an education as you can because many television companies prefer you to have at least O-levels. They may also look for someone who already knows about broadcasting and has production experience, so it may help to take a degree in film and television production, or to have worked for a television company in some capacity already.

4 How to become an editor

As stated above, you should acquire as many educational qualifications as you can, at least to O-level and preferably to A-level or degree standard. Since you must spend several years as an assistant first, which can be frustrating if you have visions of yourself as a great creative artist, some people recommend that you enter the profession straight from school. A college degree, however, particularly in English or Television or Film Production could give you valuable grounding in technique and aesthetics, as well as, in some instances, giving you the opportunity to make your own film.

There is obviously great competition for jobs as assistant editor. You must, therefore, be able to demonstrate that you are really interested. Watch films and television programmes to see how they are edited. Learn about still photography, because that can help you to understand about the composition of a shot as well as teaching you about different kinds of film. It can also help you to become sensitive to differences in colour, which could be invaluable later. Read everything you can about editing, such as Edward Dmytryk's *On Film Editing* (1984) or Karel Reisz and Gavin Miller's *The Technique of Film Editing* (1974). Finally, you should get as much practical experience as you can. There may be an amateur film-making group in your area which has access to basic editing equipment and would let you cut some of their footage. Likewise, there are many schools, colleges and community centres which have video editing equipment which may provide another opportunity to practise the skills you will need. When you have prepared yourself in this way and, ideally, have some samples of your work to show, then you should approach television and film companies asking for a job as an assistant. If your ambition is to work in feature films, then you should approach the editors directly, because they often have a big say in who is chosen to be their assistants. A list of names can be obtained from ACTT or can be found in trade directories such as *Kemps Film and Television Yearbook*.

Alex Anderson

☐ Film editor
☐ Freelance

Alex Anderson is a Canadian who settled in this country several years ago and now works in London as a freelance film editor. Many of the films and programmes which she works on are destined for Channel Four. She is in her early thirties.

» 'I graduated with a BA in History in 1977 and I went from there to do research in television. Those kinds of jobs in Canada aren't as competitive, I don't think, as they are here. So I worked in television in a very commercial sector and found it not very satisfying to work as a researcher. I was being asked to come up with ideas and do a lot of the work of putting the programme together but someone else's overview was very firmly preventing me from having any real freedom. I felt very frustrated, but while working as a researcher, I obviously met a lot of technicians. I think the thing that appealed to me most about their jobs was the fact that they were freelance, while I was tied to a job and having to kowtow to a boss. I was really

attracted to the whole freelance way of life.
Immediately, I was drawn to editing, rather than
camera or sound, because I thought you have more
time to work things out, it was more intellectually
interesting and the freedom of having a skill really
appealed to me. If you're a woman, if you're just selling
yourself on your patter, your personality, and your
ability to fit into a production team, which is what
research is about, you're a lot more compromised.
There's a lot more things to do with how you look,
how you can appear in a situation, how you can
manage other people etc. With a technical skill,
however, I thought I would be slightly more distanced
from that whole thing. I sort of nobbled the editors for
about a year while I was working as a researcher trying
to get them to teach me everything they knew. They let
me stay in the cutting room after I finished work
because they used to work late into the night. I picked
up the basics of editing from them. At one stage, one of
the editors was looking for an assembly editor and I
left my research job to do that. It lasted about six
months and by the end of it, I was actually doing some
editing. I was obviously just very, very keen. I must
have been impossible. I thought editing was the answer
to all my creative frustrations and my desire to live an
independent life and so I was badgering them
incessantly to give me more opportunities. I also
suffered from over-confidence. When I first got this job
as an assembly editor, I just thought I could do
everything. It's only since I've been doing it for all these
years, that I realise how inept I really am. By the end of
the six months, I decided that if I wanted to learn this
skill properly, I wanted to learn it in a place that
actually had a better reputation than Canada did. I had
access to work permits in Britain because my father's
English and so I decided to come here in 1979.
   'I had a few names of people from Canadian

contacts so I just got on the phone and walked up and down Wardour Street (headquarters of the film industry), going into cutting rooms and saying "Do you need any assistants?" which was horrendous. It was actually one of the most excruciating things I've ever had to do. It really is most humiliating, and the sheer terror of not being able to get a job and not being able to pay the rent, and there's nobody around to reassure you that you will get a job or you can do the job. Anyway, I was very lucky and managed to find a job in about a week. I just happened to walk in at the right time because the assistant had gotten ill that morning and this woman said, "Can you start this afternoon?" So I did. I think I was less experienced than she had hoped, but I learned very quickly.

'I think it was because I came from Canada where they didn't really have assistants, that I didn't have much patience with spending a long time as an assistant editor. I didn't see assistant editing as a professional step, which it is. I think I suffered somewhat because of it when I got into editing because I didn't have the basics all sorted out yet. But I was adamant about getting into editing and badgered practically everyone I could get a hold of. I would cut anything as well, as long as it wasn't pornography. So very quickly, I started doing corporate films and little films for the non-broadcast area. I also got my union ticket. I got my ticket in a quite straightforward way, but I think the fact that my name is Alex made it easier. I think that's why the editorial section let me in, I really do. I think if they had known I was a woman it would have been different, because I've heard that women who apply to the editorial section get all sorts of queries about their experience and how they got the job and so on.

'Shortly after that, I started editing on short films and the director was actually a former editor so I learned a lot about editing through him. Then I started getting broadcast television jobs, mainly through word of mouth. I'd meet people and show them, in my North American way, that I was dead keen. The English are a bit embarrassed to be that keen. I didn't know about that then, so I impressed people, I guess, and they'd give me work. Since Channel Four started up, I've worked almost exclusively for them.

'I think it's slightly worrying for me at this stage in my career, that I seem to do a lot of films about women. Twice it's happened to me recently that people have asked, "What are you working on?", and when I tell them, they say, "Oh, is it an all-woman crew?" It's men who have asked me that and I think they meant that if the crew was mixed, I probably wouldn't have got the job. I find that quite irritating. I get the feeling, when I talk to male colleagues, that Channel Four and the feminist sector is where I should stay. Having said that, however, I would like to work with men on films on general issues. I must say that I'm quite spoiled now and expect to go to work and be able to voice my honest opinions about things and actually be myself. I can remember the days when I was a researcher when that was a big problem. I couldn't be myself.

'In my position now, I can tell the production company how long it's going to take me to do a job, although there's obviously guidelines. It used to be about ten weeks to do an hour-long programme for the BBC. Now it's eight weeks to do an hour-long programme. When I talk to the production company, I usually say that I'm not into doing overtime. As a principle, I'm not into killing myself to get this film done. I prefer to extend the schedule by a week and then not incur any overtime on the budget. Obviously, there are times when you have to work till 9 p.m. or 10 p.m. Most people I know work like that. There are the odd occasions when you have to cancel arrangements and work late. I don't have a family, so that doesn't cause problems. I think most of my friends work in the same industry and most of them are single and everybody accepts the disruption. The thing when you're working as a freelance technician is that you actually have a lot of control over the conditions of work. Things like where I want to work, what cutting room I want to use, who I want to work with and the business of whether we kill ourselves working overtime can basically be worked out.

'The main skill required if you want to get regular employment, is diplomacy. But to be a really good creative editor you need an understanding of what effect the images have and a real sense of rhythm and how to unfold a story. It's not an in-born thing and it's not like some people can't do it. It's very much a learned thing but you've got to get into the rhythm of film. That's the artistic side of it and I'm still working on that side of it because it takes years to get really good. Yet I still get jobs, so you don't need to know *everything* right away. It can be quite a strain in terms of communication because the director is trying to tell you what her ideas for the film are, and you can't say immediately, "It's impossible". It's a question of compromising all the time, saying, "That's what they really want, but let's see if I can make it work this way." The director comes in from shooting with all the anxieties and fears of what went wrong on the shooting and you've got to appear calm. But that's the sort of challenge I love.'

Ann Coates

☐ Film editor
☐ Freelance

Ann Coates is considered to be one of the best feature

film editors in the country. She has cut such outstanding movies as *Lawrence of Arabia*, *The Elephant Man*, *Murder on the Orient Express*, *Becket*, *Greystoke* and *Lady Jane*. Now in her mid-fifties, she has three grown-up children and is based in London.

» 'I decided I wanted to be a film director when I was at school really, but it wasn't very easy to get into the industry. I started reading up books on films and studying them and editing seemed the most interesting job for a woman to do. A lot of directors had come through editing. I had an uncle who worked in distribution and he eventually got me a job in Religious Films, making *Sunday Thoughts* and sending out films to churches. Before that, I did some nursing and worked in a racing stables. Religious Films was a non-union organisation, but then ACTT came and made all of us join. Once I was in the union I was able to get a job as a second assistant editor at Pinewood. That was about 1950. Then I got a job over at Denham on *The History of Mr Polly* as a first assistant. After a while, I heard of a job for an editor on a filmed adaptation of *Pickwick Papers*. They were looking for a young editor because they didn't want to pay much money and they wanted to give somebody a break, that sort of thing. The editor I was working with at the time had been offered it and I said, "Why don't you put my name up?" So he did, and I went to the interview and got the job. I was about twenty-five then. I had ups and downs as an editor. Then I got a break and did *The Horse's Mouth* with Alec Guinness so I got the chance to do *Tunes of Glory*. All these things are luck, really. I met a friend in Harrods, towards the end of that, and he said David Lean was doing a whole week's tests of Albert Finney for *Lawrence of Arabia*. I asked if they had anybody to cut the tests and he said he didn't think so and I said, "Well, put my name up". They rang me up on the Monday and said they'd give me £50 to cut the tests of Albert Finney, which I did. He turned down the part but in the meantime, David Lean asked me if I'd like to cut the film. That was my big break.

'I didn't really mind not becoming a director. I was married to a film director and I thought that one in the house was enough. I've had one or two offers to direct but bringing up the children and editing was all I could really cope with. You've got to give so much more to be a director. I have produced one picture, *The Medusa Touch*. I liked producing but I prefer editing. But I think that maybe eventually I will end up producing.

'To be a good editor, you need a lot of patience and I think you need to be very creative too. You've very often got to build on other people's creativeness. You've got to be able to see what the director's aiming at, and be able to do that for him or her, even when they can't explain *how* they want it done, only *what* they want done. I think film editing is really a flair. Sometimes you have it and sometimes you don't. You need a lot of rhythm and a lot of timing and a dramatic kind of feeling for situations and a lot of emotion, I think, which is a thing that people lack in editing sometimes. They don't cut with enough emotion. They don't go enough for the emotion in the faces of people and in the eyes of the actors. They cut because it's a good place to cut, rather than because it's the right emotional place to cut.

'I've been away in China for three weeks and I got about five letters when I got home from very interesting people wanting jobs. My first criterion would be that they show an interest in film – that they go to the cinema and are interested in film-making. The boy I took on last time had been to college and had actually started his own film school within the college. I'd look for people that are hard-working, keen and with a good sense of humour – people that I would think would have something to contribute to the film industry. I try not to take people who are just coming in for the money or because it's a good job. I think we need to bring in new young people. In films, we're very inclined to take in people just because they've got relations who can help them in instead of taking in people who are really keen. I like them when they want to be a director. I think everybody should come in with an aim to be a director or a producer because I think that shows they're ambitious. I wish women would come in more. I'm not a particular feminist really and I have found no discrimination in my job at all. But I don't think that the women over here seem very ambitious in editing. There's enormous scope for women editors. In America, a lot of the top editors are women and in Italy and France it's the same, but in England there are practically none. If you want to be something badly enough, you get yourself there. I always saw myself as an editor and I kept putting myself forward. I really was hardly ready to cut *Pickwick Papers* when I did it. Everyone said I was mad but I said it's my one break and I'm going to hang on to it. People don't seem to have that kind of push.

'As a mother, it was my own choice not to try for directing. The whole film falls apart at 8.30 a.m. if the director isn't there. As an editor, if one of the children was ill and I went in a couple of hours later, it didn't really matter. I would always put my children before my work. But the demands of the job do encroach on my private life up to a point. You have to give and take. I've been freelance now for many years so that I can take off two or three months between films. When the children were very young, I took them on location with me and when they were older, I turned down certain films for the children's sake. If it's possible, it's best to be on the location, cutting the film as it arrives from the lab.

'The only way to get started is to write around. Everybody's doing it so you're in a long line, but that is the only way you can do it. But I think, if it's possible, that you should try to get into commercials and advertising because they have a large turnover of people. If you're lucky enough to get into a company that turns out a Hugh Hudson or an Alan Parker, they will take you along with them to feature films; or if it's a company that employs feature film directors, you can get yourself in with them that way. It's just a question of trying and trying. I'm not sure about the film schools. I think there's a lot to be said for them. But I would think that if you go to film school about twenty-four or -five, which is the usual age, then after two or three years there you won't want to be a second assistant when you come out. You're too old I think, because the job's not that interesting if you're a second assistant. But there's no way that you can get into the business really other than as a second assistant, so you want to be around eighteen or nineteen. The way to do that then is to write around or maybe even go round. If I want a trainee, then I'll go to those lists of letters, and I'll pick out half a dozen to interview.

'I love this job. It's my job and it's my hobby. I love film. I love going to the cinema. It still has the same magic that it had when I was going to school. It's worth overcoming the obstacles to get in.'

Rhona Mitchell

□ Film/PSC* editor
□ Freelance

Rhona Mitchell grew up in the North of Scotland and has worked in film editing for various television companies around the country. She has now trained as a PSC editor and is working on contract with the BBC in Aberdeen.

Now twenty-eight, she is single and has no children.

» 'I didn't start off intending to do television or anything like it, really. I suppose I was slightly rebellious at school and therefore left at sixteen without many qualifications. My first job was as a drawing office assistant, until I realised what an awful lot of my time was being taken up with dancing and dramatics, so I decided to do drama. I eventually got enough qualifications together, working in my own time, to get into a drama course at Aberdeen College of Education. It was a four-year teaching course and I got off the on-stage things very quickly and into directing *via* choreography. Then in second year, we did television as a subject and that really got me going. You were allowed to operate the cameras but it was the vision mixing that got me. I decided that this was what I really wanted to do but I really didn't have a clue how to get in. I applied for every job that came up anywhere and just kept sending CVs to people and went into Grampian Television a lot because I was in the area. In between times, I was doing temporary work backstage in theatre. Then, within months of graduating, Grampian Television actually phoned me up and said they had a job they thought might suit me and asked if I would be interested in coming in for an interview. The job was as a trainee assistant film editor. My film background was non-existent, but I did at least have the experience of knowing how a television programme was made and so on. It was a supposedly a nine-month training but they desperately needed people, so after five months, I was made up to assistant. I did quite a lot of work on my own. I think that's the main thing. You have to push and you have to be willing to work. Nobody's going to hand you anything on a plate and it's not easy. Because it was a small company, it was really advantageous for me. You did get pushed on to do editing much more quickly than you would anywhere else. After about two years, I decided to move and three jobs came up. Central Television was the first interview that came up and I went along and really liked the place. The people were friendly. It was immense and slightly frightening but I decided to go for it and I got that job.

'Luckily, I'm a very organised person which I think you have to be in film. You have to be very quick; you have to be efficient; you have to remember things. People would be gone at 10 p.m. and if I felt I didn't know how to do something, I would be in and out of the other editing rooms, finding out how each other assistant did that job. We (the editor and I) worked on immense projects. There was something like 50,000 feet of film coming into my cutting room, which I had to organise. I just watched a lot and picked up as much as I could. Central had approximately thirty cutting rooms in Birmingham. I organised the whole room for the editor. I cleaned everything – cleaned the machines, replaced the bulbs and made sure everything was working. I always got in an hour before the editor. I had to have that room organised before the editor got there, I felt. That was what made you a better assistant. All the Chinagraphs were sharpened and in their proper place, whatever colour of marker he wanted was there, rolls of film were clearly marked, shelves were labelled and I knew where everything could be got. He'd say, "Find the shot of such and such", and I'd know where to go. Really, it's a matter of getting a method that's going to work for you. I feel that anyone can be a good enough assistant by having a good organising ability, asking heaps of questions and just being there. Because it was such a big project, our room had two Steinbecks and I would do a lot of assembly editing jobs.* And then I got on to doing what was really the dubbing editor's job. I would lay track* for part two of the programme while the editor would lay part one. I even had to find out how to go about ordering sound effects. In that particular project, we were working with twelve separate sound tracks.

After I left Central, I went back to Scotland for various reasons. I'd been at Central a year, but in that year I didn't have any leave. I worked most weekends as well as working during the week from 8 a.m. till whenever. I went freelance and spent most of my days at STV and then Yorkshire Television and later at BBC, where I got longer contracts rather than odd days and weeks here and there. I seem to be on never-ending contracts now with BBC in Aberdeen at the moment. They employed me first of all as a freelance film editor but they were finishing up film in Aberdeen and going on to what the BBC call PSC production*, which is called ENG equipment at most of the ITV companies. That was a fantastic opportunity to train on that machinery because I do believe that an awful lot of the work is going to go across to that. There was somebody posted from Glasgow to get the PSC off the ground at the same time that I was there as a film editor. So, instead of going home at 6 p.m., I would go through to PSC and see the transmissions being done and if ever I had a free moment I would be through watching the editor doing his job. I told them I was very interested in doing this and I believed I could do it if I was given more time.

'It is becoming more and more an engineering job. At the moment, it's about half-and-half editors and engineers. You could become an editor, particularly on PSC, without any technical knowledge at all. But I'm the type of person who would like to know as much as I can. I am being sent on an engineering course at my request. It won't be easy for me because I don't think I was ever that way inclined. But I believe you can incline yourself to do anything you want to. That's probably the key to the whole thing – just glean as much information as possible.

'I strongly believe, however, that you need the right personality – the ability to deal with people and a strength to know what you want. You need imagination and a certain amount of creativity, even in terms of sound. People often forget about sound and think it's only the picture that matters, but it's not. There's an awful lot you can get from books to begin with, but after that there's a sense of "Well, let's see what we can do by going against all the rules". I love that special buzz you get from a news edit. You have to have all your faculties about you. You're looking at four monitors at once; you're trying to judge the quality of the picture; you're thinking about the sound at the same time which is very different from film. In a news edit, you have to edit it all at once because there's no time.

'I've never encountered any discrimination, but perhaps there is a general feeling of always looking to you as the little girl of the department. That's a common one and you feel that you have to break out of that. I don't feel that I have to prove that I can work harder because I'm a woman, although I'm the type of person who would do that anyway. At Central, there must have been about fifty in the editing department, but there were only four females and they were all assistants. I do believe, however, that if I'd stayed at Central very much longer, there certainly were opportunities for editors' jobs which I'd been told of.

'It would be very difficult for me to have a boyfriend who didn't understand this business – it would be impossible, in fact. Some days, I come home and all I can do is sit around open-mouthed for a whole, with nothing in my brain whatsoever. The stress can be incredible in the job and there's also the amount of hours I work. I can go for weeks without a day off. So a personal life becomes very hard. But I certainly wouldn't like to give this job up.'

Glossary

assembly editing   when the various scenes of a film are joined up together in the right order but are not yet finely edited.

lay track   to synchronise and edit the sound track to match the corresponding picture.

PSC production   this is a BBC term which stands for portable single camera production.

9 The lighting electrician

1 Job description

Lighting electricians are the people who wire and set up the lights used for illuminating a studio or location set. Most studios have what is called a lighting grid, which is a criss-cross structure of metal bars overhanging the studio space, from which brackets holding the lights can be hung as required. The brackets allow the lights to be tilted to almost any angle. Some lighting grids can be raised and lowered to attach the lights, but often the electricians have to work on the grid at considerable heights from the ground. Lights may also be placed on portable stands. These may be used for outside broadcasts and on location, although the lights may also be set up on scaffolding or on a gantry, which is a framework rather like the arm of a crane from which lights can be suspended overhead. The lighting electrician may also have to hold and operate a small hand-held light if, for example, she is sent out with a news crew which has to move fast and which must, therefore, use portable equipment. In addition to rigging lights, the electrician might also operate a lighting console, from which all the lights in the studio can be controlled. (The job of deciding *where* the lights should be set up and how they should be used to create mood etc. is usually done by a lighting director on big productions or by the lighting camera-woman or man.)

2 Hours and working conditions

The hours can vary enormously, depending on the job. In television, most electricians work on a shift pattern and will be expected to do overtime as required. If they work on outside broadcasts or on location, they may have to travel away from home and be gone overnight. Electricians working on feature films could be gone for months at a time, working in all weathers, far from home. It can be a very challenging job, particularly when you have to use your initiative to solve difficulties you encounter when a production is shot outside the studio. There can also be a lot of pressure on electricians when, as often happens, they have to work to a tight schedule so that they don't hold up the rest of the crew. Another potential source of stress is the fact that most female electricians work in an all-male environment. The union which organises in this grade, the EETPU (see p.33 for more details) has only two female lighting electricians amongst its members, although there are many women working as electricians in other areas, including the theatre.

3 Qualifications and characteristics required

Occasionally, television companies will advertise for trainee electricians, but more usually, jobs are for qualified and experienced electricians. So it is advisable to obtain City and Guilds qualifications. (Your local technical college probably runs courses for these.) Then you should get some work experience, preferably in the theatre.

A lighting electrician needs to be both meticulous and a fast worker. The safety of others as well as the quality of a production depend on her work, but she will probably have some tight deadlines to meet if she is not to hold up the whole production. She needs to be a practical person with some initiative, who can confront problems and methodically set about solving them. She may have to work on her own at times, but she should also be someone who can work as part of a team. Lighting can often only be done on a trial and error basis, as the electricians, camera operators and lighting director strive to obtain the effect that is required. So the electrician needs to be patient, as the director changes her mind for the umpteenth time about what she wants, and the lights have to be moved yet again.

It is a fairly 'physical' job, which involves lifting equipment and climbing up to the grid or on to scaffolding. So you need to be reasonably fit and active and able to cope with heights, although you don't have to be outstandingly strong.

4 How to become a lighting electrician

Get as good a general education as possible, with at least an O-level in Physics and preferably in Maths and English as well. Then write to all the television companies and enquire about openings for apprentice electricians. If you do start as a trainee, then it will take about four years, combining periods at college with on-the-job training before you will be qualified. The ITV companies accept trainees at age sixteen. A list of addresses can be found in Appendix B, p.333. If you aren't accepted for work with a television company, you should enroll for a course leading to qualifications as an electrician. Many technical colleges run classes leading to City and Guilds qualification. When you graduate, you can apply again for jobs with television companies or try to find work in the theatre, where you can gain valuable experience. Jobs may be advertised in your local press or in publications such as *Stage and Television Today*, *Broadcast* or *Audio*

Visual. In the meantime, you may find the following books will provide a useful background to lighting techniques: *Professional Lighting Handbook* (1984) by Verne and Sylvia Carlson, or *Television Lighting Methods* (1982a) and *The Technique of Lighting for Television and Motion Pictures* (1982b), both written by Gerald Millerson.

Nuala Campbell

☐ Lighting electrician
☐ Freelance

Nuala Campbell is a freelance lighting electrician, working mainly in television and based in Bolton. At thirty-two, she is a single parent with a teenage daughter who attends boarding school.

» 'I left school at fifteen and I went to a technical college to try and get O-levels. Not that I got any. My father took me away after about six months because he thought it was a waste of money because I was a girl. My father actually left home just after that, so I could have gone back but by that time I'd already broken with it. For a long time, I did a lot of jobs in factories as well as bar lounge work on the ships and working in restaurants. Basically, it was unskilled women's work and I did that for years. I used to sit on the factory line, packing goods or whatever, and watch the men. They were maintenance workers, electricians and things and I used to think I'd really like to do that, but I never actually thought it was possible. I lived in the South of England while I was married and had my daughter. Eventually, I moved up North, having made up my mind definitely to leave my husband and become a single parent. It was at that point that I realised that I was going to need some sort of skill or trade that would last me till I retired if I was going to have to keep the family. I'm not academic, and eventually I decided to become an electrician because that combined using your head and your hands. I didn't know anything about electrics. I'd never used an electric drill. I hadn't a clue how a house was wired or anything like that, but I met a woman electrician who worked in the theatre and basically I thought well, if she can do it, I can do it. I went to the local technical college for a three-month introductory course on electrics, electronics, metal work and all that sort of thing. It was for unemployed young people basically. They were all young lads of about sixteen and I was twenty-two by then.

While I was on that course, I applied for a government training scheme and the time that I spent on the course was knocked off the waiting period. In the meantime, I went back and started working in a pub until I got back into the Electricity Board training centre. That lasted about ten months, then I got my City and Guilds and got a couple of distinctions and credits. When I left there, I tried to get a job. That was a joke, an absolute joke. I was short-listed for about a hundred interviews. I think they just wanted to see what a woman electrician looked like. They kept telling me it wasn't possible for a woman to do it. Some of them just laughed. Some of them said they didn't have women's toilets. Some of them just said it wasn't the right place for a woman. They were the usual sorts of reasons. So I started working for myself, re-wiring houses and things. Although I got quite adept at that, I realised I wasn't actually learning very much. So I decided to apply for jobs again. This time I got a job quite quickly, with a local industrial contractors who were really good. They didn't ask any stupid questions like, "Do you mind getting dirty?", "What are you going to do with your children?" – all this sort of business. They just accepted that if I thought I could do the job, that was that, and they'd take me on. They were great. So I worked for them for a few years doing industrial contracting work. I got quite a wide experience on quite large jobs. Eventually I felt it was time to move on, however, so I went back to being self-employed again and was doing light industrial contracts. Then the employment situation in the North got a lot worse and there were a lot of electricians coming on the market because they were being made redundant. I was not earning very much money, which is what you expect when you start a business, but I could see that the future did not look very rosy. I applied to Granada Television a few times. I didn't get anywhere. But eventually, I was telling somebody I was interested in doing television and it turned out a friend of hers was a producer, so she said, "Oh, I'll mention it to her". A couple of days later I got a phone call because they were looking for a woman electrician. So that was how I started.

'You have to be strong and not frightened of heights because you go up on cat walks. You have to be able to get on with all different sorts of people. I did encounter discrimination but the union backed me up. I think women would be much more welcomed into the industry now, but obviously there was a lot of resistance to a woman lighting electrician – funnily enough, more so than I ever encountered on building sites or in a factory. I find it quite hard to figure out why. I think it's something to do with the fact that, in the film industry, electricians and grips are the macho element. I think that somehow the idea of a woman doing that job disturbs quite a lot of them. But the men that I work with, have always been great. Once they've worked with me or seen my work, they've been very accepting. I'm very thick skinned. I'm not a lady. My language is quite capable of being just as coarse as theirs and I can swear along with the best of people. I do find pin-ups and calendars a bit distasteful but obviously, over ten years, I've got used to them. I mean, every time I go into our tea room and I see the calendar, I turn the face to the wall. Occasionally, if I can work up the energy, I'll write graffiti on it. They know I don't like it, but they laugh. It's hard to explain. They're nice blokes, but all men are sexist. I don't expect anything else of them. But they're okay. I do tend to separate my social life from my work life quite severely, though.

'I'm very lucky because I've actually got a council grant for my daughter to go to boarding school. It's absolutely brilliant and I can't feel grateful enough. I was having to get child minders for her to live in the house while I was going away to work. She resented them, even though some of them were friends that she's known before. She gave them a terrible time and she was unhappy because everything was unsettled. That was when I was working freelance, so I might get rung up and have somebody say, "You've got to be in Huddersfield tomorrow morning by 8 a.m." So I got to the stage where I had to choose between carrying on working and trying to get her into a boarding school which she really wanted to do, or giving up my job totally. Somebody told me about applying to the local education people for a grant and I did that. It takes a long time, but they were great and they gave me the grant. So she's really happy. Childcare is a real problem in a job like this. The main thing about this job is that you don't know what you're going to be doing, so it's very hard to make a date to see friends. I might leave the house at 6.30 a.m. and I might not get back till after midnight. An eight-hour day is very rare. The hourly rate isn't that different from other electricians' jobs (about £4.75 an hour), but you make it up in overtime. I earn a lot of money, yes, but I work very, very hard for it, with very long hours.

'If you're a woman and want to be an electrician, it's much easier to get to be an ordinary electrician first. Now there are men who go straight into lighting, but I think it's easier for the men to be accepted like that. I would advise any girl who wants to become an electrician to apply to the BBC, because they, as far as I know, do not have one female electrician. It's about time.

'I got where I am now through the support of my women friends, who were wonderful. They taught me my sums for my City and Guilds, they taught me how to drive, they gave me the confidence to keep going when I felt really depressed. I think it makes a really big difference if you've got that behind you. I wouldn't have done it without them and it's a great job for a woman and I want more women to do it.'

Pat Smith

□ Lighting electrician
□ ITV

Pat Smith is a thirty-six-year-old lighting electrician with Thames Television at their Euston studios. She is single and has no children.

» 'The one thing I did not want to do when I left school was work in an office, so I found myself a job as a laboratory technician and came to London in 1969. I needed additional income, however, and because I had an interest in theatre, I was looking for a part-time job in the West End. The job that I eventually found was a job as a follow spot operator. [A follow spot is the light that follows the main character wherever they move on stage.] Gradually, I got more and more involved in theatre and decided I'd like to make it a full-time job. It's supposedly a closed shop but I don't think it is anymore. There were already women working as electricians in the West End at that time. There is a City and Guilds Installation Electricians Course which is run by a London-based college which is especially adapted to theatre electricians. The full-time course was one year's duration and the part-time course was two years' duration. This particular course also included attachments to various theatres. I got a job in one of the theatres that I was attached to.

'In the theatre, the house electrician looks after everything, including the central heating, the air conditioning system etc. You can be called on to do quite a lot of things. In television, it's much more strongly unionised – it is a closed shop, in fact – and the job isn't quite as diverse. It requires a different sort of knowledge, really, because you're working with different equipment. The essence in television, really, is speed and efficiency. In the theatre, if a rig is staying for a long time, it's usually put in very carefully. If you're filming or putting something in for television, you have to work quickly. The equipment is heavier and I don't have to do any maintenance work.

'I got into television because I knew an electrician who worked for Thames TV and they employed me on a couple of occasions when they required an all-woman crew. That way, I found out about the requirements of television and film and so I didn't come into it cold. I think my technical background helped. I'd done Physics and Maths which helped with the college work. It's desirable to have a fairly calm temperament because things can get a little bit fraught. You can end up working under quite considerable pressure. Usually, time is your greatest enemy. You always run out of time, no matter how carefully a production is planned. It is by no means terribly complex technically, but that sort of background is necessary for safe working practice, I would think. You have to think in terms of electrical loading. You have to think in terms of how much you can use from a particular electrical supply. You may also have to work on rigs which are quite high off the ground. The grid on Drury Lane Theatre is eighty feet high, and when we're on outside broadcasts, we work off ladders or off high gantries. I don't mind heights. It's not something I've ever really bothered about. Even if you don't like heights, I think you can get used to it. It's probably better though, if you can cope with heights.

'I think there was a certain amount of reservation when I joined Thames, mostly due to the fact that the men were concerned that there might be physical limitations in the amount of work that a woman was able to do. "Can she carry 5K lamps or .2 cable?" These are the sort of questions they ask. There's not very much that I find I am unable to do, actually. Anyway, there are always a lot of people on the crew and it's not reckoned to be necessary for one man to carry a 5 Kilowatt lamp on his own. It's reckoned to be a job for two. I can just about carry one on my own, but I'd never be expected to do it.

You have to learn to cope with what I call "men talk". They tend to swear a lot and their humour can be a little coarse at times, but the spirit in which it is intended is not malicious. I really don't notice now. When I first went to Thames, also, I felt very unhappy about using the crew room so I tended not to bother. Then, after a short space of time, one of the men that I worked with said, "Why don't you come and sit in the crew room? What's the problem?" I think they were a bit concerned that I felt unhappy about being in there.

'At Thames, it's a thirty-seven hour week – two long days and two shorter days. The maximum number of hours you can be called upon to work in one day is thirteen, but that is very unusual. Coming from the theatre where I used to work five evenings a week –

you worked in the morning, had the afternoon free and went back and worked in the evening – I don't find these hours particularly unsuitable. It's sometimes difficult to organise long-term arrangements, because we're only rostered three weeks in advance here. When I moved from the theatre to television it almost doubled my income so it's very well-paid with respect to other lighting technicians. So there are compensations.'

10 The engineer

1 Job description

The engineers are vital to the television industry. They are responsible for advising on the purchase of equipment, for maintaining and operating it. Engineers cover a number of different functions. They may be assigned to work solely on the operations side. This might involve lining up the cameras to meet the very precise standards required for broadcasting, as well as controlling exposure settings and the colour balance so that each camera matches all the others and is correct. It's no use having the picture so dark it can't be seen, or having the announcer's face appear green on one camera and red on another, when it should be flesh-toned.

Engineers may also work in the video tape recording area – often known as 'VT' or 'VTR'. In many television studios, all the video tape machines which record or playback programme material (except those used for editing) are kept in one central area. Engineers are responsible for operating the equipment in VTR, playing back tapes on cue, recording material which is sent from another broadcast company, or recording programmes as they are made. They may also be assigned to Telecine, where they operate equipment capable of transmitting ordinary cine film or slides so that it can be viewed on a television screen. Engineers may also be sent out with outside broadcast units to perform many of the tasks outlined above.

One extremely important engineering section deals with installation and maintenance. Much of the equipment in broadcasting is heavily used and maintenance staff often have to work hard to keep it operational. They may have to be extremely ingenious to overcome last-minute faults in machines that are essential. In addition, they may be asked to invent new technology or modify existing equipment to meet the needs of the company, although, more and more, this is being left to specialist firms who can do it more quickly and more cheaply.

2 Hours and working conditions

Since there must always be some engineers on duty as long as the station is broadcasting, you would probably be expected to work shifts, possibly with overtime too. Those assigned to installation and maintenance could find themselves working through the night because that may be the only time that essential equipment is not in use and can be dismantled for inspection and repairs. You may also be rostered to work public holidays because, even if everyone else has the day off, the television station will probably still be broadcasting.

This is a profession which is dominated by men. According to recent ITCA figures, out of 1374 broadcast engineers only 12 were women. Similar statistics can be found at the BBC. This discrepancy is partly due to discrimination as there is still a strong prejudice against female engineers in certain areas. It may also be partly caused by the fact that so few women apply for such jobs. The BBC report that, in 1984, 36 per cent of women who applied for engineering jobs were selected, compared with 34-5 per cent of male applicants. The fact that relatively few women applied meant that a correspondingly low number were actually appointed. It can mean, for those who do get jobs, that they will be the only woman working on a particular crew. It can be lonely and difficult, or it may present no problems at all, depending on the attitude of the men in that section. One side effect of working in a male-dominated area, however, is that you may be confronted with explicit pornographic material stuck up on the walls. Many firms supplying electronic parts and equipment issue 'girlie' calendars, which the engineering staff duly display. It is something you should be prepared to face, although, as more women enter the profession, such difficulties should become lessened.

3 Qualifications and characteristics required

Most companies require applicants to have a good general education with at least O-level Maths and Physics. It is also desirable to have some qualifications in electronics. These might be a TEC certificate or diploma in Electronics with an emphasis on television or communications, or a college degree in Engineering, Electronics or Telecommunications. Many local colleges run such courses. There may also be relevant government training schemes which you should enquire about at your local Job Centre.

You should be at least eighteen before you begin applying for engineering positions. Normally, if you get the job, you would enter as a trainee or as a first year engineer and progress from there.

As well as having some affinity for this kind of technical work, you should also meet certain physical requirements. You must have good colour vision (i.e. you can't be colour blind) and good eyesight (with or without glasses), because you may be expected to work with minute circuitry. For the same reason, it is important to have good eye-hand coordination. Certain jobs may require a degree of brute strength, but, in general, no one – whether male or female – would be expected to lift very heavy equipment and it is usually moved around on trolleys or fitted with caster wheels. Occasionally, engineers may be expected to work at some height from the ground on outside broadcasts, but this is relatively rare and it is unlikely that any man or woman would be forced to undertake such an assignment if the height made them uncomfortable.

As far as personality goes, you should be reasonably even-tempered and able to work as part of a team. You must also be able to cope methodically and calmly with technical breakdowns, because at times you may have to carry out urgent repairs to enable the station to keep broadcasting without a break.

4 How to become an engineer

Get a good general education with at least O-level Physics and preferably Maths as well. You can try applying for trainee engineering positions at this stage if you are at least eighteen years of age. The BBC will consider applicants who have no previous training in engineering. If you are unsuccessful at this stage, however, then you should consider taking some course in Telecommunications, Electronics or Television Engineering. Write to companies, even before you have graduated, to let them know that you are interested in working for them. You should address your letters to the Head of Engineering at each of the ITV companies (there is a list of addresses in Appendix B, p.333) or to the Engineering Recruitment Officer, BBC, Broadcasting House, London, W1A 1AA.

In the meantime, you should find out everything you can about television production and electronics. Write and ask if you can visit the engineering department of your local television station and observe engineers at work. Many schools and colleges have audio visual technicians who may be willing to let you watch and perhaps even help them out, if you show that you are keen. You may also find it helpful to read books such as *Television* (1963) by Hugh Pitt, or *Using Videotape* (1981) by J.F. Robinson and P.H. Beards. Then, when you have done all that, keep on applying for jobs and don't give up until you get what you want.

Janette Grabham

☐ Engineer
☐ Educational technology

Janette Grabham is a production technician, which is an engineering position, at Brighton Polytechnic. She has a post graduate diploma in film and television production and full City and Guild certification in radio and television and electronics servicing. She is twenty-nine and lives in Brighton.

» 'When I left college, I knew I wanted to work with video, but I didn't want to work in broadcasting. So I got a job as a technician in education and soon realised that I knew very little technically and if I wanted to make a career out of it, I ought to find out more. So I just set about learning what I could, then persuaded my employers to send me on this day release course to learn about electronics. That was at the local technical college and took five years. I felt it wasn't any good just to know how you made a television programme, I felt you ought to know how the equipment worked and be able, if anything went wrong, to at least understand it. I also felt you'd be in a better position to operate the equipment. I started my first job at Brighton Poly on a temporary contract about ten years ago. I lasted six months, then the contract ended and I got a job at Manchester University doing the same kind of thing and after two years that got boring. There happened to be a job going here and I came back.

'I do all kinds of things in my job. Basically I need to be able to know what signals should look like when they come out of a camera or out of a video recorder, be able to know if the signals are right or not, and hopefully be able to do something about it if they're not. Because we have very little money to buy equipment, some of my time is spent making the stuff we can't afford. I don't design it, however. I just sit at a bench with a soldering iron and put the components together. I think this job is wider-ranging than a job in broadcasting because there you just do one thing all the time and I didn't really want that. I wanted to be involved in the whole range of production. Working in this area, you end up knowing about lighting and all kinds of things.

'I did encounter difficulties at Manchester University just because I was a woman. I was particularly interested in VTR's and asked the VTR engineer (who kept saying how overworked he was) if I could do this or that but he just would not let me. If I asked any technical questions of the two main studio engineers they would just tell me to go and look it up in a book or say that if I didn't know that what was I doing there. They were generally very unhelpful. All the time I went on the day release course, I was the only woman there. It was mainly eighteen- and nineteen-year-old boys who kept on telling me that I should be at home or shouldn't be there, but when they got to know me after about six months, they realised it was just a waste of time. I think if it was someone a lot younger who was doing a course like that it would be more difficult for her to stand up for herself. I deal with that kind of harassment and discrimination by making sure I'm better, making sure I do know what I'm doing. All the time I was at college, I'd work hard to be better than the lads because if I didn't, they'd laugh. They could quite easily make you look a fool.

'I have fairly regular working hours. Location work involves travelling and sometimes staying overnight. Video takes up an awful lot of my private life as well. I'm obsessed with it. I think when I meet people outside, they're quite impressed to start with because they think that becoming an engineer might have been difficult. Last week we worked on location in a factory but something went wrong with our equipment and I just walked in with my tool box and fixed whatever it was. Apparently the blokes on the factory floor just stood there with their mouths open, just looking at me. I suppose it does come as quite a shock to people who haven't seen women fix anything or use a soldering iron before.

Lynne Collis

□ Transmission engineer
□ ITV

Lynne Collis is a transmission engineer with Tyne Tees Television in Newcastle. She is single.

» 'I studied French for two years at Lancaster and then went to work in France as an assistant teacher. Then I did various jobs to do with community work and was employed on a community project for a year. Eventually I reached a point where I was unemployed and looking for something to do which would give me a better chance of finding a job. I was assessed by the skills centre and got into electronics, because "women are good with their hands". That was their line. I went to a government retraining centre and they had just started a new course in industrial electronics. It was a ten month City and Guilds course. It started from scratch. I had given up Physics at the age of fourteen and hadn't done it to O-level. The course catered for people of all ages and backgrounds. Towards the end, I was applying for various jobs in industrial electronics which was quite difficult because I specifically did not want to do defence work. There are very few electronics companies which do not have anything to do with military hardware. Then I saw an advert in the Job Centre's professional and executive recruitment newspaper which was for a maintenance engineer at Tyne Tees. They said they would consider a trainee, so I applied but didn't really think that I stood a very good chance of getting the job because my background wasn't television at all. They said, "We don't really think that your knowledge of television is detailed enough for you to work in maintenance, but we have a job as an operational engineer and we're willing to take you on as a trainee in that area." That's the job I'm still doing.

'To do this job, you need the electronics knowledge, but in the particular work I'm doing, you also need to be able to organise things well. I'm in a central transmission area where you have to do video tape recordings from the network, at a particular time, so you have to remember that. [For example, another television company may broadcast a programme which Tyne Tees didn't want to show until later. In that situation, Lynne might be asked to record the programme at the precise time it was broadcast by the other company so that then it could be kept till later.] You may also have transmission controllers shouting that they want this programme, that tape, or this bit of film. There's different things going on all at the same time, and you've got to be able to juggle all these. I might put on a tape and make adjustments if there's some minor fault. If you have a problem with the tape, then you have to judge what the difficulty is – whether it lies with the machine, in the setting up of the machine, with the tape, or whether it was a fault which was recorded on to the tape. You have to judge whether that tape looks any better on another machine. If it does, you would call down maintenance to repair the particular machine that was faulty. You are making judgments all the time on technical quality.

'I am viewed as unfeminine, but I think that is as much because I do not defer to men in a traditionally feminine way, as well as because I'm doing something that's not considered a woman's job. I've had a supervisor sitting next to me at the tea table saying that he really dislikes women who try to be men and he obviously means me, so I've obviously upset him about something. There are three female engineers now at Tyne Tees, but we're in very separate areas. I tend to take it for granted that I get left out a bit. Sometimes the men are having conversations that I really don't want to join in with, talking about women in a derogatory, sexual way, or about who did what to whom last night. I do know men who strongly dislike pornography, but even if a man dislikes pornography on the walls of his workplace, it does not affect him personally in the same way that a women being portrayed in that way affects other women. When men at work have said that all women are stupid slags, that women should be barefoot, pregnant and at the kitchen sink, they are reflecting on my right to be there. Now they've taken to putting headlines from newspapers on the walls. One says, "Men must be dominant", another says, "Women should obey their husbands in everything", and a third says, "Women *are* the weaker sex". My attitude is to leave them there because I think it makes them look stupid, but it's taken me a long time to come to that. I've got to a point now where I make jokes about it, but I still don't feel any more comfortable about living with pornography. At the beginning of the year, their calendar had a woman astride a log going backwards into a vertical saw. That was the worst. It would be much easier if there were more women in the department. There are twenty-five people in the department – three of them women. Individually, there are some of the men who are sympathetic, but when they're all together at the tea table and someone is telling a sexist joke, they all laugh. We get on well in other things. I wouldn't want to portray a situation of total conflict. It's only when we come to their attitudes towards women.

'It's a better paid job than I've ever had. That makes my standards different. I can put up with a lot for that. I work what's called "The Alexandra Palace" shift, because it was originated there. [Alexandra Palace was one of the original BBC broadcasting stations.] I work Monday, Wednesday, Saturday, Sunday, Tuesday, Thursday and Friday, over a two week period. I work a fortnight of lates, then seven days of earlies. "Lates" is midday till 1 a.m.. "Earlies" is 8 a.m. till 8 p.m. My social life is always very disjointed because some weeks I'm virtually out of circulation. It's difficult to plan anything a long way ahead.'

11 The floor manager/ production manager

1 Job description

The jobs of floor manager and production manager are quite distinct, but the skills and experience required for both are often similar and the same person may end up doing both jobs. An experienced floor manager may also go on to become a production manager.

The floor manager's job exists only in television and then only on productions shot in the studio or on outside broadcasts (OBs) where the studio set-up is replicated by using a mobile 'gallery' or control room. On a film production, many of the functions of a floor manager would be carried out by an assistant director, who would call the actors to the set as required, cue the artistes by yelling 'Action' to start a scene, or 'Cut' to end it, and who would organise the extras for crowd scenes and so on.

The floor manager is the director's representative on the studio 'floor'. She will relay instructions from the director, who may be in the gallery where she can monitor all the cameras and watch everything that is going on. In such a situation, the floor manager is connected to the gallery *via* headphones so that she can hear what is being said. Alternatively, the director might be present on the set and can communicate with the floor manager in person.

It is the job of the floor manager to make sure that

everything happens as it should in the studio – that the props are there, the actors are ready when required and the crew are working smoothly. If there is a studio audience, then she will be responsible for seeing that they are in their places and know exactly what is expected of them, and that every precaution has been taken to ensure their safety, as well as that of the cast and crew. She must also make sure that the actors, interviewees, presenters and performers are cued at the appropriate times. Once the production is over, then the floor manager would supervise the clearing away in the studio, checking that everything is returned to its proper place, that all members of the audience have departed and that the studio is ready for the next production to move in.

The floor manager will be helped in her work by various members of staff. She might have a floor assistant, who would go round the dressing rooms to summon actors when they were needed, who might fetch and carry for the cast and crew (getting a glass of water for the leading lady, for example) and who might help to cue the various performers. An assistant floor manager usually has the responsibility for seeing that the props are assembled and arranged according to plan, although the props will actually be moved and put in place by someone from the props department.

As mentioned above, the floor manager is primarily concerned with what goes on during a production. If there are extensive rehearsals, then she might sit in on one or two, to get some idea of what will be happening, but she may not be involved in organising those. Often rehearsals will be held in a large hall which is hired for the purpose, so that valuable studio time is not taken up. Usually a stage manager will be employed to book the facilities, make all the arrangements and carry out the floor manager's functions during this rehearsal period.

Production managers work on both television and film projects, but their role varies considerably from one company and job to another. Generally speaking, however, while the floor manager is concerned with what happens in the studio during a programme, the production manager is concerned with the organisation of the film or programme as a whole. It is often she who arranges for location catering and transport, who makes sure that the crew gets the agreed number of breaks, who pays bills which have to be taken care of on the spot, and who hires extras and possibly some of the crew. In such a situation, she can be quite powerful, with enough clout to tell the director that she doesn't have time to re-shoot a particular scene without incurring overtime charges and going over budget, or to say that there isn't enough money to hire a certain piece of equipment. If this *is* the production manager's role and she is primarily concerned with the finance and planning, then she will probably be fully occupied arranging all the details. The job of actually 'running the floor' in the studio, or organising what happens on the set will be done by the floor manager or assistant director.

There are situations when the production manager's job can be quite different, however. For example, at the BBC there are production managers employed in the Drama and Light Entertainment departments, although they may be loaned out to other sections if required. Whereas someone working for a smaller company might have to obtain facilities and services from outside contractors, the BBC is such a huge corporation that much of the work is done in-house. Thus, to arrange transport, the production manager would simply call another department which would then make all the arrangements. This system means that she is less involved in handling money and paying bills, since much of the cost will be kept within the corporation. Production managers at the BBC are, therefore, much more likely to be involved in 'running the floor' or organising the location for the projects in which they are involved. They would probably be helped in this by an assistant floor manager and other staff, if required.

Another variable which affects the role of the production manager is the size of the crew. That may depend on what has been agreed with the relevant union. If it is a large crew, then there may also be a location manager, who will arrange for location facilities, such as routes to and from the site, transport, parking, toilets, catering and so on. If there is no location manager, then the production manager may end up being responsible for all of these details.

2 Hours and working conditions

The hours which a floor manager might work will depend on which productions she is involved in. If she is employed by a local television station which produces only a few, technically uncomplicated programmes of its own, then her duties may be fairly light and routine, with long breaks between shows. She would probably be expected to work shifts, however, as well as her share of weekends and public holidays. On the other hand, she could work for a large company and be assigned to a drama serial or variety show. In that situation, she might have to work long hours to get everything ready on schedule and to cope with any last minute requirements. If the production takes longer than planned, then she must stay until shooting is finished for the day, which could mean a very late night.

If the floor manager is assigned to a fairly simple programme and works at a small station, then there may be relatively little stress involved with the job. There are not many female floor managers – although the numbers are increasing – and she may encounter difficulties with men who don't like being told what to do by a woman. If, however, she works on a complex production, then her job can be extremely stressful. She may have to keep track of a multitude of details – always with one eye on the clock. She may also find herself having to deal with all kinds of personalities, settling differences and mediating between the director, the cast and the crew.

Depending on how much preparation time she has been given, the production manager can work extremely long hours, particularly when a programme or film is actually being shot. She must stay on the job for however long it takes to ensure that everything is ready for the next day's shooting or studio session. There can be a lot of stress in this job because so much depends on the production manager's work. If, for example, she has not arranged for adequate catering facilities, then the crew might mutiny and the resultant delays could cost many thousands of pounds. She must reconcile many competing demands on her time, keep track of a myriad of details, and cope with lots of different artistic personalities to ensure that everything runs smoothly. She might become the object of other people's anger if, for example, she refused to let the director go over budget or asks a disgruntled crew to work late. This is also a job which is more often carried out by a man and she could encounter various forms of sex discrimination and harassment.

3 Qualifications and characteristics

The most important requirement for both jobs is that you are familiar with film or television production. For this reason, many companies hire from within. Thus a production assistant may apply for, and get a job as an assistant floor manager and move up through the grades to become a production manager, if she so wishes. Some trainee floor managers may previously have obtained degrees in Film or Television Production or in Drama. Others will have theatrical experience.

In order to become a production manager, you may first become a floor assistant and then a floor manager.

Alternatively, you may begin as an assistant to a producer or production manager until you have learned how films are budgeted and organised, then you can apply for jobs as a production manager. It may be easier to break in to the independent sector – perhaps with a small company making programmes for Channel Four – than to get into the BBC, which has a more formalised career structure. If you want to work for the BBC, it is probably advisable to get theatre experience first, then apply to become a floor assistant.

Whichever job you choose and whichever route you take to get there, you must be someone who is good at organising not only yourself, but other people. You should be able to remain calm under stress, particularly since you might have to work on a live programme where there is no room for mistakes. You must also be good at handling people. If you are irritable with an artiste, then you may upset him or her with the result that the performance is bad. If you antagonise the crew and lose their cooperation, then the whole production could come to a standstill. It is also useful to have some business acumen if you're going to be involved with budgets.

4   How to become a floor manager/production manager

It is helpful to get some theatrical experience before applying for a job as a floor assistant or as an assistant floor manager. You may also wish to take a degree at a university, college or drama school which would provide some training in stage management or film and television production. Even experience gained in amateur theatricals is useful and you should become involved helping backstage with local drama, opera or dance productions and concerts.

Learn all you can about how films and television programmes are made and about the job of the floor manager. Write to production companies and ask if you can observe their floor manager at work, or at least visit and talk to her. Some of the larger television companies produce shows for which an audience is required. Write and ask for tickets for any of these, because it will be an excellent opportunity to watch the floor manager and see how she works. You can gain much useful information by reading general texts such as Gerald Millerson's *The Technique of Television Production* (1985) or Steven Bernstein's *The Technique of Film Production* (1987).

Once you have learned as much as you can about the role of the floor manager, you should start applying for jobs. Advertisements for work in the theatre can be found in publications such as *The Stage* or *Variety*, or you can find a list of repertory companies in *Contacts* and approach them directly. Vacancies with television companies are usually advertised in the local and national press, including the *Guardian*'s Creative and Media section published on Mondays, or in trade magazines like *Broadcast*. Vacancies at the BBC usually appear in the *Listener* too. Unless you have a great deal of prior experience, you would probably expect to apply for jobs as a trainee or assistant floor manager or as a floor assistant. You may decide to apply for a clerical or secretarial job instead, in the hope of transferring later on, but obviously, it is better to enter the profession as far up the ladder as possible, and this could be a very long route to your goal.

If you wish to become a production manager, you may choose to follow the advice given above for would-be floor managers, and then, once you have some experience in that area, move on to become a production manager. Alternatively, you can write to freelance production managers and film and television companies and try to get a job as an assistant. Once you have learned as much as you can about production methods and how a film is organised and budgeted, then you can begin to apply for jobs as a fully-fledged production manager. ACTT publishes a directory which lists all their members working in this job, and you can obtain the names and addresses of production companies from directories such as *Kemps Film and Television Yearbook*.

Jenny MacArthur

☐ Production manager
☐ BBC

Jenny MacArthur is a production manager in the drama department of BBC television. She is single and has no children. Now in her early forties, she is based in London.

» 'I left school at fifteen, after taking two O-levels, then trained as a secretary and worked for a charity before spending a brief period at drama school. After that I worked in the theatre for six years, either as an assistant stage manager or as a stage manager. The first two years were in repertory in the provinces, the last four were in the West End of London or with touring companies. I started with the BBC as an assistant floor manager in the Plays department and became a production manager about four years later.

'Drama and Light Entertainment are the only departments to have production managers permanently attached to them at the BBC. Other departments, such as Music and Arts, will usually borrow one of us if they are doing a drama-type programme or a documentary with a drama element. Production managers in Drama and LE will usually run the studio floor for their production but otherwise the job is different from that of a floor manager. A production manager starts on a programme when the director does and is the liaison between him or her and everyone else. We also find locations, cast extras or supporting artists, keep an eye on the budget, liaise with the police and the public, write film schedules or recording orders and any other bits and bobs that are not the job of anyone else in particular. Floor managers, on the other hand, will attend one or more rehearsals, if the programme is rehearsed, but will not usually go on location or be expected to perform any of the other duties I've just described.

'I would think that women make up roughly 50 per cent of production managers in Drama Departments and probably slightly less in LE. I do not think there is any outright discrimination in my area, but to get on you need to be just that bit tougher, and fight harder and have plenty of self-confidence. Women seem to find it harder to progress beyond the grade of production manager. I've never been sure of the exact definition of sexual harassment and we don't seem to have any casting couches. But the hardest thing for a young woman to put up with is the constant teasing, which isn't usually meant unkindly, but can be exasperating when you are tired. It is fatal to get upset. It hasn't worried me too much because I've always been able to give as good as I've got or ignore it or laugh at it, but I have seen (and tried to defend) other women who were badly upset.

'As a production manager, you mustn't mind being unpopular. You must be able to bawl people out if they've fallen down on the job. You must put a stop to shooting if they've gone over schedule and it's going to mean penalty payments all round. The director won't love you for that either. On location, you are probably going to have to ask your crew to work far more hours than are reasonable. It is a waste of time to try and blame anyone else for what goes wrong. It is much quicker to accept the blame for everything and get on with the show. I once heard a harassed production manager accept the blame for the fact that the sun had gone in.

'It is almost impossible to become a production manager without relevant experience in the television or film industry. A number of secretaries and clerks have made the transition to assistant floor manager and then on to production manager, but I wouldn't really advise anyone to go this route because it can take years. It is better for a young woman to try to get theatre experience first.

'The hours of work vary enormously. An office or rehearsal day may be no more than 10 a.m. till 6 p.m., but a studio or film day is more likely to be at least thirteen hours and may be much more. It is not unheard of to work through the night and the next day as well. Days off are also irregular. I live with a colleague from a different department and we can go for weeks without having a single day off together. This makes it especially difficult for single parents. A friend used to have to rush her son to her mother the night before she went filming – which is usually a rather hectic time anyway – then rush back for the filming and rush off again as soon as she'd got a day off. The long hours also make child-minding difficult to arrange, and the salary is not high enough for most people to be able to afford a full-time nanny.'

Josephine Dunn

☐ Production manager/floor manager
☐ Freelance

Josephine Dunn left college in 1979 and went to work at an ITV station. Later, she worked at an independent facilities house* in London before going freelance. She is twenty-eight, married and is expecting her first child. She is based in the London area.

» 'I went to art school for four years at St Martin's to get a BA in Fashion and Journalism. It didn't really qualify me to get into television, but then nothing really does. It was really just my determination that did it. I decided that I wanted to work in television. In my final year there was actually a job going at Southern Television (now TVS). It was literally a case of them saying, "What do you want to do?" and me saying, "I don't care. What have you got?" They said they had this job as a floor assistant. I got an interview and then they went on strike for three months and then I had a second interview and I got the job about two days later. But I pestered them. Once I'd got one interview, I actually rang them up every other day throughout the strike and said, "Have you gone back yet?"

'My training was, "That's the floor manager. Go and assist him." You stand around and watch for a bit, waiting to be told what to do and you go and fetch a bit of paper or you cue actors from behind the scenes and act as "call boy". In theory, in ITV, a floor manager only works in the studio. You do have a certain amount of things to control, such as when to call people for make-up or wardrobe and see that the crew don't work past the meal break. You do things like getting cabs for people but you shouldn't have any responsibility for money.

'A production manager, again depending on the company, can be responsible for an awful lot more. You can be anything from merely a production accountant who holds the money, pays facilities' fees, out-of-pocket costs on the location and things like hiring extras on the day, or you can be incredibly powerful where you're preparing the budget with the producer, as well as going out and finding locations (if you haven't got a separate location manager), and also keeping an eye on production costs. The production manager will come out to the set to make sure that things are ready, that there aren't any problems between the director and the cast or crew. She's the person who will come along at six and say, "That's a wrap.* You're not having any more time because we don't have any more money." On a lot of small productions and commercials, the production manager is the person who will liaise between the company and the client, hire in all the crew and be responsible for negotiating fees and paying them. Then they'll hand over the control of the studio or the location to the floor manager or assistant director.

'You need an immense amount of tact and the ability to tell terrible, terrible lies and sound convincing. For instance, the classic case of what not to do was told me by a producer who had started out as a floor manager. He was working in light entertainment and there was a singer who was not very bright and she could not hit her mark at all.* He was being terribly patient and relaxed with her and was coaxing her through it. The director was in the control room swearing. At that point, you don't repeat what you're hearing through the headset from the director, but this floor manager finally lost his cool and repeated some of the insults. The singer took offence and walked off the set.

'You need a sense of humour and a great deal of patience and the ability to listen to about six things at once and do ten. You need to be able to plan very well and very efficiently and delegate wherever possible. You need to be able to think faster than the director, always, and be able to come up with possible solutions to the problem. They may not be the best solutions, but they must be fast solutions, so you must be able to think on your feet and improvise – especially if you're sixty miles from the nearest telephone box. People will turn to you and if you don't know what's going on, everything collapses. So you need the ability to inspire confidence in people, to be calm and assured, even if you're only thinking from one minute to the next. I suppose you need to be able to make yourself understood, although I would disagree with the opinion of some men that you need a loud voice.

'There are advantages and disadvantages to being a woman. I find that when I'm working, I get a lot of things done because I'm a woman. It's not just enough to be a woman, though; it'a being a woman with the right attitude and the right way of asking. You mustn't ever tell people what to do. You have to ask them and I suppose it's easier in a lot of ways for a woman to ask. When a crew is very tired and stroppy (for instance, when they've been messed about by a director), I'll quite often get people to do things that they wouldn't otherwise do. The disadvantage is that there are still some very difficult attitudes that women have to overcome and it's not only from men. The person who did the worst harm to my career at the beginning was not a man but a woman. There do tend to be two types of women – the ones who are very willing to help other women, and then those few who look on other younger women as a threat in a much worse way than a lot of men do. But there are some intractable men who are impossible. There are also some who mean well, but get it all wrong. My previous boss wouldn't let me go and work on *Spearhead* because he thought it wouldn't be nice for me to work with all those rough types. He thought he was protecting me, but at the same time, he was preventing my career from advancing, because that was a good drama to work on. The guy who did work on it got the next film manager's job.

'I never wanted a nine-to-five job, but there are times when you turn down work because you'll be away for six months even though you know you'll get home at weekends because you'll be so tired that you're not going to be civil to the person you live with. I have to continue working when I've had my child because I'm really the breadwinner in this family. I think that my husband will be doing quite a lot of babysitting and I'll be going out to work.'

Glossary

an independent facilities house   a company which provides full studio facilities and equipment for hire to independent producers or anyone else who needs them.

a wrap   a slang term meaning that that's the end of production for that day.

to hit her mark   often an unobtrusive mark will be made on the studio floor so that an artiste knows where she must stand or the point she must finish at after she has been moving around so that she is correctly placed for the cameras.

Ann MacLelland

☐ Floor manager
☐ ITV

Ann MacLelland is a floor manager with Ulster Television. She is married with a three-year-old child and lives near Belfast.

» 'I got eight O-levels and two A-levels and then I went to the College of Business Studies in Belfast, to take a secretary's certificate. After leaving there, I worked for a professor at Queen's University in Belfast for maybe two or three years. Then after that, I got a job in Ulster Television as the secretary to the news editor. I was in that job for about a year before I got a job as production assistant and did that for five years. From there, I became a floor manager and now I'm a senior floor manager.

'It was on-the-job training. You work with another floor manager on the whole spectrum of programmes and then, when they think you're ready to go on your own, that's what happens. I do all the programmes that we do in the studio and with the outside broadcast unit. If I'm in the studio, I sort out things like if there are any captions or any guests and I make sure everything's as the director wants it. On outside broadcasts, it's much the same thing only you're more remote from the director so your job is that much more important. In the drama that we did, I was dealing with the actors, passing on information from the director, making sure they'd got their call times and that sort of thing. Before the drama started, of course, I had to work out my props list, liaise with the designer etc. You're dealing with people all the time.

'You have to be an organiser and be able to think clearly and pass on the instructions that you get from the gallery to the people on the floor. You have to be able to mix very well and get on with the people you work with and that, more than anything else I feel, is a matter of getting to know them. Once you know how they react to different situations, you can tailor what you're going to say to them so you present it in a way that you know they'll respond to. But I don't have many problems like that because it's a small company so I know everybody that I work with quite well. I'm a quite straightforward person and if I think there's a problem I'm not going to back away from it. I'll simply say to the person involved, "Look, we've got a problem here. What's wrong? Can we sort it out?" It doesn't really matter whether they're male or female.

'I remember when I first became a floor manager and was working with a lot of men. I wasn't just sure how to issue instructions and I'd end up not saying to anybody in particular to do something. I'd say, "We'll have to move that flat* three foot back" or whatever. And it just got done. I didn't actually ask anybody in particular to do it. And then when I got more into the job and got to know the people better, I was able to say, "Look (whatever their name was), could you move that flat three feet back?" But that was all just a matter of getting to know the job and the people.

'The hours vary of course. We work a thirty-seven hour week. It can vary in that you may be working weekends, but in that case you get two days off sometime else. If you're doing a late night news thing, you could start at 4 p.m. and not finish till 11 p.m. but I know in advance what my hours are going to be. I've got one small boy who's three. I have a lady who comes to look after him three days a week. My mother looks after him two days a week. My husband has his own business and if I start at 4 p.m., for example, he makes sure that he's here to take the girl who looks after Alan home. So between my husband and myself we work it. It's a question of just making sure we both know what we're doing all the time. At the moment, I'm wondering about having another child.

'There are two ways of going about becoming a floor manager. We've just employed a new floor manager who had done a degree course at the University of Ulster. Also, a lot of production assistants coming in at the moment seem to have degrees so either you go ahead and get a university degree in something like Media Studies, or the other way is to come in as I did and work your way up.'

Glossary

a flat   this is a term for a piece of scenery which, although it may depict a three dimensional landscape, for example, is actually a painting done on a flat sheet of canvas or board.

12 The journalist

1 Job description

Television journalists are the people who put together the news bulletins, reporting from the scene of a topical event, appearing as newscasters, working behind the scenes to write and edit scripts for the bulletins and producing news and current affairs programmes.

The journalists who work 'in the field', reporting on events, carry a great deal of responsibility. They may be sent out to cover a news story with only the scantiest information. Once there, they may have to decide who should be interviewed and what the issues are, as well as formulating in their heads a plan of how all the bits will fit together into a completed news item which gives all sides of the story. On return to the television studios, they will probably supervise the editing of the film or tape that was shot of that event.

Other journalists work as newscasters and are usually based at the studios. They may spend the time when they are not in front of the cameras writing scripts or editing film or video tape which has been sent in from abroad and which must be made into a coherent package of information, perhaps with an added commentary. Some journalists may be employed as sub-editors, to re-write and check the accuracy of news items which will have come in from a variety of sources.

News producers, or editors, decide on the content of the news programme and bulletins as well as the order in which items should be placed in the final script. They are responsible for coordinating all the different elements of the story. There are also some journalists who work as researchers on news and current affairs programmes whose job it is to collect background material for news stories.

2 Hours and conditions of work

The hours can be long and exhausting in almost any news journalist's job. Some companies ask news staff to work twelve hour shifts, others demand a ten-hour day. You may be rostered to work public holidays (*someone* has to do the news on Christmas Day) or early mornings, or late nights. If you work for a national company, such as ITN, you could be asked to go literally anywhere in this country or around the world at a moment's notice, and be gone for several days at a time. Journalists get sent out in all weathers under all conditions. It may be physically rigorous at times or, occasionally, dangerous. Some of the events you might have to report on could be distressing, for example, a car accident in which people have been killed. You could also have to deal with people who are hostile to the media, and you may find yourself in some ugly situations as a result.

In the past, women have been discriminated against as newscasters and journalists because they were said to lack 'authority'. This prejudice against women has now been remedied, largely because of pressure from groups like 'Women in Media'. We are now accustomed to seeing women reading the news and reporting on world events. Some female journalists still feel, however, that there is a tendency to assign them to 'soft' stories – stories about mothers and babies, children's health, puppies rescued after three days stuck down a rabbit hole etc. – rather than sending them to cover industrial and financial topics, or stories about politics or war.

3 Qualifications and characteristics required

Competition to become a journalist is now so fierce that many newspapers and training schemes will no longer accept candidates who are not university graduates. It is therefore advisable to obtain a degree first. It may not be particularly important which subjects you study, although English, Politics, International Relations and Economics, for example, would be particularly relevant. Having obtained a degree, it is possible to go straight into the BBC or ITN as a graduate trainee, but in practice, literally hundreds of people apply for a very few places and only a small number make the grade. In fact, since television journalists have to work alone much of the time and carry a great deal of responsibility, many companies try to hire staff who have already had some experience on newspapers or radio and who can be relied upon not to make basic errors.

If you are going to appear on screen, rather than be a sub-editor or researcher, then you should have a clear voice and good diction. Your accent doesn't matter as much nowadays. Television companies – even the BBC – are moving away from uniform, upper-class accents and are accepting regional variations as long as they can be understood by the average viewer. You should also be well-groomed and reasonably smart – and conventional. They probably wouldn't let you read the news if you had an orange Apache haircut! If you are appearing on screen, you should also be someone who can remain calm, no matter what is going on around you. There may be technical breakdowns, last minute changes to news scripts may be passed to you as you sit in front of the camera, and there may be a great deal of activity going on in the studio which *you* can see, but which the viewers can't. Throughout all of that, the newscaster must appear unflustered and in control.

A good journalist is someone who is genuinely interested in news and current affairs around the world. You must be able to assimilate and process information quickly, because most of the time you will be working to a deadline. You must be assertive and confident enough to walk into any situation and approach anyone, no matter how famous or infamous, unpleasant or antagonistic they may be, and ask them questions. Sometimes people will refuse to answer or else dodge the question, and you will have to be very persistent to get the full story. At times, you must be capable of a softer approach also, because you will have to gain people's trust and persuade them to talk about events which may have been quite harrowing. Lastly, you will need a great deal of stamina, to cope with this very demanding, but rewarding job.

4 How to become a television journalist

You should begin by getting a good general education, preferably to degree level. Subjects like English, Economics, Politics, International Relations and Communications or Media Studies would have some relevance to a career as a journalist. The competition for trainee schemes and jobs is fierce, so you must be able to point to activities which demonstrate your interest in the profession, your initiative and your experience in journalism, even if it's only at amateur level. Something like working on your school, college or university newspaper would count. Read your local paper carefully and see what kinds of things they publish. Often they are keen on regional history and characters. Perhaps you know of some older person with vivid memories of what your community was like several decades ago, whom you could interview. Think of what you've got to offer that is unique. Do you have any unusual hobbies or have you had particularly interesting holidays or experiences? When you have come up with several ideas, you can approach the editor. He or she will probably be unwilling to commission an article from you if you haven't worked for them before, so you may have to offer to write something 'on spec' – i.e. you will only be paid if it is accepted for publication and they don't guarantee that it will be.

You should also approach your local radio station and find out if there are any opportunities there. At the very least, they may allow you to go in and watch the news staff at work, or they may give you a job as a dogsbody for the summer, or they may agree to take occasional contributions from you. There is even the possibility that you might be allowed to present a programme, particularly if you are willing to work late at night or at the weekends, when regular staff would prefer to be off.

Being able to point to activities such as these is almost essential if you want to be considered for any job as a journalist. As stated above, the BBC and ITN, as well as some of the independent television companies, will accept trainees straight from college or university. But competition for places on these schemes is very tough. If you aren't accepted for one of these, then there are other training opportunities you can try. Some colleges offer courses in journalism and many newspapers have training schemes. There are also opportunities in local radio. Any one of these will give you valuable preparation and experience should you then wish to apply for a journalist's job in television. You may also find it helpful to read books such as Ivor Yorke's *The Technique of Television News* (1987), or Robert Tyrell's *The Work of the Television Journalist* (1981).

Whichever route you take, it is vital that you prepare carefully for a job or traineeship interview. Make sure that you are well-informed about topical events and issues. Most importantly, study that day's newspapers and listen to local and national television and radio news broadcasts. With that preparation behind you, go into the interview remembering that they may harass you to see how you react under pressure, so remain calm, confident and assertive.

Pamela Armstrong

☐ Newscaster
☐ ITN

Pamela Armstrong graduated with a diploma in Media Studies and Communications from the Polytechnic of Central London and then went to work at Capital Radio. After several years there she became the presenter of the *Well Being* programme series on Channel Four, before she was offered the job of newscaster with ITN. (Since the time of this interview, Pamela Armstrong has gone to work at the BBC.) She is thirty-five and lives in London.

» 'My job involves working in the team that puts *News at Ten* together. We have a meeting at 3 p.m. and we're given stories to work on. We then go away and write the scripts and edit the film. Newscasters are effectively script writers up until 10 p.m. when they become newscasters. So there are many people contributing to the programme. I tend to do a lot of editing of film that comes in from around the country or by satellite from abroad. It's material that has to be shaped "in-house".

'The kind of skills required for newscasting are the same kind of skills that any journalist would use in any broadcasting medium, i.e. an ability to present information clearly. That is the most obvious skill. All journalists, however, regardless of which medium they work in, use the same skills to collect information, digest it and understand it and then re-present it. What's interesting about the job is that it can be different every night. I love the journalistic side which is immensely satisfying. On top of that, I also enjoy dealing with the technical challenge of broadcasting in a live situation. We are all cogs in an immense machine. When it works smoothly and goes well it's exhilarating.

'The timing is done so carefully that you're very aware of what you've got on your script and how long it will take to read. If you know your script is too long you either cut words out as you're going along, or you speed up or extend it. You can be flexible within the discipline. There are various people making a tally all the way through the programme – the production assistant and the programme producer and the programme editor are all looking at the timings so they let you know how it stands. The whole programme is timed in total and it's only at the very end that you're given so many seconds to go.

'There's only one person who has total editorial control, that's the programme producer. In a newspaper it's the editor who has final responsibility. All journalists work within that framework and it doesn't bother me.

'In the past, I think it was difficult for women when they were first taking up high profile places in front of the camera. But now that there are so many of us on television, fewer and fewer of us are singled out for attention. That makes it easier for the bulk of women journalists in television to just get on with the job that we're doing. Previously, the excessive media attention which was focussed on women turned them into a sideshow. They were looked on almost as novelties. In a sense, that marginalised and devalued the work they were doing. Those attitudes have changed. I certainly have been very clear about how I think women should be interviewed. If you are ever in a position of being put in front of a camera and are asked to do publicity, then be as careful as you can about the manner in which people choose to describe you.

'It's a good time for women in television, however. There are lots of women directors at ITN. At one point, we did have two programme editors also who were female, but one of them has now gone to the US to do some work for ITN there. The thing that struck me when I came to work for ITN was that the whole institution pulls together as a team, and that goes for the men and the women.

'If you're doing the sort of job I'm doing, it's futile to pretend that appearance isn't terribly important. What matters to me is that, however I look, I'm unobtrusive enough not to get in the way of the news and information that we're trying to get across in the shortest possible period of time. Simple and plain clothes look best. I found out what works for me and now that I have got those clothes sorted out I don't think about them any more.

'When I was working at Capital Radio years ago, I was on an evening programme. Later, when I was working on *Well Being*, I was travelling all round Britain and the US, so that was what people would call disruptive to my private life. But I think, basically, if you're in our industry, you're going to be working those kind of hours and I don't even think about it – really it's just work. It's also quite important to remember that one third of the British population work a shift system. There are a lot of us. It's not a job to get into if you are going to quibble about the hours. I come into work about 2.30 p.m. in the afternoon and we work until we have our lunch break between 6 p.m. and 7 p.m. and then go all the way through till 10.30 p.m. I get a schedule a month at a time. Sometimes I work five days a week, sometimes it's four days a week, sometimes it's three, sometimes it's two – it's never regular.

'When I signed my contract at ITN the amount of publicity that came with the territory was well known. If I hadn't been prepared to take it on, I didn't have to sign, so I don't feel I can cavil at my situation now. The fact is I don't find all the publicity an intrusion but even if I did, I couldn't, in all honesty, complain about it. If you don't feel like handling that kind of thing, then you really shouldn't be in this kind of work.

'I have to say though, that I would never advise anyone to plan to become a newscaster and a newscaster alone. You need a broad horizon to project your ambitions on to. In my experience, becoming a newscaster happened by chance. Basically I'm a journalist. Being a journalist is what I've done in the past, what I'm doing now and what I'll continue to do in the future. This is just one of the different forms of journalism that I'm doing at the moment. If you talk to any journalist about how they got into the industry, everyone has a different story. Some people get in through either local radio or local television. Regional newspapers are a very good way of doing it. Increasingly, you can do it through college courses, which are gradually becoming more and more respected throughout the industry. You should consider becoming a journalist if you're interested in meeting people, talking to people and dealing with an immensely wide amount of subjects and information. It's a great job. I wouldn't have any other.'

Liz Ramsay

☐ Senior duty editor, news
☐ BBC

Liz Ramsay is the most senior woman in television news

at the BBC and is the first woman to edit the *Nine O'Clock News* – ever. She is thirty-five, married with two young children, and lives in London.

» 'I applied for the BBC Journalist Training Scheme straight from university in Aberdeen. I was lucky with both interviews. The first interview was at 2.30 p.m. and my last lecture was about 11 a.m. I thought, "I've got this interview. What will I do about it?" and I decided, "I'll read a paper". So with that fresh in my mind I went into the interview and the first questions were, "What newspaper did you read this morning? What was the lead story? What was the lead on page two? etc." I still think that had my interview been at ten o'clock in the morning, I wouldn't have read a paper and I wouldn't have got any further.

'It's important to know what's happening in the world. I don't really think it's a question of forcing yourself to do it. You're either interested in news, and therefore in journalism, or you're not. I've always read newspapers. I've always been interested in what's going on. For the second interview, I had to make the long trip to London. I just remember being very, very angry at the interview. They seemed to be making a whole lot of derogatory statements about Scottish students being apathetic, Scottish education not being very good and they just went on and on. I finally lost my cool. I think that's why they remembered me – because I answered back. The competition was enormous and I didn't expect to be selected at all; but I was. Six of us were selected and two of us were women.

'I would recommend preparing for those kind of interviews as I would for any interview at any stage. Be very up-to-date with current affairs, know what's happening in the world, know who the leaders in the world are and also know about the output of the organisation to which you are applying. It's not the least bit of good applying to BBC or ITV if you admit at the interview that you don't actually watch the *Nine O'Clock News*, or saying, "Oh yes, I watch television but I never listen to the radio", if you're going to a radio interview. Know what their output is and be able to comment on it, offer them ideas, say why you don't like something. I think all that's terribly important. You have to know a lot about the people you would like to employ you.

'My official job is number two on the editorial board, which means that I'm deputy to the editor of the day. The great joy of the job though is that you do act up a grade and you do edit the *Nine O'Clock News*. As editor, I am the person who decides the form and the content, but that doesn't mean I have free rein. I am one of a large group of people all working towards the *Nine O'Clock News*. For a start, there is the News Intake Department which decides how to cover stories, which reporter to send and how to get the pictures back. So the editor of the day must liaise very closely with them. There is also a team of writers, reporters and, of course, newsreaders. A lot of the job involves talking to them and trying to stimulate ideas and working out how best to present a news item so that it is clear and informative. But the editor of the day is, finally, the person who decides what the lead story is and how it should be presented, and what else should be included or dropped. As editor, you're where the buck stops when it comes to accuracy or the fairness of what you present of the world news on the day. It's a crucial role. A lot of it is very rushed and last minute and you have to stay very calm.

'I work a six-day fortnight which to me is a great joy. They're very long days, from 9 a.m.-9 p.m. or later, but I work two days together and then I'm off for two or three days. So for someone like me with a family, it's absolutely ideal. I couldn't ask for anything better. It gives me the opportunity to have a full-time job with a lot of responsibility and still have a lot of time at home with the children. If I had been on a five-day week, I suspect that I would not have stayed at work. I would have hated it. I would have resented the time I was at work that I couldn't spend with my children.

'I don't really think there's any conscious bias against women but I wonder whether once they get to the stage where there's 50 per cent women and 50 per cent men that they won't say, "Oh God, we've got rather a lot of women here." I don't know. I would say there tends to be a bias against the older woman. As far as people appearing on the screen is concerned, they do not appoint the craggy fifty-five year old woman, whereas the Alistair Burnet figure is entirely acceptable. Women, as reporters, may also face unconscious discrimination. I think that anything like a 50 per cent female reporting staff could be a long way off. Reporters tend to be more aggressive and extrovert, women tend to be less so. Therefore, I think women will just have to learn to assert themselves in their own gentler way – not necessarily in a macho way – and keep their confidence up. It can be daunting when you start out in a man's world.

'I think, also, that our ideas of what is news is biased to some extent. One supreme example is in our coverage of male athletes. Women athletes always get treated as second best. It's happening less and less because most reporters have enough savvy to realise they can't be blatantly sexist. Often, though, the language is biased against women. I heartily detest the use of "girl" when you mean "woman". We still talk about "400 men" being made redundant from a factory when, almost inevitably, there were some women amongst them, or we say, "Three people were killed, one of them a woman", that sort of thing. I've seen gradual improvements. They've employed more women and there are more women on the screen. But just last year [1985], the then editor of television news asked at the morning meeting, "What did you all think of yesterday's lunch-time news – two women were reading it." He obviously thought that was remarkable. Everyone else looked blankly back at him. As far as they were concerned, two newsreaders had done their job professionally and well. Their gender was immaterial.'

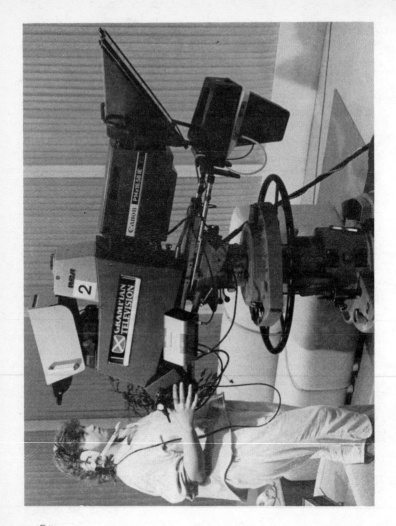

Figure 1 Carrie Watt operating a TK47 camera on the studio floor (Courtesy of Grampian Television)

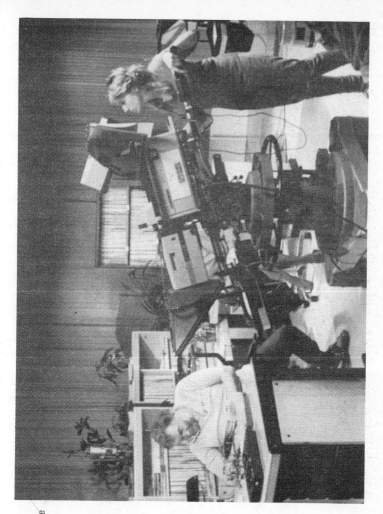

Figure 2 Joanna Turner operating an electronic camera (Courtesy of Yorkshire Television)

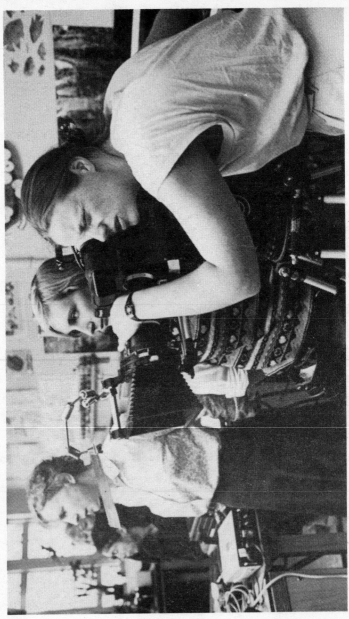

Figure 3 Belinda Parsons, camera operator (Photo: Raissa Page. Courtesy of Format Photographers)

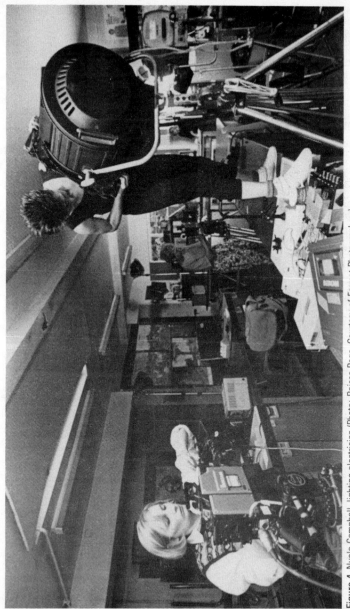

Figure 4 Nuala Campbell, lighting electrician (Photo: Raissa Page. Courtesy of Format Photographers)

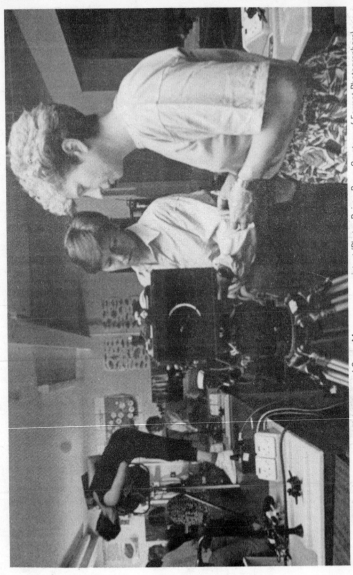

Figure 5 Erika Stephenson, camera operator, and Caren Moy, camera assistant (Photo: Raissa Page. Courtesy of Format Photographers)

Figure 6 Moya Burns, sound recordist (Photo: Raissa Page. Courtesy of Format Photographers)

Figure 7 Engineer Irene Watson working with a 1″ Editor and Digital Effects Unit (Courtesy of Grampian Television)

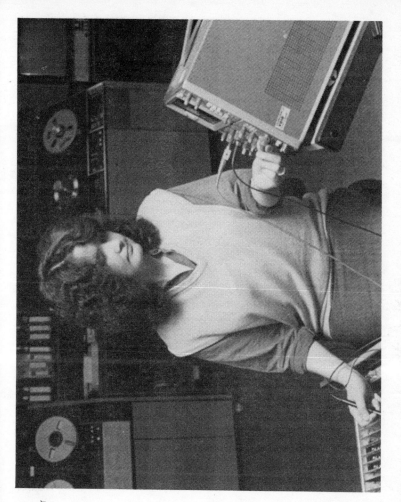

Figure 8 Engineer Irene Watson performing an electronic line-up on a 2" Quad Video Tape Recorder (Courtesy of Grampian Television)

Figure 9 Val Lawson, floor manager (Courtesy of Yorkshire Television)

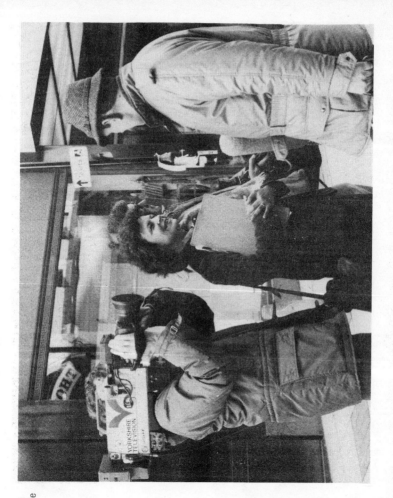

Figure 10 Ruth Pitt, television journalist (Courtesy of Yorkshire Television)

Figure 11 Beverley Anderson, presenter (Courtesy of London Weekend Television)

13 The laboratory worker

1 Job description

The laboratories were originally set up to handle the processing, cutting and printing of films to send out to cinemas and other exhibitors. Some labs are now expanding into video production, however, because the future of film as a medium is uncertain. Video tape may take over from film completely in the future and there have been redundancies at several film labs.

Although there are a number of different jobs within the laboratories, they are included here in one section, because very often employees enter at a low grade and then progress up the scale from job to job. The following is a list of some of the work areas and what goes on there:

Developing	The original film is developed;
Negative breakdown	The original film is cut into individual scenes prior to being edited.
Cutting	The shots which are to be used in the completed film are edited together to conform exactly to the instructions of the editor.
Frame counting	The number of frames required for special effects is counted out and

	translated into instructions for the printer.
Printing	The original film is printed so that a copy is made which can be projected and viewed.
Grading	Different scenes are studied closely to ensure that colours and exposures match as required. If they don't, then the printer will be given instructions to correct the error and make a new print.
Contact	This department acts as a liaison between the clients and the lab.
Marketing	The services provided by the lab are marketed to prospective clients.

Those who wish to work in video will find that job categories vary from one lab to the next, but the following are some examples of what you might be expected to do:

Cassette operator	Operates video cassette machines similar to those found on the domestic market. Might, for example, be involved in making copies of popular videos for home market rental.
Technical operator	Would operate cassette machines and receive training in operation of broadcast quality equipment.
Technical assistant	Would operate broadcast video machines for playback and record but would do so under supervision.
Video tape operator (VT operator)	Authorised to do playback and recording on all machines but would only perform minor editing jobs.
VT engineer	Operates all equipment and carries out editing.

VT engineers .	Would operate all equipment but
(operations and	also be responsible for maintenance.
maintenance)	

As you will see from the descriptions above, there is a distinction made in video production between broadcast and non-broadcast quality equipment. In general, those machines used to record and playback material intended for broadcast must meet higher technical specifications than those intended for playback on closed-circuit television or on home video machines.

2 Hours and working conditions

Most laboratories expect employees (except for clerical and administrative staff) to work shifts. Some are unwilling to assign women to night shift work, however, citing various reasons, such as concern for their safety, or deference for any family committments they might have, such as making their husbands' tea! Many women feel, however, that whatever the reasons given, they are effectively being barred from earning the higher wages given for night shift work.

Moreover, there are very few women employed in the higher, better paid jobs. Some companies do seem willing to hire women if they are qualified, but find that very few actually apply for jobs. Other companies seem to discriminate against women and refuse to promote them beyond a certain level, or to accept that women might have career ambitions in this area. Women in the labs are organising, however, and have the backing of ACTT, so that, hopefully, these barriers will soon be overcome.

ACTT effectively operates a closed shop in most labs, which means that in practice all employees belong to that union (see p.30). Many of the labs are also experiencing financial difficulties at this time, particularly those which specialise in film work. There have been a number of redundancies because of this, which not only means that there may be very little job security for those who do obtain work, but also that there may be few vacancies for new staff.

3 Qualifications and characteristics required

It is essential to have clear vision and good colour sight – that is, you can't be colour blind because your work may involve assessing the accuracy of the colours on a piece of film or video tape. You should also have good eye-hand coordination because you will probably be required to handle fragile equipment, film or tape. It is also essential to be a careful, meticulous worker, because the slightest error can mean ruined film or tape and cost hundreds or even thousands of pounds.

The qualifications required vary from one job to the next. Some companies ask for five O-levels, although some of the lowest grades of work are relatively unskilled. If you wish to work in a video lab, then the higher your qualifications in electronics or engineering, the better your chances of obtaining a higher grade job. Often new staff are recruited at the lowest grades and then promoted within the company.

4 How to become a laboratory worker

You should obtain the best general education that you can. If you wish to work in video, you should then take further qualifications, such as a Higher National Certificate or Diploma, or B/TEC in Electronics or Television Engineering. Books such as *Videotape Recording* (1981), written by J.F. Robinson and revised by Stephen Lowe, *Television* (1963) by Hugh Pitt or any of the technical manuals which can be obtained by writing to the British Kinematography, Sound and Television Society, will help to provide you with a good background knowledge.

If you wish to make your career in a film lab, then you may find it helpful to study still photography and learn to process and print your own pictures. In this way, you can learn a great deal about different kinds of film and about how images are made and film is processed. In addition, you may wish to read L. Bernard Happe's book, *Your Film and the Lab* (1983), or Dominic Case's *Motion Picture Film Processing* (1985).

You can also contact the labs directly and ask if you can be given a tour to observe the work done there. A list of addresses can be found in directories such as *Kemps Film and Television Yearbook*, or by looking in the Yellow Pages for the London area under 'Film Laboratories'. Any job openings will be advertised through ACTT and in the local or national press, such as the *Guardian*'s Creative and Media section on Mondays, or trade publications like *Broadcast*, *Television Weekly* or *Audio Visual*.

Debbie Findlay

□ Shift leader
□ Visnews Laboratories

Debbie Findlay is aged twenty-nine and is married with no children. She is now based in the London area, where she works for Visnews Laboratories.

» 'I'm a shift leader in the video department of a company that also has a film lab. On a daily basis, I supervise all the jobs that are done in this area, such as dubbing work or news editing, and I also look after the out-going and in-coming land lines and satellite lines and do quality control. This means making sure that the signals are up to technical specifications. This job is very rarely done by a woman. Generally it's people with Higher National Certificate or the equivalent who do this job. Apart from an obvious interest in electronics and television, it requires a cool head.

'I started out in Australia as a junior video tape operator with Channel Nine and I worked there for about four years. Then I came to England and applied for a job as a video tape assistant, which is about four or five grades down from where I am now. From there, I just applied for the next grade up and then the next grade and so on. It's a relatively well-paid job, although to get a good rate of pay, you usually have to do night work and a certain amount of overtime as well. I always work at the same place, so there's no travel involved with the job. I'm fortunate in that my husband also does shift work so that we're not dependent on one another doing a nine-to-five schedule. There are great advantages to doing shift work in that you get time off during the week when everyone else is at work.

'In a male dominated industry, you will face some form of discrimination, however slight, everyday and sometimes it may seem harsh to label it as that. After several years of working on a day-to-day basis with such attitudes, however, I find myself less able to excuse them. I work with guys who've been in the business for twenty or thirty years and they don't see much of women except for their wives, and I don't think that what they say or do is an attempt to put women down, but just an attempt to establish some sort of difference. What I deal with on a daily basis is generally not intended or malicious, it's just there. I suppose they know I'm there to do my job and I'll do it to the fullest of my ability, and I'm not prepared to take any hassle. Management would back me all the way down the line. I made sure of that when I took on the job of shift leader. I just said, "If ever I come to that sort of situation where I have to insist on something, you'll be there to support me?" and they said, "Most definitely."

'Women are most likely to be working in clerical and administrative jobs here. My job is not designed for people with children because of the shift work, but we are trying to organise a crèche at the moment. That could take up to forty years to establish, however, and then it wouldn't really cover shift workers anyway, because crèches usually run from 9 a.m. till 5 p.m.

'Anyone who wants to do this job should get as much technical background as they can so that, when they go to an interview, they feel confident in what they're saying. Even if a job doesn't sound very good to start with, it's better to get a foothold and then work your way up. If you get into a job you can at least then prove that you can do it and get on. When I started I was in one of the lowest grades but now they've created even lower grades to cope with cassetting (the dubbing of video cassettes). They're all male in those grades and I don't know that any women apply for those jobs, which I think is a pity because they're the people that they take the next stock of higher grade technicians from.'

Jenny Hooley

□ Supervisor
□ Rank Film Laboratories

Jenny Hooley is a day shift supervisor in the framecount department at Rank Film Laboratories. She is thirty-five, married and lives in the South of England.

» 'The women here are mostly employed in the lower grades, such as positive assembly, viewing and negative breakdown. We're also employed in negative cutting which is a middle grade. Sex discrimination has been operating in the laboratories for years. To my knowledge, there are no women graders or contact persons in England, nor have there been in the last twenty years. We are also discouraged from working in printing and developing because those areas are also male-dominated. When we queried that, we were told that women don't generally like going into those areas. At an interview I had for a vacancy in the contact area, I was asked, "Do you realise that we might expect you to start at 6 a.m. and work till 6 p.m.?" I said that I knew that and wouldn't have applied for the job if I hadn't been willing to work those hours. "Well, what about cooking your husband's tea then?" they asked.

'When we were in the Soviet Union as part of a union delegation, they couldn't believe that there were no women graders in England, because over there all the graders are women. Our colour eyesight is far superior to men's. The colour blindness in men is 8.5 per cent and in women it is only 0.5 per cent. The union put all these facts and figures forward, but we still haven't got a woman grader. I have applied for seventeen grading jobs. We'll make headway one day. We do have one woman in marketing, though.

'Only 25 per cent of the workers at Rank labs are women and most are working class. A lot of the women who work here are not ambitious and just want to work in the lower grades and save to get married and leave for motherhood. There are many, however, who want to make a career at the labs and there are a few who come back into the industry when their families are grown up and they want a career again.

'If you do want a career in the laboratories, you just have to be strong and keep trying. Now they are asking for five GCEs and there is no way you need all that. You just need to be practical and willing to learn.

'Most of the day shifts are from 8 a.m.-4.30 p.m. or 8.30 a.m.-5 p.m. and the clerical shifts are from 9 a.m.-5 p.m. There are three shifts, days, evenings and nights. Evening and night shift workers get paid time-and-a-half. There are only two women on those shifts. The plant runs twenty-four hours a day, five days a week.

'Vacancies are always advertised through the union, because it's a closed shop. Recently the labs were employing youngsters straight out of school in the lower grade jobs. There have been redundancies at other labs, however, so the policy lately has been to take on redundant workers from elsewhere first.'

14 The make-up artist

1 Job description

Most television companies employ at least one make-up artist on staff and many film and video production companies hire free-lance make-up artists to work on television commercials, films and programmes in which actors or performers appear. The role of the make-up artist varies enormously from one production to the next. At a small television company she may simply re-touch the make-up of interviewees and programme guests and tidy their hair. Many of those whom we see on our television screens, such as continuity announcers or journalists, usually do their own make-up and don't require any help. For drama productions, television commercials or feature films, however, the make-up artist's work can be very complex. She could be required to make the actors or performers look glamorous or dowdy, older or younger. She may have to create special effects, such as wounds or burns, or reproduce physical abnormalities like those in *The Elephant Man*, or alter the actor's features by, for example, changing the shape of the nose. The production may have a certain 'look' to it, as in the movie *A Clockwork Orange* in which the gang members were distinguished by their bizarre make-up, and the make-up artist would have to collaborate with other departments to create the desired effect. If the production was set in a particular historical period, she would have to carry out research in order to design a style of make-up appropriate to that era. For example, Barbara Daly had to look at paintings and drawings of the period before creating the make-up for *Barry Lyndon*.

2   Hours and conditions of work

Again, these vary greatly, depending on the job. You could be employed with a production company and work an average eight-hour day with little or no travelling involved. If you worked for a television company, you would probably be expected to work shifts, since there is often at least one live programme which goes out in the evenings. You could find yourself working very long days, however, and if you are sent on outside broadcasts or on location, then that could mean dealing with adverse weather conditions and being gone from home for extended periods. This is particularly true of work in the feature film industry where you could be sent to the Amazon for six months while a film was being shot there.

It can be a fascinating and creative job, but it can also involve periods of boredom. There may be long hours hanging around a studio or set, waiting to powder the actors' noses between takes. It can be physically tiring also, because you are on your feet most of the time, bending over to apply make-up.

The majority of make-up artists in television are female and there is little discrimination against women in this area – although some crew members don't always take the make-up department seriously and can be dismissive of their work. In the film industry, however, the majority of make-up artists are male and many women claim that it is difficult for them to obtain work in this sector.

3 Qualifications and characteristics required

Many television companies hire trainees. They look for applicants with a background in Art, the theatre or hairdressing, or perhaps someone who has already acquired DATEC or City and Guilds or some other qualification in make-up. A good general education is required, particularly in English and History, because there may be historical research involved. Both the BBC and ITV prefer trainees to be at least twenty-one. Training lasts for approximately two years, at which time you would become a make-up assistant, provided your work was satisfactory. After a further two years at an ITV company, you would be eligible to become a make-up artist, at which time you would be given a great deal of responsibility and be expected to be able to work on your own with little supervision. At the BBC, the make-up assistant could, after four years experience, apply for a job as a supervising assistant, and after a further year in this role, she could apply for a post as a make-up designer, at which stage she would be responsible for researching and designing the style of make-up for a variety of productions.

A good make-up artist will be meticulous in her work, because any sloppiness will be magnified on the screen. She also needs to be creative – able to design a 'look' or visualise how to create an effect using make-up. She will meet all kinds of people, from the famous to the obscure, and she must be confident enough to deal with all types of personality and be able to chat to them and put them at their ease. This is particularly important because the make-up artist may be the last person an interviewee or actor sees before going in front of the cameras and she may have a crucial effect on their mood. She must be a fairly calm person who is able to cope with the tensions of working to a tight schedule in less than ideal conditions – possibly with artistes who are uncooperative.

4 How to become a make-up artist

While at school, you should concentrate on getting a good general education, working towards at least O-levels in English, Art and History – although A-levels are preferable. At the same time, you should learn as much about make-up as you can. Most women's magazines feature articles on this subject, and there are many books, including several by Barbara Daly as well as Vincent Kehoe's *The Technique of Professional Make-up for Film, Television and Stage*. Volunteer to help local drama groups or dance companies with the make-up for their performances. You may be able to get a job with a local hairdresser, helping out on Saturdays or holidays, which would give you valuable experience and demonstrate your interest to future employers. After you leave school, you should consider either going to art college, or training as a hairdresser, or studying make-up. Several drama schools include make-up as part of the curriculum, or you might consider a course like that at the London College of Fashion which specialises in the skills of the television make-up artist (see Appendix A, p.328). Write to television companies and ask if you can observe the make-up department at work and learn as much as you can about television production and about lighting. Keep practising on anyone who will sit still long enough for you to apply make-up and if you show that kind of perseverance and committment, then you should be an impressive candidate for a job as a make-up trainee.

You can also try contacting freelance make-up artists directly and ask to be taken on as an assistant. A list of names can be found in trade directories such as *Kemps Film and Television Yearbook*, *Contacts*, *Film Bang* (applies to Scotland only), or the *BFI Film and Television Yearbook*. You may also be able to contact some make-up artists through ACTT.

Elisabeth Armstrong

☐ Make-up artist
☐ Freelance

Elisabeth Armstrong is one of the most experienced make-up artists around, having started in the early days of television. Since going freelance, she has worked on several films, including *Girl in the Picture* and *Restless Natives*. She is sixty-two, separated from her husband, has no children and lives in Edinburgh.

» 'I had started a brief course in hairdressing just before the war broke out but because of that, I became a driver at the War Office. Then I did a course in hairdressing and make-up – beauty culture, it was then. I applied to the BBC because it was the only television company at that time and I was given an interview and a test, then went into the school they had just started. There were about four of us. Then commercial television opened up and the BBC department lost a lot of people to commercial and there was some fairly rapid promotion. I was promoted to be a supervisor within about eighteen months. In normal circumstances, it might have taken eighteen years. I stayed with the BBC till 1973, marrying a cameraman in the meantime. Then we both gave up and came to Scotland and ran a guest house in the Highlands for three years. After that, we came down to Edinburgh and I've freelanced ever since. I've worked for the BBC and practically all the ITV companies. In the last two and a half years I've done three films.

'When I joined the BBC, there were only about nine of us and now there are about a hundred and forty in the make-up department. The best thing you can do is hairdressing and beauty culture. Hairdressing will get you in. You've really got to have a reasonable standard of education, especially in English and History for period productions. The BBC are unlikely to interview you if you haven't got A-levels in English and History and Art. It's just as well it didn't happen in my day because I haven't got that.

'You need a good eye for colour, obviously, and you've got to have enormous patience and good manners as well as a steady hand. To begin with, in make-up, you're a trainee for two years. Then, depending on the size of the department you're in, you might be given little jobs to do absolutely on your own, whereas in the bigger companies you won't be put on big productions and you'll be doing a lot of watching. Make-up assistants are left on their own to do small programmes for children or schools – things like that. Then you are promoted to make-up artist or designer. That is a whole different thing because you are absolutely responsible to the director or producer to interpret what she wants, how she sees the character and how, indeed, you do. So you work very closely with her. The last costume production I did was *King's Royal*. I had to go to planning meetings, then when the artists are cast, you get them together and decide on the styles and the wigs and all that sort of thing. You work very closely with the costume department when it's a period production, but not when it's modern. As a make-up designer, you are totally responsible for the look of the make-up on the screen. If the hair lace shows on a wig, you're the one who takes the can, and if they have to cut that bit of the film out because the hair's not right, then you *really* take the can. There's a lot of diplomacy needed. Perhaps an actress doesn't like the style of that period even though she's accepted the part, while the director wants it absolutely, categorically 1920s, so you have to get something in between that looks right, with a lot of compromise on her part and a bit of pulling the wool over the director's eyes and saying that's how it was – that sort of thing.

'I haven't encountered any discrimination because there are very few men in television make-up. They've only recently been allowed in. So we weren't batting in a man's world. We were batting in a woman's world. That's not so in films.

'This job has ruined my marriage. Obviously there were other problems. When we were first married there was about nine months before we had a weekend off together. Now that was very trying, especially as my husband was in the studios and I was out filming, so not only couldn't we get weekends together, a lot of the time I was away. It's not good to constantly come home and your wife's not there. Eventually, I decided it was the job or my marriage and gave the job up in 1973. Shortly afterwards, he decided he'd had enough of the rat race in London. We did the guest house, then came to Edinburgh, but unfortunately I got a great deal more work than he did, so eventually we separated. And I am not alone. Any married colleague has problems, especially if your wife or husband isn't in the business and doesn't realise how taxing it can be. You film for twelve or fourteen hours a day. It is very difficult and it has been the cause of a lot of marriages breaking up. But I'm very fortunate to be one of the people in the world who go into work very happily.'

Barbara Daly

☐ Make-up artist
☐ Freelance

Barbara Daly is one of the leading make-up artists in the country, working not only in films, but also creating the make-up for television commercials and magazine features and writing about one book a year on the art of make-up. She is based in London.

» 'I did Fine Arts at Leeds College of Art, before working

as a photographer's assistant for a few months. Then I went to work for the BBC and trained in their make-up department for two years before going freelance. Now I do photographic work, television commercials and some film make-up. I've actually done all sorts of make-up and I could be called on to do anything. For films, I do all the conceptual work and figure it all out, but I don't actually carry it through on the set. Someone else takes over, mainly because of time pressures. Filming can take anything up to six months and my schedule doesn't allow me to go on a film for six months, like I did with *Barry Lyndon* some years ago. Then I worked out how the whole look should be and then actually carried it out on a practical level. You work out what someone would look like in the eighteenth century or whenever and then try and reproduce it. I don't actually do the actors' hair because the hairdresser does that but I'm very involved. You don't just do your thing and let somebody else do their's. It's all got to work as a unit.

'When I was training, you did absolutely everything from learning how to do very straight make-up to sculpting and learning how to build up people's noses, how to make prosthetic pieces and blood – all that good stuff. I think you have to be extremely visual. That's why I think people who've got art backgrounds are suitable, because by inclination they're visual people. I think you have to develop terrific technical skills and you have to be extremely meticulous. You also have to be able to get along with people. I think it's quite important to be tactful. I think art school is quite important and I was lucky to get into the BBC because the training there is fantastic. Most people I know have come from television because you've got to get your training somewhere. The thing is, if you haven't spent years practising on your own because you're motivated, then you're not going to be any good anyway. Like all crafts, you've been doing it all your life anyway. It's something you can't not do. It's like being an actor – you're just interested. You are naturally motivated. People who're good make-up artists often can illustrate and they've been making people up or drawing since they were old enough to hold a pen.

'There are quite a lot of men in make-up. It's changed a lot over the years since I started. When I first started to try and get my union ticket, nearly all the people in film make-up were men. But if anybody ever discriminated against me because I was female, I was too naive to ever notice it. Of course, they're not allowed to keep women out now so it's all changed a lot. Many of the people still working in film are men and a lot of them are very good. Of course, film is so technical. It's not necessarily just doing glamour make-up. You could have the most extraordinary special effects to do. It's quite a craft. They have huge workrooms and it's very interesting. I love it. I can't think of ever doing anything else than this or something connected with it.'

Jane Jones

☐ Make-up artist
☐ ITV

Jane Jones has worked as a freelance make-up artist and now has a staff job with Grampian Television. She is thirty-five and is married with three children aged five, eight and ten. She lives in the Aberdeen area.

» 'I've got a degree in English and a lot of make-up artists are graduates. Mostly you can come in through Fine Art, or through pure Art, or English and Drama. I don't actually know anyone who has come in from the hairdressing side although I know you can. I did Art at school and was quite keen. At university, I did a lot of drama and I tended to gravitate towards the make-up side of it. When I graduated, I was unemployed. Then my husband got a lecturing job in Aberdeen and I walked through the doors of Grampian Television and said, "Gie's a job". They said, "Well, what can you do?" and I said, "Everything". They had a vacancy for a make-up artist and they said, "We don't suppose you know anything about that do you?" and I said, "Yes". I had an interview and they made me draw a picture of a face and asked me to try and age somebody, which I did in a very stagey way because I knew nothing of television make-up. And they said, "Okay".

'Then the training began and I was sent to other companies for experience in a big studio and that went on for about two years. Then I was allowed to be on my own. It's learning as you go, really. There's so much that can't be taught. Then I had my first child and went on the freelance market.

'All make-up is based on lighting. The most important person in the make-up artist's life is the lighting director. This is why it's difficult for someone who's new to television to understand that they might have one style of make-up on one day, and then the next day it might be different. You explain that the lighting's different. A good lighting director can help you 80 per cent of the way.

'The art background is very necessary but anything like that can be taught. If you practise it long enough, you can get it. The tricky thing is that you are often dealing with very famous people and you've got to be confident with them without being pushy. You've got to be a calming influence. They're very vulnerable. They come into a make-up room and they sit there and take off all their make-up. They've got to believe that you're going to make them look good. You can make anyone look good, but you can't always make them look like them, which is the trick. I can sit you down and make you look like Bo Derek, but if I can't make you look like yourself, then I've failed, because successful people always project themselves on to the screen. They can't pretend all the time. They have to try and be themselves – a glamorised version of themselves, but them nevertheless. I would look at you. Are you a "lots of make-up" lady? Are you a fairly natural lady? Are you a feminist and don't want to look made-up? Or are you very sweet, or do you want to look glamorous? It's catching the essence of you and giving you a face that's you and that you like – that's the clever bit.

'If you're nervous, then I've got to calm you down, because this is the last place you visit before you enter the studio. The mood you leave here with, is the mood in which you do the programme. If you're calm and confident, you can forget your appearance and do a great job. If you're anxious about your eyes or mouth and think you look hideous, then you're going to be upset. I guard the artistes a great deal.

'It's quite hard to get into film as a make-up artist if you're a woman. Yet I think women are more aware of body language and are more sensitive, and can spot if somebody is nervous. I think it's mostly women in television because you're not so threatening and women like to be made up by other women. The only barriers you encounter is that occasionally people imagine that make-up isn't important. I think it's very important because I know that it can make the difference between a good and a bad programme. I don't think I get waved aside because I'm a woman. Most women in this business are pretty strong and if you're dealing with Cabinet Ministers and fairly well-known people all day and every day, you don't get crushed very easily.

'You've got to be able to talk to people. You may be

left alone with someone for twenty mintues and you've got to be able to talk to the poor person. I got this job in January with Grampian and I'm the only make-up artist so there's no one to turn to and say, "Do you think that's right?" You just have to get on with it. I don't know how the make-up artists in any of the bigger companies combine the job with children because there are literally twelve and fourteen hour days. You just work as long as the light is there if you're outside, or for as long as a production is running in the studio. I went freelance when my children were young, because then I could plan my work around them and it's also possible to cancel. My husband's a lecturer so he has school holidays. Now I work a thirty-seven hour week. Today it was a 10.30 a.m. start and I finish at 6.30 p.m. Monday, I didn't start till 2 p.m., but I finished at 7 p.m. It's very rarely nine to five. Nights can be till midnight but then you don't start till late the next day. I find it suits me better because I can get my household organised between the gap when they go to school and I go to work. In the afternoon I have a daily woman who comes to meet the children from school and stays till my husband gets home at 5 p.m. He does actually do a good 50 per cent of the household work and does half of the shopping, that sort of thing. I couldn't do it unless he was as supportive as he is.

'I get about ten letters a month from people, a lot of whom are graduates who are out of work. I think the only way to get into television is to walk through the door to get your face known, to hang around, to pester, to be there in person. A beautiful little letter with your CV is wonderful, but it will be filed. To be taken seriously, you have to appear through the door, ask to see people and when people are filming, hang around.'

15 The presenter/ continuity announcer

1 Job description

It is the presenter's job to introduce a programme, provide links between items and perhaps interview guests or participate in the programme activities in some way. She is a sort of 'Mistress of Ceremonies' for that programme. Continuity announcers may appear on screen, or may simply be heard as they announce what is coming next and provide brief links between programmes. They may also be expected to read news bulletins or even present short programmes. Both presenters and continuity announcers may be expected to write their own scripts. Presenters may also be involved in developing the content of the programmes they present, coming up with ideas and suggesting how to approach certain topics etc.

2 Hours and working conditions

Although presenters may be able to record programmes in advance, some shows, like *Breakfast Time*, are still live. Continuity announcers are always live. That can mean working very unsocial hours. It may mean having to be ready in full make-up when the station goes on the air at 6 a.m., looking your brightest and breeziest. It can also mean that you would be the last person to appear on screen before closedown, around midnight. In between, continuity announcers can be stuck by themselves in the presentation studio, which is often a very small, windowless room. Even though they may only be on screen for one minute every half hour, they usually have to remain at their posts, in case there is a fault and they are required to tell viewers what has gone wrong.

Many presenters and continuity announcers are hired on short term contracts of one year or less, which means that there may be very little job security. Great emphasis is placed on personal appearance and personality and companies may discriminate on the basis of age, preferring younger, rather than older women – all of which makes presenters and announcers even more vulnerable. At the moment there are very few black or asian women on our screens, but pioneers, like Beverley Anderson, have shown that there are opportunities.

3 Qualifications and characteristics required

It is important for a presenter or announcer to have a clear voice and good diction. For this reason, preference is often given to those who have had drama or speech training. In general, you should be well-groomed, although certain programmes may require their presenters to have a particular image. For example, they would expect the person who fronts a rock music show to look young and dress in the latest styles, whereas someone introducing a nature programme might wear rubber boots and casual clothes with no make-up and a windblown hairstyle.

Presenters and announcers are drawn from a variety of backgrounds and there are no specific educational requirements. A good grounding in English is advisable, however, since you may be asked to write your own scripts. It is important to be articulate also, because announcers and presenters are often required to *ad lib* in front of the cameras.

Since the job of a presenter is to grab the audience's

attention and hold it throughout the programme, while an announcer not only represents the television company but must persuade viewers to stay tuned to that channel, the best ones are those who convey a strong personality and identity. You should be able to come across as a warm, engaging, lively human being. At the same time, you must be able to cope with the unexpected without becoming flustered.

4 How to become a presenter and/or continuity announcer

If you feel you meet the personal requirements in terms of personality, speech and appearance, then you should obtain the best education that you can. Since most television companies are reluctant to hire anyone in this capacity who is under twenty-one, it would be wise to study for a degree or for some other professional or vocational qualification after leaving school – particularly as the job of presenter/announcer is notoriously insecure. In addition, you might find drama training useful not only to improve your diction but also to learn confidence and performance skills. It is helpful, also, to learn about television make-up, since this would be a feature of your job. Any of Barbara Daly's books will give useful hints, or you could read a professional guide such as Vincent Kehoe's *The Technique of Professional Make-up for Film, Television and Stage*. Write to television companies expressing your interest in becoming a presenter or announcer. Jobs may be advertised in the local press and in national newspapers, like the *Guardian*'s Creative and Media Section which is published on Mondays. Alternatively, you should watch the credits of programmes which particularly interest you, and note the name of the director and/or producer. Then write to them at that television company explaining your interest, pointing out any special qualifications you might have for presenting that kind of programme (i.e. that you are a Physics graduate, if it is a scientific series). You should accompany your letter with a copy of your CV, a recent photograph which shows you at your best, and perhaps a tape of your voice. Since the latter can be very expensive, however, you may not wish to send out your cassette until you have received some sign of encouragement from the producer or the company management. You may even be able to sell your ideas for a programme to a television station and persuade them to hire you as the presenter.

Beverley Anderson

☐ Presenter
☐ Freelance

Beverley Anderson was formerly a full-time presenter for the BBC current affairs programme, *Sixty Minutes*. In the autumn of 1985, she decided to return to teaching at the Oxford Polytechnic. She is in her early forties, separated from her husband and living in Oxford with her nine-year-old son.

>> 'I was born and brought up in Jamaica and then went to university at Wellesley College in Massachusetts, where I read Politics and History, graduating in 1962. At that point, I went into the Jamaican Foreign Service as an administrative trainee. Later, I became a Third Secretary, which is the lowest rank of diplomat, and was posted to Washington for two years. Then I decided that I would rather be a primary school teacher so I came to England. I just thought that I didn't want to spend the rest of my life as a diplomat. It wasn't a sufficiently involving job for me. I wanted something really absorbing, that would stretch me fully. Primary teaching seemed to suit my dilettante interests since I liked both the Arts and Sciences and in fact, it proved to be a sensible decision. I loved it. I did a post

graduate teaching certificate and taught in East London for four years.

'I hadn't really meant to stay here, but I married an Englishman and moved with him to Oxford four years later. I taught in Oxfordshire for a long time. Then, about three or four years ago, I became a Labour city councillor in Oxford and almost immediately a head teacher. As a result of the publicity, Thames Television asked me to do one of the *Sit Up and Listen* epilogue things that they do. Now this coincided with the start-up of Channel Four and Trevor Phillips was looking for a presenter for his new show, *Black on Black*. He saw the epilogue and thought I might be suitable. I said, "You idiot. I'm a full-time teacher" and he said, "Ask them if they'll give you one day off a fortnight as unpaid leave because I think we can manage with that plus the weekend." I teach for a smashing county and they said, "What a good idea."

'Now, I have to say, that it was clear to me after a little while that there were certain disadvantages to television presenting, but since it was merely a delightful hobby, I didn't worry about them too much. After a year, however, the BBC rang and said they were starting this new show, *Sixty Minutes* and would I be interested in taking part. Although I wasn't at all sure it was the right thing to do, for various reasons, I decided to leave my headship and *Black on Black* to go and do *Sixty Minutes*. That proved to be a very bad decision, because none of the things that were described to me came to pass and I had a very unpleasant and unhappy time there. After six months, as soon as I had enough money to survive on, I left. By that point, they had decided that they would make me a reporter even though, when I was initially approached, I had said I wasn't interested in a reporting job. Almost immediately after leaving that, I was asked to write a book for teachers. Then, last November, *Black on*

Black asked me to come back to present the last series, which I did. In the spring of 1985, when I wasn't sure what I wanted to do, this very nice job at the Polytechnic swam into my ken and I grabbed it. So I am now really back in education. If any television work comes up that I want to do, however, and I have the spare time, then I shall do it.

'One of the curious things about being a presenter is the way that you have to put forward a *version* of yourself to the world. So what the audience sees isn't you. It is you, constrained and behaving in particular ways because that's what's required for the camera. You have to learn to act in a way that will make you appear natural on the screen. For example, you have to move gently because any movement is exaggerated on screen. That's not objectionable, but it was odd to have to do that. For me, the really unattractive thing is that, as a presenter, you have to understand that you are the face of someone else's mind and heart. It may be that there are presenters around who have acquired sufficient power to dictate the manner and the matter of what they do, but I have never been in that position. I have always had a lot of control over what I did as a teacher and I don't really find it congenial to have to submit necessarily to someone else's editorial judgment – especially on politics and things of that kind about which I do have my own views. Now I didn't fuss and it wasn't that anybody was particularly picking on me, but I don't find that a very attractive way of living.

'I was well paid and one of the things that persuaded me to go to the BBC was that the salary they were suggesting to me was several thousands more than I was earning from my combined teaching and *Black on Black*. Also, it was going to be a three-day week and since my son is only nine, I really wanted a chance to have a bit more time to be his mother because I've always had to work full-time. I was given a two-year

contract (which is very unusual for the BBC), because I
said I couldn't give up my security for less than that. I
would say, however, that for people to whom
independence is important, it is a good idea not to
regard broadcasting as your sole occupation. If you go
into presenting full-time, you are made very vulnerable
to other people. One of the things I found uncongenial
was that, unlike teaching, if you do good work, that is
not in itself a guarantee that you will be able to move
on or get higher in the presenting side. A presenter is
much more vulnerable to whim, and it seems to me
that there is a great deal of irrational, fashionable
whim. Someone would decide that I would be useful in
a particular slot. I was never consulted about whether I
agreed with the representation that was being made of
me and they wouldn't have thought it appropriate to
consult me. I felt, really, like a sort of Brussels sprout –
like a vegetable. I think they really had difficulty seeing
presenters as full human beings. In broadcasting they
might say, "We seem to be seeing a lot of Beverley
Anderson on the screen. Shouldn't we use somebody
else?" That would be somebody deciding that they'd
had enough of you. They wouldn't be deciding that
because you were doing your job badly. It was simply
time for a change.

'I now think that the people who invited me to come
to *Sixty Minutes* were trying to get themselves some
cheap credit for employing a black woman, and one of
the things that happened was that they behaved much
more carelessly towards me than I had anticipated. I
don't think there's anything wrong with someone at the
Beeb deciding they're going to have a black woman in
current affairs, provided they are going to see that the
person is properly prepared and they committed
themselves to that person. I don't actually object to
tokenism if it's something that someone is doing
responsibly and as a step towards something more

substantial. But if all you're saying is "We'll get some easy Brownie points here for being seen to employ a black woman" then that's worse than doing nothing.'

Margaret Donald

☐ Presenter/news reader
☐ Freelance

Margaret Donald is a freelance presenter and news reader currently working on contract for Grampian Television. She has also recently developed a children's programme which has been produced by Scottish Television. For this, she has created the characters and written the scripts and songs, as well as presenting the programme. She is now aged forty-seven and is married with an eight-year-old son. She lives in Aberdeen.

» 'I did a teacher training diploma in primary education to start with and from there went on to do an associateship because I had a special interest in working with little ones. That was a four year course – not highly academic, but certainly communication was the crucial focus of that kind of work. From there I went on to teach children for several years, finding that music had a special significance in my life. I felt that a lot of my teaching could be done through music and very soon, I was invited to be a teacher of music, which I did for two years, covering nineteen schools. I travelled from one school to the next and it was a wonderful time. Then I was invited to the US to work for the summer at San Jose University as an early childhood specialist and again my strength in music seemed to be a tremendous asset. I did that for seven summers. Somewhere during this phase, the local college of education were short of early childhood staff and I was approached. I accepted a job there, although this meant giving up the music teaching. I started doing an MEd at the university part-time because I wanted to be more academically qualified and I was doing fine. Then the principal of the college asked me if I'd like to take up a lectureship in primary education. I knew I couldn't do the full-time lectureship and the MEd at the same time because I'm not made that way. The demands made on me on the domestic front were too great. I'd have cracked because I'm very, very conscientious. So I gave up the MEd. I did seven years of the lectureship which were exceedingly hard. I wasn't sure that I was well enough qualified in all the subject areas. I was conscious of certain gaps which, needless to say, all other eighteen members of the department had but seemed not to worry about. I required perfection of myself. So that, in a sense, was a weakness of mine. I think it was one of the reasons why, when the Thatcher regime took a grip, I was one of the first to volunteer for redundancy. There was also the fact that as a married woman, it was assumed I was supported by my husband, when in fact I wasn't, and the single women in the department felt that I should be the first to go. That was very suffocating so I left.

'I was very, very lost in the first six months without the lectureship, after fourteen years of professional life. I loved being with my baby, but I had a thirst for intellectual stimulation of some kind. One day, I took a long look at my personal resources and concluded that these were essentially in the realm of communication. I'd always been interested in broadcasting. The head of Radio Scotland sent me to Glasgow for a voice test. He then advised me to go to my local station and offer ideas. There was no training. I learned to use the Uher (the tape recorder) very quickly. I found that success came, not because of my skills but because of my specialist knowledge. My first ever tape was done at the local music school. Steadily, commissions began to come in. Then a position came up at Grampian Television as a continuity announcer and, much to my surprise, I got it. One of the reasons for accepting was that the pay was just so much better. Also, I'm embarrassed to admit that the demands of the job, compared to rushing around as a radio broadcaster, were just nil. Once I mastered the job, there was nothing to it. When this job dies, as it will, I'll have to go back into radio, unless my STV series grows. But I think the precariousness of being a freelance broadcaster can make you better at the job. Staff can plod along, but you have to be better than that to sell your work.

'The basic requirements for presenters vary from company to company. This particular one requires youth and attractiveness. You have to have a pleasant voice and you're expected to have considerable skill with English. A drama background is often accepted instead of an academic one. I think that someone who is jumpy and edgy is really no use because it comes across and all the work is done live. You have to be able to look serene even if you're not. So, a really strong centre is required – you have to be quite tough and courageous. You're up there live, on your own, and you have to be able to take your failures – which are inevitable – look at them, learn from them and then forget them.

'You need to be exceptionally good at grooming and be able to maintain that grooming throughout a twelve-hour day. You also have to find yourself a good hairdresser. People who have come to this job and not cared enough about their appearance, have not had their contracts renewed. I think it is because I've studied make-up techniques etc. in some depth, that I am still working on camera at the age of forty-seven.

'The system here is that four members of staff will be on relatively long contracts of about a year. Since I'm freelance, I'm sometimes on a daily, sometimes a weekly or even a monthly contract. There's no such thing as a life-time job in continuity. There's a great deal of anxiety because it's a job that's desirable and perceived as glamorous. Therefore other people have often come along and knocked on the door and said to my employers that they can do better than me. That adds to the precariousness.

'From my experience here, I would say that women don't fight as aggressively for their contracts as men. My situation is unique because my husband is a theatre manager and really comes to life late at night. Freelances are used here for day shifts and I find I have to be in at a reasonable hour. I'm up in the morning drying my hair when he wants to sleep. That's probably the major handicap. On the social scene, you have to say, "No" to certain social events because you know it will leave you tired. You have to put your appearance first, and say "Goodnight" early, because you are a sitting duck on the screen. Some viewers can be quite rude. There are moments of panic when I think I can't possibly expect to continue because of my age. But I console myself with the thought that many of our viewers are old and housebound. I must seem young to them!'

Debbie Rix

☐ Presenter
☐ ITV

Debbie Rix was formerly the newsreader on BBC's *Breakfast Time*. Recently, however, she has become the presenter of ITV's programme, *Game for a Laugh*. She is single, aged twenty-nine and lives in the London area.

» 'I left school at eighteen and considered going to university to read English and Drama, but decided that

I would rather get on with the career that I wanted to do which was broadcasting. So I went to the BBC and asked if they had any production courses but was unable to do any of them because I wasn't a graduate. They said I could be trained as a production secretary which filled me with horror at the time. I had never expected to be a secretary and I told them so and they said, "Well, you could be a producer in five years if you worked really hard." Well that, as it turns out, isn't true. I joined on that basis, however, and trained as a production secretary, then worked in the science unit in radio for two years. Fortunately, I was put with a producer with whom I got on very well and he allowed me to do a great deal of research. That's where I got my first taste of what broadcasting is really about. Then I moved to television and I worked on *The Body in Question* for two years. I was still a production secretary, feeling very frustrated and wanting to be a researcher or whatever, but, nevertheless, fairly contented to be working on a very good series like that. Then I became a production assistant and eventually went to work on *Everyman*. I fell in love with it. Its output was exactly what I was interested in. After two years of that, I began to do research for people and got researcher credits although I wasn't actually a researcher. But I felt that this was what I wanted. At the same time, I started to diversify slightly. I decided that I wanted to get on in television and that although I would still pursue the producer strand, I would also tackle it from another angle. I did an audition at BBC Bristol and was given a little job presenting a music series. That was great fun, but they couldn't afford to take on extra staff, so I came back to *Everyman*. Occasionally, I auditioned for other things, but there were a lot of disappointments along the way. For example, the film programme decided they liked me very much then changed their minds. Eventually, I got a researcher's job and then *Breakfast Time* began to happen. I wrote them a letter with a photograph and said I'd like to be a reporter and thought no more about it really. I then applied for a job at Channel Four as a researcher. The day of my first interview, I had a phone call from *Breakfast Time* asking me if I'd like to audition to be a newsreader. I was flabbergasted because I'd never thought about doing that. We arranged to do the audition in a couple of days and I went off for my interview. I knew I was going to get the job at Channel Four – you know how sometimes you just know – and in fact I was offered the job. I thought, "I don't really want it. I'd rather be on *Breakfast Time*." So I did the audition and I was dreadful. I thought about it overnight and next day I phoned up and said, "Please give me another audition. I know I can do better." The producer kindly agreed. I then phoned up Channel Four and told them I didn't want the job, at which everyone said, "You're mad. You're never going to get *Breakfast Time*. Why are you throwing away this really good job?" But I just had a feeling it was the right thing to do. I'm afraid that's how I always live my life; and I got the job on *Breakfast Time*. When Ron Neill, the editor, called me into his office and told me, I staggered out of the office and just whooped with delight. It was amazing. It must have been one of the happiest days of my life, I should think.

'I have to be honest and say that I have two interests in broadcasting. I like performing. I also like producing. You can very rarely do both. I have an organisational ability and a fairly strong editorial feeling for things. I decided to try to be a presenter, however, because it was something I really wanted to do. I just have a natural performing desire. As it happens, I love being a presenter for now, but in the end, I think I would like to combine the two.

'After reading the news on *Breakfast Time* for two and a half years, I felt I'd done it and I couldn't go on like that for ever, because I wasn't developing. I would never have come up with the idea of going to *Game for a Laugh* but when it was offered, I thought about it very seriously and I realised that it was perfect.

'Being a presenter is rather a broad term. It can encompass so many things. I think you need to be unflappable, and within that you have to be naturally calm, otherwise you've really had it. It's also important to be able to write reasonably well because no one can express things the way you want to say them. When it comes to interviewing people, I think you have to be somebody who is prepared to listen and not talk. I know that sounds very obvious, but it's very easy to interrupt people all the time, especially on live television, because you become nervous about spaces and gaps. I think you have to have a lot of common sense – that's what interviewing is all about really. I'm a great believer in preparation, because all that matters at the end of the day is your performance, and you have to be perfect when the camera's on you. I think it's very important to get it right first time, so it's never your fault that they have to do it again if it's recorded.

'I have no idea how other people become presenters. The way I did it was very hard. It's been very hard work these eleven years with many disappointments *en route*. I wouldn't recommend the way I did it as an automatic way up. You've got to be able to believe in yourself on the way and know that you are capable of more than they say that you are at that moment. There is no automatic way of becoming a presenter. Some have never worked in production in their lives. As it happens, I'm glad I did, because it gives me an enormous background knowledge and I think it helps me a lot. I understand what everyone's problems are and that makes me feel more confident about what I can do in the future. I mean, a presenter's life is a precarious one.

'I was never, I believe, pushed back because I was a woman. I think I was pushed back because I was an assistant and it's true to say that, as a rule, women are assistants in the BBC. I think they wanted to keep me as a production assistant desperately. Some people say that you can be too good at your job. If you are good as a floor manager, then they will keep you as a floor manager. I know. I've heard too many testimonials from people who've sat on the other side of the interviewing panel. If you're good at what you're doing, they want to keep you at that level because otherwise they'd have to find someone to replace you.

'As it happens, I have a boyfriend who works in the business and who does understand the demands of my job. I don't know how easy it would have been if I had been going out with a banker or something. Perhaps they would find it very inconvenient that I was always going away or that they never knew when I was coming home. I love my job so much that I never think about it interfering with my own desires. If I can't come home to go to a dinner party because I'm working, then that's that. There are days when you are working all the hours God gives you and days when you might not be doing anything at all and then you have time to yourself. That's the other thing I love about it. Nobody's clock watching on this side of the business. I love it.'

16 The producer

1 Job description

The role of the producer varies from one work situation to the next. In broadcasting, the producer usually has the overall responsibility for a production and often has the final say in all decision-making regarding the film or programme. She will probably decide on the content of the programme – perhaps from a range of ideas put forward by many different people. She then determines how that content will be presented – whether the overall tone will be humorous, serious, hard-hitting, or low-key and whether the style of presentation will be documentary, or fictionalised, or involve skits or song and dance routines or whatever. A decision may also have to be made about whether the programme will be shot in a studio or out on location. With the help of the researcher (if there is one) and the director, she will decide who will appear on the show, who will present it, what information will be given and, if actors are required, who will be cast in various roles. In some companies, the producer will have very little leeway in the choice of crew and director as these may be simply assigned to her according to which staff are available. The director will usually be responsible for the actual creation of the sound and images and for coordinating the activities of the cast and crew, but the producer will often be present throughout to ensure that the effect created is the one that she had envisaged. She will also supervise most of the administrative details, such as the preparation of the budget, making sure that expenditure does not exceed that amount, and that the production is completed on schedule. She will have checked that all legal and union requirements have been met, that contracts for cast and freelance crews are in order, and that copyright clearance for music or other original material has been obtained.

In the feature film industry, the producer may, or may not take a creative role. She may be responsible for the business and financial side only, raising the money, overseeing the budget, and then marketing the finished product. On some productions, a big name star may usurp the power of the producer and call the shots; on others, it may be the director who has the clout and the producer is hired to stay in the background and handle the business and administrative side of things. There are other producers, however, who do have a creative input into the films on which they work. They may come up with the original idea, hire someone to write the script, or even co-write it, choose the director, sign on the crew, cast all the actors and select the locations to be used. Often such tasks are carried out in collaboration with the director, however. In some situations, the roles of the producer and director overlap and may be carried out by one and the same person. This frequently occurs in small companies or university film and television departments. In the film industry, many producers are independent and work for themselves. Since it may take several years for a project to get off the ground, and since many never get into production at all, most producers will have several films in development at any one time, all of them at different stages.

2 Hours and conditions of work

The hours that a producer works vary from one situation
to the next and may depend on what stage a project is at.
It can take up all your waking hours, particularly during
shooting, and the more money is involved, then the more
time it can take up, in general. The only advantage is that
it is usually considered to be a high-level job and
producers can plan their own schedules, working when
they please. Unless you are working on small, locally
based or studio productions, you could be expected to
spend long periods away from home. Your work schedule
could also be very unpredictable, dependent on the
requirements of the production, the vagaries of the
weather etc., which could make it very difficult to cope
with domestic commitments also.

It is a high pressure job because, generally, the buck
stops with the producer. She takes ultimate responsibility
for even the tiniest details and can be held accountable for
the work done by those she supervises on the crew. If you
are involved in raising money, that can be a dispiriting
experience and the job, as a whole, requires a great deal
of stamina. The attraction for many people, however, is
that this is a job in which you can have some impact on
the final product and make some creative contribution.
That can be an exciting and ultimately rewarding
experience. The producer is also one of the most highly
paid members of the crew, in most cases.

Since it is such a high-level job, it is, predictably, one in
which there are relatively few women. Female producers
who work as independents complain that it is difficult to
persuade financiers and backers to trust women with
large sums of money. Many of those working for
television companies find it hard to become promoted to
producer. Thus, many women find it a struggle to reach
this level, and once there, they may have to battle against
prejudice. This is a situation which can only improve,

however, as more women enter the industry and work their way up through the ranks and demand equal opportunity.

3 Qualifications and characteristics required

In the feature film industry there are no formal qualifications required, although it is probably helpful if you know something about film-making. The same is true if you wish to become an independent producer. There are those who become involved because they are accountants or financiers who get caught up in raising money for a film. Others may simply have come up with a good idea or an excellent script which they have then been able to persuade a television company, or someone else with money, to back.

It is usually a much slower and more complicated process to become a producer with a television company, however. For example, news producers will probably have begun their career as journalists and have spent many years working at different jobs within the news or current affairs departments. Drama producers may have theatrical experience, music producers may have worked with an orchestra before going into television etc. Generally, however, one becomes a producer by working one's way up through the organisation. Typically, one might be promoted from being a researcher or a director or an assistant producer to become a fully fledged producer. (At the BBC, an assistant producer very often functions as a director.)

Whichever route she takes, however, a producer has to be someone who can organise events and people. She must have the personality and the energy to sell an idea and create enthusiasm in backers, those responsible for programming (if it's a television show), cast and crew. She must be good at handling people, because she will have to reconcile conflicting artistic egos, or persuade hardheaded business investors to part with money. She must be able to cope with a myriad of details efficiently, as well as a multitude of demands on her attention and all the resulting pressures. Most producers have to be highly creative and resourceful, because it is they who either come up with ideas, or choose from other people's suggestions, and who must be able to visualise how the original concept can best be developed into a film or programme which will attract and hold an audience. Last, but not least, you should also have a good head for business, or you won't last long as a producer!

4 How to become a producer

If you wish to become a producer with a broadcasting company, then you will probably be expected to have some previous experience of television production. That may mean working as a researcher or director for several years before applying for a job as a producer. At the BBC, the general rule is that you become an assistant producer first, having previously worked in another grade. You may have to work as a floor manager, or researcher before applying for promotion to producer. If your ambition is to produce news and current affairs programmes, then you would get as much journalistic experience as possible first, and would probably have worked as a television reporter or sub-editor or director in the news department for several years before becoming a producer.

It is still possible, however, simply to come up with a good idea and sell it to a television company or to backers. But a word of warning. Many a budding producer has come up with a brilliant concept, taken it to someone whom they thought could help get it produced and then had their idea stolen. Television companies are not exempt from this practice. If you can, prepare a treatment or preferably a full script and then get advice about copyright before submitting it to anyone else. Channel Four is possibly the most receptive to ideas and the least likely to steal them since it relies on independents to produce its programmes. It may require great perseverance to get in touch with the appropriate staff member there, however.

In the feature film industry, you can try selling your idea, or apply to grant bodies such as the Scottish Film Production Fund (if you live in Scotland), or the British Film Institute or regional Arts Councils. Alternatively, you may be able to persuade a film company or a producer to take you on as an assistant and go from there. A list of companies and producers can be found in *Kemps Film and Television Yearbook*, which should be available through your local library. There is also a directory of producers and assistant producers which is published by ACTT. In the meantime, as well as learning as much as you can about production techniques, you might do well to read a manual such as *The Independent Film and Videomakers Guide* (1984) by Michael Wiese which gives an introduction to the making and distribution of an independent film, or Danford Chamness's *A Hollywood Guide to Film Budgeting and Script Breakdown* (1983). You might also enjoy William Goldman's book, *Adventures in the Screen Trade* (1984), which gives a fascinating insight into the way films are produced in Hollywood.

Jan Mathew

☐ Producer/director
☐ Educational technology

After graduating from the Guildhall School of Music and Drama, Jan Mathew then spent two years teaching for the Inner London Education Authority (ILEA). It was this experience of London schools that helped her to get her first job in educational technology at the ILEA television centre. Following that, she decided to obtain a second degree, this time an MA in Television and Film at the Royal College of Art. She is now thirty-seven and works at Brighton Polytechnic where she is a producer/director. Because of the recent budget cuts to education, the unit in which she works is required to cover some of its costs by doing work for outside bodies. For this reason, 60 per cent of her time is spent on industrial projects and only 40 per cent on educational productions.

» 'Generally speaking in education, there's one grade of producer/director which involves doing both jobs. It means managing the money for projects and seeing the production through from beginning to end as well as doing all the actual direction. Sometimes I include script-writing and sometimes I don't – it depends very much on what the project is. I would say that I write my own scripts 50 per cent of the time. I don't do any of the hands-on work for editing.

'The job covers a wide range of topics. I am employed to make programmes within the area of social and cultural studies. Aside from that, for the last couple of years, we've also been required to make training films for industry. About half of my programmes now are programmes about electronics. I think ed. tech. has always had to struggle for survival, but I think it will survive. With the changes in the industry, I think that in future there will be more work in ed. tech. and not less.

'I encountered a lot more difficulties with sexual harassment and discrimination as a younger woman than I do now. It also happened more recently in this job, however. I was working on my own in an edit suite, which obviously had no windows, and the man came into the room and he just grabbed me. I threw him off and went and found friends in the building. The first time something like this happened I was much younger and I didn't tell people. On the second occasion I did tell everybody and I reported it. Recently staff and students at Brighton Poly have collaborated in starting a working party on sexual harassment. Our unit is extremely sympathetic and there are men as well as women who are interested in having women work here.

'I think it would be possible to combine this job with family commitments and I am, in fact, pregnant right now. But it won't be easy. It would be particularly difficult for a single parent. Obviously the wages in ed. tech. aren't as high as in other parts of the industry, but if you're working at producer level, then they are high enough to manage with children. I think it would be a very different matter for someone who's working in, for example, a technician's job, because there is a big divide in terms of earning.

'In a sense, I got into the kind of work I do by accident and you could say that about every producer working here. There is no one prescribed route. It's certainly less pressured in ed. tech. than in broadcasting – less well paid, but less pressured, although there certainly are times when I am under pressure. Another advantage for me is that the people I work with are committed to the ideology of education and that makes them very different from the kind of people who work in mainstream broadcasting. That's one of the main reasons that I've stayed working in education. In the kind of job I'm doing at the moment, there doesn't ever come a point where someone's putting pressure on me to say the product is more important than the people. It's my choice which is more important. I work with a small team, the same team each time, so we know each other and we have good relationships with each other. That's very important to me. There's never any question of me being challenged as a producer because

I'm a woman, because I work with the same people each time and they know that I do my job to the best of my ability. If I worked in broadcasting, I'd be working with a different crew each time and I think that the stresses of that – particularly for a woman – are much greater. The other thing is that we have a split crew of women and men which, again, is fairly unusual. That makes it different from the type of crew I might work with in mainstream television.'

Lynda Myles

☐ Producer
☐ Feature films

Lynda Myles is the producer of the recent cinematic success, *Defence of the Realm*, made while she was working for David Puttnam's company, Enigma Productions. She is in her late thirties and is based in the London area where she has now formed her own independent production company.

» 'When I was at university in Edinburgh in 1967, I was involved in movies through the university film society and I was very unhappy about the state of the film festival [The Edinburgh International Film Festival]. At that point it was being run in a rather ramshackle way with part-time people. So a friend and I attacked it in the *Scotsman* newspaper and later it turned out that Murray Grigor had just taken over as director so he asked this friend and me to join the staff. Gradually, I became more and more involved. I went to work for BBC for about eighteen months, but basically I wanted to work in movies more than anything else. In 1972 we did the first *Women and Film* event in Europe at the film festival. What's frightening about it is that that was 1972 and we were yelling about the shortage of women directors, but nothing has changed. In 1973 I became the full-time director of the film festival and, over the next eight years I wrote *The Movie Brats* with Michael Pye and I taught about film at the National Film School. I also did some lecturing and broadcasting. Then, in 1980, I went to America to the Pacific Film Archive and decided I really wanted to produce. Sean Connery knew that and also that I didn't know how to start. He'd promised to do a film about his relationship with Edinburgh so he suggested I produce that and that was great. While I was in America, I was flown back to accept an award from the BFI (British Film Institute) and it was presented by David Puttnam and I told him I wanted to produce. He said, "Well, we could use producers more than anything. You should come back." That was in 1981. So I started thinking about a way of getting back and Jeremy Isaacs offered me a job as a film consultant at Channel Four. I was there for a year.

'Then I went to see David Puttnam one day and he said, "Why don't you come and work here?" So I went to work for David in 1983 as a so-called creative producer, which meant I was commissioning scripts. I read the script of *Defence of the Realm* which David had agreed to produce and absolutely fell in love with it. One of the things Puttnam taught me was that you've really got to be willing to kill to make a film. Unless you care about it as much as that it's pointless because it's going to be two or three years of your life.

'I think there are lots and lots of different kinds of producers. There are some producers who are just wonderful at doing the deals. There's this notion of "the art of the deal" and some people structure deals so delicately and elegantly that it takes other people's breath away. That's not what interests me at all. I tend to be on the set all the time, because my interest in production is very much the Puttnam model. Ideally, I would have the original idea, maybe a one line story, then bring in the writer, bring in the director and work with them staying very closely involved with every aspect. I couldn't understand why anyone would be a producer just to deal with the money.

'I think it's been an advantage to me having twenty years of theoretical experience. I used to see about 500 films a year so at least now I know whether something is innovative or not. It's very easy, especially for young directors, to think they're doing something startlingly new when, in fact, Godard did it ten years ago. I tend to think that it helps to be female. This is a sort of dodgy area, but I think that I don't like working in an atmosphere of friction. I don't believe people work best that way. That's one of the reasons I hang around the set all the time and talk to everyone to stop problems before they arise. I think sometimes being female helps with that – that you care more about that side of the production. I'm very reluctant to plug traditional female virtues, but I think maybe one does care just a bit more. Obviously, the producer doesn't hire everyone on a crew so if you're a female on the set for the first few days, most people will think I'm the hairdresser or the producer's secretary. I find it quite funny really, to see their faces when they find out I'm the producer. It's just a reflection of the way women generally turn up in the industry. It would be pointless getting angry. I just make a joke out of it. I don't believe in intimidating people. It's going to be very different after this when I'm working as an independent producer because I think that's when the real trouble starts when you're trying to raise money. I suspect that that's when my being female will start to be a bit of a problem, because I think that most men traditionally don't trust women with money. Sometimes one feels slightly condescended to. I don't think I've ever felt harassed. If anyone actually tried anything like harassment, I can be very frosty.

'There's no clear cut way into producing. I would recommend going to the National Film School or I would suggest just trying to get involved – perhaps by forming a team with a director and a writer and trying to set something up. I think it's very hard to come from nowhere and get a couple of million. I mean I've never heard of anybody doing it. If I were a novice producer and had an interesting idea then I'd certainly take it to Channel Four or to one of the many companies around now who're making low budget things. You might have to accept that for the first film you'll have a co-producer. Every new project, you start from scratch.

'I think there's no point in doing it unless you're prepared to make your personal life come second. I just don't see how you can do it otherwise, because last year, 1984, is virtually obliterated for me, because we were struggling to get *Defence of the Realm* financed. It's going to eat up every minute and you've just got to have understanding friends who put up with the fact that you'll disappear for three months and that you'll probably cancel 90 per cent of the times you arrange to see them. I don't think you can produce on your own terms. You've just got to go and do whatever needs to be done. Having said all that about the agonies of it all, however, I must say just how fabulous it is. It's worth it.'

Esther Rantzen

☐ Producer/presenter
☐ BBC

Esther Rantzen is the producer and presenter of the highly successful BBC programme, *That's Life*. She is married with three children and lives in the London area.

» 'I always wanted to work in the BBC. I'm second generation BBC. My father was the head of engineering design and I suppose that through him I became aware of the role that BBC played as an enormous patron of journalism and the arts. I thought it would be a marvellous place to work. I just tried to get in in whatever capacity I could. I did a secretarial course, but it turned out I was hopeless at that. In those days, they went round the universities, Oxbridge particularly, looking for two kinds of people. They wanted general trainees who were bright young men – just occasionally a bright young woman, but really so occasionally that it's not worth thinking about, and studio managers who worked in radio. It was at least a way in, so I did both sets of interviews. I came nowhere in the general trainee's one, but got a job as a studio manager. I did that for two and a half years and it was valuable experience. It's important that you do a job that isn't right for you because then you appreciate a job that is right for you. Personally, I found the studio manager's job very difficult because you were working with producers and actors whose work was obviously creative while your job was simply to provide a technical service – producing the correct sound effects, playing in the tapes or mixing the sound. I wasn't very good at it, so it was doubly frustrating because I felt unstimulated by the job and unable to produce any of my best work. After two and a half years, I resigned and spent three months on the dole, so I know about being unemployed and how utterly soul-destroying and brain-knotting and demoralising it is.

'Then I pulled a string, a university contact I'd had when I was at Oxford. I knew that the mother of a student I'd met there was somebody important at the BBC. She ran a small revolutionary movement getting women into the BBC. An awful lot of creative women in the BBC only got their jobs because this woman,

Mrs Joanna Spicer, had eased them in through that implacable portcullis. She eased me into a clerical job in her programme planning department. From there I heard that Ned Sherrin was looking for a researcher. I applied and I knew it was going to be the biggest break in my life. It was. Ned took me on, on a six-week contract for £20 a week with not even a screen credit because he forgot about me. It was absolutely wonderful. He was the kind of boss who, once he realised I understood how to do something, kept throwing more and more difficult work at me. From then on, one contract led to another. I worked as a researcher, then a trainee director, then as a researcher in vision for Bernard Braden. I never thought that would lead to any more work in front of the camera but eventually it did. That was in 1968.

'It's difficult to generalise about women, but if one must, I think women suffer from a lack of self-confidence. If you get a man and a woman together applying for a job, a woman is aware of her weaknesses. A man may be aware of his, but doesn't talk about them. He'll bluff and catch up later. I also think that women are frequently content with jobs in which they are underemployed because it's safe and they're happy within the limitations. Comparatively recently, a colleague of mine in this very office showed enormous talent and then quit to go abroad and have a series of much less demanding jobs. I argued with her till we were both purple in the face and tried to tell her about the opportunities that I felt were open to her. Eventually she said to me, "Yes, I've seen those tough old hags in the canteen, and I don't want to be one of them." Now the tough old hags she's talking about are senior producers, women who have gone through this grindingly slow promotion process and done so with courage, some of them trying to be wives and mothers at the same time. She couldn't see what creative people these were. She only saw them as tough old hags and so I gave up at that point. Sadly, I think a lot of women might agree with her and limit themselves by saying, "I'd rather be the blossom with the dew still on my petals. I choose not to brave the fierce heat of the sun and try for a difficult job in a man's world"; and they could be right, I could be wrong.

'There's a thrill that you can't analyse in this job, which is a show business thing. Television is in the entertainment business. You have to be able to present programmes well to an audience. No matter how serious or intellectual a programme is, you have to be able to attract and hold the viewer. So a producer or presenter has to be able to tell a story well and that is an instinct which I don't believe can be learned. It can be developed, the eye can be sharpened, but in my view, the basic skill is something that you've either got or you haven't. So when I'm talking to young people who want to join television, I'm always interested to know what they did at school, what they do at university, whether they're interested in performance of any kind, whether they're interested in journalism and so on. These days, there are a lot of opportunities for non-professionals to gain experience – hospital radio is one, university radio is another. There are a lot of closed-circuit television places, university magazines, local newspapers and so on, where you don't earn a lot of money, heaven knows, but you do get terrifically valuable experience. They demonstrate your skill in communication. So that comes first and foremost. Then you have to have the curiosity to watch what other people are doing and learn from them. I think you also have to have stamina, determination and guts to do this hideously demanding job which can use up your whole life during the period of apprenticeship. Your social life goes to pot. During that time you have to be able to travel, to spend long hours in the office. It does ease off a bit, but it is never a nine-to-five job in the office. It's never predictable. It's never safe.

'Nobody ever combines home life and work to their satisfaction. A vast proportion of my salary goes on the many support systems that a working mother needs. You have to be quite schizophrenic. You have to make time. It's even difficult because the work gets between my husband and myself. We have to make dates with each other over the phone. Our drives together are much treasured because nobody can interrupt us.

'But I think it would be insane to plan to postpone marriage and children because of one's career. I think you have to be who you are. I was a late emotional developer always. By having my children later, I felt no conflict between a social life and them, because I'd done all that socialising and I was aware of its limitations and I very much valued time with the children.

'I think that building a career is harder for women. I don't think people much like other people's success, and I don't think people like success for women at all really. Sometimes survival goes not to the most talented, but to the one with the most stamina. The answer is, if you do do it, if you pick yourself up for the umpteenth time and you do get the job and you do make a success of it, you will make it easier for the next generation of women.'

17 The production assistant/ production secretary

1 Job description

The job of a production assistant is often viewed as being secretarial, although it is much more than that. The production assistant is the right arm of the producer or director with whom she works and in many companies will be assigned to work with one producer or director, so that they become a permanent team. She will perform some secretarial tasks, such as answering the telephone, arranging appointments and typing letters, but she will also type scripts and keep track of most of the paperwork to do with each production. Many of the administrative details may be left to her, too, including perhaps arranging accommodation and travel for the crew when they go on location.

During a television production, the precise role played by the PA (as she is usually called) will vary depending on the size of the crew and her relationship with the director. Generally, however, she will sit next to the director and time the programme as it happens and cue the technicians so that, for example, the vision mixer knows when to superimpose a caption over the picture on the screen, or the engineering staff know when to start the video tape machine so that the required pictures are ready on time. During a filmed production, the PA will assist the producer and/or director, acting as liaison with the crew and helping with the many administrative details which have to be dealt with. For example, if there are script changes, she will note those down, re-type the script and make sure that everyone has a copy. Some PAs will also do continuity. (See p.272 for an explanation of this.)

The production assistant, along with the producer and director, may be the only person who follows a film or programme through from its conception to completion. Thus, she is a pivotal member of the crew. At times, she may be the only person who is able to provide information to one technician about the work being done by another. The job of a production assistant can, therefore, be both demanding and very satisfying.

Frequently, the PA's job overlaps with that of the production secretary and both jobs require many of the same skills and experience. The precise role of the production secretary varies enormously from one situation to another, however. In some companies, she may perform only secretarial duties, typing scripts and letters on behalf of the PA, the producer, the director and other members of the crew. She can also have a very crucial role to play, particularly on a big production. She may take on many of the administrative duties of the PA and assist the producer and production manager with the organisation of a production. But unlike the PA, she would not normally be on the set or in the studio to assist while a film or programme was being shot.

On many smaller productions, however, the job of production secretary and that of PA would be done by the same person. Some companies even consider that being a production secretary is a stepping stone to becoming a production assistant. Therefore the description of working conditions and skills required which follows would be applicable, in many instances, to both jobs.

2 Hours and working conditions

The hours which a PA works vary not only from job to job, but from one production to the next. She could be expected to start early, if the crew is going out on location, or she could have to work late, typing up notes which are essential for the next day's shooting or editing. She could also be expected to work shifts if there are early morning or late night programmes or recording sessions to be done. The job may, or may not, involve travel. Some PAs always work in the studio, others – particularly those on feature films – may be sent to distant locations and be away from home for days, weeks or even months at a time. The key is to find the work situation that suits you and your lifestyle.

It can be a high-pressure job, because the PA has to keep track of so much important information, work to deadlines and cope with the many different personalities amongst the cast and crew. It is also a job which is often under-valued. According to the ITCA figures, all the PAs in independent television companies are female and this is probably also true of the BBC. You can end up feeling like the general dogsbody in this job.

Production assistants can also be poorly paid for the amount of time and effort they put into their jobs and the amount of responsibility which they undertake. It is possible to earn a very good income as a PA, however, particularly in the feature film industry and at some independent television companies.

3 Qualifications and characteristics required

A production assistant should have a good general education and secretarial qualifications. Some women who have degrees take jobs as PAs with the goal of transferring to other grades within the company. But although this is a job in which you learn how a programme is made, it is also a job which is frequently undervalued and many women have found it difficult to convince employers that they are capable of doing other jobs. A university degree is not essential for this job and those who hope to move on to other grades may find it a dead-end.

It is important to have good organisational skills because much of the job involves administration. You should be able to process information and set it out clearly. When you take notes or write something up, it must be understandable to any member of the crew. You must also be resourceful because you will often be expected to cope with details and minor crises by yourself.

Since the production assistant is at the hub of the activity, you should be able to cope with all kinds of people and be confident enough to deal with celebrities and various personalities. It helps to be good-natured, because you will be juggling lots of different tasks and be expected to remain calm and pleasant when there are half a dozen people all asking for information or help at the same time. It is particularly important to remain unflustered during a live production because if the PA loses track of what's going on, then the whole thing can fall apart.

4 How to become a production assistant

Get a good general education, with at least 5 O-levels at a high grade. It would probably be helpful if one of those was in English. Then you should acquire good secretarial skills, including fast, accurate typing and shorthand. While you are doing that, find out as much as you can about film and television production. Write to companies and ask if you can visit their facilities and talk to their PAs about the job, as well as observing them at work. There are a number of good textbooks which give general information about production techniques, such as Gerald

Millerson's *The Technique of Television Production*.

When you have acquired the basic qualifications, you should write to film and television companies telling them about yourself and expressing an interest in becoming a PA. It may be easier at first, to obtain temporary secretarial work with a production house, studio, or television station, because they may be short-staffed during the holiday period or because someone becomes ill. In this way, you can get the opportunity to prove yourself and become known to the management, as well as gaining valuable experience, so that when a job does become available, you have a better than average chance of getting it. Jobs are likely to be advertised in your local press and in publications like the *Listener* (BBC only) or the *Guardian*'s Creative and Media section published on Mondays. They will also be advertised through ACTT and BETA. A list of major production companies can be found in trade directories such as *Kemps Film and Television Yearbook* or you may be able to locate any in your area by looking in the Yellow Pages.

Anita Cowan

□ Production assistant
□ ITV

Anita Cowan is a thirty-seven year old production assistant with Scottish Television. She is divorced with one child aged twelve and lives in Glasgow.

» 'I got into this business by chance. A girl I knew, who's now a director, worked for the head of Light Entertainment as his assistant and they were looking for a production secretary. I had been doing temporary work. She told me they were holding interviews so I just came along and luckily the producer and I just clicked. Up until then, I had just been a typist and I didn't know anything about television at all, but he was so helpful. He sat me down and explained about outside broadcasts etc. I was very lucky because when they were in the studio or on outside broadcasts, he would tell me to come along and watch. Because of that I got to see what the PA did and I liked the idea of that. You've got to be a certain type of person to do this job, but I find it totally fulfilling.

'It's not easy being a single parent, but part of the skill of the job is organisation and if you love the job as I do, then you organise your private life around it. I don't think it's a job that you can go into thinking you'll only give it 50 per cent of your time. You have to be prepared to give 99 per cent to it. You have to organise your private life around your work because that's what pays the mortage at the end of the day. It's a bit like military manoeuvres. You have to have a good back-up team, and I'm very lucky in that I've got a very good back-up team of parents and other people who're prepared to do that for me. If I didn't have that, it could be difficult. Because the hours are relatively flexible, I can take my daughter to school. She goes to another house with a little girl after school till I can pick her up which is usually about an hour and a half later. I have to make sure she's not shunted about, though.

'Being a PA is a well paid job if you work in ITV, especially in comparison to equivalent jobs outside the business. In our company we don't specialise. It's part of the enjoyment of the job that you don't know what you're going to do next. You have to be able to go from sport to documentary to light entertainment. You must be prepared to travel. You also need the ability to organise and the skill to juggle a number of things at once because not only are you typing a script, you're arranging transport, you're arranging hotels for the crew and you have an awful lot of paperwork. I don't think you can afford to be too moody. You're dealing with an awful lot of personalities. You do a lot of public relations and you have to be able to talk to people whom you've possibly never spoken to before.

'I really do think getting secretarial training is a great help because it gives you the discipline of having to get things done, of accuracy, of taking care with layout, and of planning. I also worked in a travel agency before this, so the experience of trying to organise people moving from A to B helped a great deal. I think that if you have no "in" to the industry, then brass neck might help. I don't think that companies would ever knock people who came up and said they'd really like to learn more about a particular job. I think you have to be aware of all the problems and the not-so-glamorous side of it when everybody else goes home and you're sitting typing a camera script on Friday night till eleven, then you're in on Saturday and Sunday as well. Then that's not so glamorous.

'I don't see any sex discrimination in this job, although possibly PAs tend to do a little more of other people's jobs than we ought to. But then you organise and you anticipate. This job gives you an overall knowledge. I think it's probably one of the few jobs that you start with an empty file and you follow the programme through, do the payments at the end and put it to bed in the filing cabinet. For that reason, I think that being a PA can lead to other jobs. There are a couple of girls in my experience who've gone on to be a floor manager and a director.

'A lot of people say, "What do you want to do afterwards?" because since you're a production assistant, they assume that you assist somebody and are a deputy something. They don't actually see it as a career in its own right. In fact, you don't have to go on to anything else when you grow up. It is very rewarding as it is.'

Gemma Fallon

☐ Production coordinator
☐ Freelance

Gemma Fallon is Irish, but works in the UK also, on a wide range of productions, including feature films. She is based in Ireland and, at forty years of age, she is currently single and has no children.

» 'I left school at sixteen because my family needed the money. I went to work with my father's old employers and stuck it for two years although I hated every minute of it. I looked for something more adventurous and colourful. So I went into the blood banks – I became a vampire. In those days, the only other alternative you had in Ireland was the bank or insurance. I decided to shun both of those. After four years in the blood banks, I did a stint in London. I just had basic secretarial training at that stage. Then I came back to Ireland and got a job with an architectural company. I was with them for nine years. After that long working for one man, you actually begin to bitch. So we agreed that I would leave but he said he'd help me find something I'd like. Eventually, he said that the managing director of National Film Studios was looking for an assistant and would I go and see him, so I did. I got that job and that's how I got bitten by the celluloid bug. I was about twenty-nine. I wasn't very long working for him when I realised that I wanted to go freelance, so I had to resign the position with him, find an opportunity to get union membership and wait a year for my trainee membership to come through. In the meantime, I worked for various businessmen and got totally fed up with boardroom politics. I had £200 left and I put an advertisement in the *Irish Times*. I took a four inch column, "Young, single, creative woman needs a change after sixteen years. Would consider anything." I got amazing replies and I went round the country visiting them all. They varied from little old ladies in garrets writing their memoirs to dirty old men in big houses or widowers with seven children looking for Julie Andrews. I took a job with someone who lived in a Norman castle because I wanted to live in a castle and I did his correspondence in the morning and cooked in the evening. This was all while I was waiting for my union membership to come through. It takes a long time in Ireland, although that's changing slowly. I got a phone call towards the end of the season to go and work on my first feature and I never looked back

'I've been working freelance in the business ever since with some success and some disaster because I've been depending on producers all the time. Very often they don't have the money they say they have, and they disappear leaving lots of debts behind. So I've had a couple of those. It's been embarrassing and very soul-destroying. Fortunately, the last two years have been wonderful and I'm just hoping now that I'll go from strength to strength. The opportunities in Ireland aren't that great when you consider that if you get one feature a year, you're lucky. So having the flexibility of ACTT membership which allows me to work in Britain has been wonderful.

'I'm a production coordinator. It's a new title. It started in America to distinguish between production secretaries who worked for small companies and people like myself who work on location on features. If somebody rang up the union and asked for a production secretary they could be given the name of somebody who had only worked in a small production house and wouldn't be able to cope with it. On a feature, depending on the size of it, there could be anything from forty to three hundred people. So this requires a different kind of skill – a great administrative skill.

'When I went into the industry, there were several considerations for me. I wanted a career in which there was no retirement age – I wanted to work till I dropped – with as little discrimination as possible. I wanted something which would have a lot of flexibility and in an area in which I was fluent. I was fluent in administration because I'd been working in that all my life. So that was how that happened. The only chance I had, without spending years as a trainee, was to go into production coordination where I could practise my skills.

'A production coordinator is hired by the production manager and between us we hire all the crew, we transport them, house them, we equip them, pay them and feed them. The job involves the coordination of all that as well as the day-to-day running of the show as well as the reports back to the producer. There have to be production reports every day, script changes have to be supervised, everybody on the unit has to be informed every day of what's happening and this is a huge volume of paper.

'The hours are horrendous. I have worked on shows and put in a fifteen-hour day, seven days a week. You know that you can only do it for a certain length of time, then you climb into bed for a month.

'We have union agreements in Ireland but they're much more flexible than here in Britain. If there's a show to be done, then you go in and state your fee. You've got to know enough about the structure of the show to be able to build into your fee all the possibilities that you might have to work long hours, but then you've got to be satisfied with that regardless of what is demanded of you – provided it's not extreme. So the hours are long and the commitment is huge. I've seen relationships fall apart and you put your friends in a file under "pending" until you're free to see them all again. But it's a great buzz and I wouldn't want to be doing anything else. I think it's what I always wanted to do but I didn't discover it until I was thirty.'

18 The production designer

1 Job description

It is the production designer's job to consult with the director and then to create the 'look' of a film or programme, as near to the director's intentions as possible. For example, if a film is set in the future, the production designer would try to create a visual atmosphere that was innovative in design, or if the setting was in, say, the eighteenth century, or in some far flung corner of the world, or in an English manor house or a modern British city, the production designer would strive to re-create that time and place through visual detail.

She begins by reading the script to determine the emotional mood and the physical location of the setting. She would discuss her impressions with the director until they are both agreed on an interpretation of the script. Then the production designer would consider all the visual elements of the film and how they could complement and contribute to that interpretation. That might involve designing sets or helping to select suitable locations and devising ways of modifying them to meet the requirements of the script. For example, an Elizabethan manor house might be an ideal setting for a historical drama, but the production designer might have to disguise modern additions such as telephone wires or electric lights. She would also collaborate with other members of the crew to achieve a consistent visual style throughout the production. It would be essential that costumes and make-up not only complemented the sets in terms of colour but also in terms of style and period. It would be no use having modern make-up or futuristic clothing for a seventeenth-century drama. The director of photography would also be consulted to ensure that the sets allowed sufficient room for the cameras and technicians to move about. The production designer must be aware of the camera angles (i.e. the position of the cameras and their angle of view on the set) so that the furniture, props or scenery are arranged to form a pleasing picture from that viewpoint, and that there is nothing to block the camera operators' line of vision. It is also important that the style of camerawork is appropriate to the general visual theme. For example, a slow, atmospheric film might be ruined by fast-paced camera movements, while modern techniques or special effects would not be suitable for a period piece.

The production designer might also be involved in creating the graphics, so that the style of the credits and titles fit with the theme. For example, in the *Superman* films, the opening titles zoom out of the sky in the same way that Superman appears from Outer Space. The type of lighting which is used could also contribute to the visual effect, so the production designer may also collaborate with that department. A drama concerned with deep, brooding emotions which takes place against a dark, gloomy background would be ruined by harsh, glaring illumination. Last, but not least, the production designer would communicate all these ideas and intentions to the editor, so that she could continue the visual style in the way that she cuts the picture. Throughout all of these discussions with other crew members, however, the production designer would work very closely with the director, who would probably have the final say on anything to do with the visual content of the film or programme.

The bulk of the production designer's work will probably be the creation of sets, however. Unlike the scenery used in the theatre, film and television sets must be three-dimensional because they will be photographed from every angle and they may also have to be built so that walls can be removed easily to allow cameras to move around. Some sets may have to be constructed for special effects such as explosions or fires. With help from her staff, the production designer will begin by preparing simplified architectural drawings from which costing estimates can be made. If it is a historical drama, then she may have to do a considerable amount of research in order to create an authentic setting. She might also make a rough groundplan of the studio with the dimensions of the set marked on it to make sure that there will be enough room for the actors to move around and for the cameras and other equipment. If the costing estimates demonstrate that the sets can be built within budget, and provided the director has approved the designs, then construction begins. In the meantime, furniture, props and accessories are hired or purchased or brought out of storage. The whole process will be supervised by the production designer so that the final 'look' makes an important contribution to the effect which the director wishes to achieve.

There is often a great deal of confusion about the role of the production designer and that of the art director. If there is no production designer assigned to the crew of a film or programme, then the art director may fulfill many or all of the functions outlined above. If, however, there is both a production designer and an art director working on the crew, then the latter will probably concentrate on the sets and graphics, although she may assist in other areas, while the production designer is responsible for coordinating the work of all departments to achieve a consistent style and 'look'.

2 Hours and working conditions

The duties of the production manager vary from one job to the next. On one programme, she may work regular hours and be based in the studio. If, however, she is assigned to a drama series or works on a feature film, she may end up toiling day and night to ensure that sets and locations are ready on schedule. Those kinds of productions may require that she be away from home for weeks at a time in some far-flung part of the world.

If the production does take place in some remote location, the designer may have to struggle with the problem of getting supplies and equipment and have to function in very primitive conditions. The climate may also cause difficulties. High winds can make exterior construction hazardous or destroy a set overnight, but it is the production designer's job to ensure that there is little or no delay in the shooting schedule.

As well as dealing with practical problems, the production designer must collaborate with the other crew members and work to translate the director's concepts into visual detail. This may involve some compromise and having to cope with a variety of artistic temperaments.

This is an area of work which is still male dominated. The majority of production designers in both television and film are men, as well as many of the craft workers you will supervise, such as carpenters and painters. This situation is gradually improving, however, and women are demonstrating that they have much to offer in the area of production design.

3 Qualifications and characteristics required

You must have good eyesight and colour vision in order to be able to perceive minute details in a set and assess colours and their impact. You must also be someone who is both visually creative and able to translate concepts into concrete designs. In other words, you must not only be able to think up designs which convey the right mood, style and period, but you must be able to draw up plans which are feasible and can actually be built. It is important, therefore, that you have some skill in mechanical drawing and know how to use a scale rule and so on. You should also have some talent for drawing, as well as a dramatic sense of shape, colour and style and the effects they can have. It is helpful also to have a knowledge of the history of art and architecture and most companies require that you have a degree in a subject like Interior Design, Art and Design, Stage Design or Architecture. Since you will be working with a variety of other departments, it is almost essential that you be familiar with all the production processes. In addition, it helps if you are knowledgeable about construction techniques, as you will be required to supervise the building of sets.

There can be many stresses associated with this job and you must be able to work calmly under pressure. You must be resourceful and ready to improvise if you encounter last-minute difficulties at some remote location. You will be dealing with many varied personalities and having to collaborate with other members of the crew, so you must be able to get along well with people and cope with differences of opinion diplomatically. Since much of your work will be administrative, it is also helpful if you are well-organised and have the ability to balance figures and keep within a budget.

4 · How to become a production designer

While at school, you should develop your drawing skills and take classes in mechanical drawing, if possible. Volunteer to help design, build and paint the sets and props for school productions or for local theatrical, pop music or opera groups. You will probably find it useful to read books such as Edward Carrick's *Designing for Films*

(1950), Doris Zinkeisen's *Designing for the Stage* (1938), Gerald Millerson's *Basic T.V. Staging* (1982a), or Terence St John Marner's *Film Design* (1974). By taking classes in still photography, you can learn about the composition of visual images and the effects achieved by using different filters, types of film and lenses. You should also learn all you can about film and television production. You may be able to gain access to equipment at your school or college which would enable you to get some practical experience. Read some of the basic texts, such as Steven Bernstein's *The Technique of Film Production* (1987), or Gerald Millerson's *The Technique of Television Production* (1985). Write to television and film companies asking if you can observe their design departments at work and talk to their staff.

After leaving school, you should, ideally, obtain a degree in a subject like Art and Design, Stage Design, Interior Design or Architecture. Work hard to build up a portfolio of your work, collecting photographs and plans of sets you have helped to design and construct or, if you have not had such an opportunity, then read the script for a play that has been published and prepare drawings and models for the sets you would design for that production.

You may be able to find work with a professional theatre, opera or ballet company as an assistant production designer, which would provide invaluable experience if you wished to move on to film and television later. You may, however, apply directly to companies or freelance production designers for a job as an assistant. Such openings are often advertised in the local and national press, including the *Guardian*'s Creative and Media section which is published on Mondays, or the *Listener* (BBC only) or *Stage and Television Today*. The names of production companies and of individual designers can be found in trade directories such as *Contacts* or *Kemps Film and Television Yearbook*. ACTT also publishes a list of its members according to their profession.

Hazel Peiser

☐ Production designer
☐ Freelance

Hazel Peiser is a freelance production designer who has had more than twenty years experience in the feature film industry, working in all areas of production design. She is forty-seven, single and based in the London area.

» 'I was a sculpture student at St Martin's School of Art and I didn't really know how I was going to make a living as a sculptor. While still at art school, I was offered work surreptitiously to make bits of monster for monster movies. The reason it was surreptitious was because they could get me, as an art student, to do for a fiver what would have cost them four times as much if it was made by studio staff sculptors or model makers. Eventually, one vacation I wanted to go to Italy, hadn't got any money and realised that I could earn enormous amounts doing these bits for films. I hitch-hiked to Pinewood (one of the big film studios), walked past the security man (who ignored me completely) found the model making department and more or less informed them, "Here I am" and that I wanted work. It just happened that it was a time when they needed somebody. So I was taken on by the Rank Organisation for the princely sum of £16/1/9d a week – I remember that vividly because it was a fortune to me.

[She stayed in that job until she had saved enough money to go to Italy, after which she returned to art school.] 'By then I'd had to become a member of NATTKE and as a result got a call to go and work at MGM about six months to a year later, doing some bits of sculpture. That was the beginning of *Cleopatra*, which I remained on for the following year and a half. Although I thought I didn't really want to be making sculpture for films, I realised I was quite interested in what was going on.

'One of the people I'd been working with then moved on to another low budget film and took me on as a set decorator. I was delighted about this, although I'd no idea what the job entailed. Amazingly, about a week before shooting began, he announced that he had been offered something much bigger and much more splendid elsewhere and was going. Suddenly, I was left with the whole thing. I realised that I didn't know what I was doing. People don't give you much credence in this industry. You can either do it or you can't. He'd told me, "Never ask questions, never let people believe that you can't do it, always make it sound like a mystery and more difficult than it really is." My attitude has totally changed over the years, but maybe it worked at the time. I wandered around, kept very quiet and didn't ask anybody anything and I didn't know where I was going wrong. It was very exhausting as well. I think I went back to set decorating after that!

'It was the early days of television commercials at that time and there were a number of art directors who were very well established who did commercials. They would say to me, "Draw up a kitchen" or whatever it was and they would sign their name on it with a big flourish and rush off to the meeting and be there on the morning of shooting. Occasionally, I would be put in the role of minder (making sure there were no problems with the set while the commercial was being shot), and they would get the fee – I certainly didn't. I was grateful to be doing it. I thought it was all part of the job. What I did get was experience and eventually the day came, as days do, when somebody asked me to do a job and they didn't ask the big splendid art director whom I'd been working for. That was very useful because commercials are a good grounding in working fast, working with a lot of very different people, learning to use the tricks of the trade and being able to organise and delegate – all the things that one doesn't realise, as a beginner, are really what the job's about.

'In essence, whether you are an art director or a production designer is not a huge amount of difference. It should be, in as much as, theoretically, a production designer has a very broad area of control of the visual aspect of a film. It means that one is certainly responsible for the sets, but also for areas such as costume and make-up. What you are is a coordinating influence so that the thing has a bigger strength as a whole. Whether you call it art director or production designing is the same difference to me, except that assistants don't like being called assistants, they like being called art directors so everybody gets legged up a bit.

'I think it's very important that a designer is not just a visual person. It is very important that one is an interpreter so that what one is trying to do is do more for the script. I think part of my job is to make the ladies look lovely and the gentlemen look handsome. I think that's what the public wants to see on the screen. One does everything one can to set up the circumstances where their appearance on the screen is enhanced by where they are, what they are wearing and how they're looking and to get that right I think one has to have a very strong feeling for a story.

'The other qualifications for the job are quite different. You've got to be able to work with a wide variety of people. When talking with directors, you've got to be able to understand what they feel about the film and what they wish, because I think any orchestra can only have one conductor. Even if the director is taking the thing at a pace and in a way that personally I don't feel comfortable with, I still feel if I've agreed to do the thing, that I must try to make the most of whatever character that individual is imposing. It's important to be able to work with the construction people, the accounts people and the production managers. One has to understand that it is, after all, a commercial venture, that we are trying to get things done in the time and for the money and if we don't, they won't be asking us again. For me it's very important to try to make a team out of the people I'm working with and to pull out of them what they do best, because there's always all kinds of things they can do better than me and the sum of them is better than one of me. Films aren't made by one person, no matter who it is.

'You have to have various areas of knowledge. If one is making a film that is set in Georgian England or in a Chinese goldmine, you must know how to find out about those things and also you must have a sympathetic feeling for them. You've also got to be able to set this thing down on paper. Even if I'm not a great draftsman, I've got to be able to get the information down well enough for those people who are good at technical drawing. It's no good if it just exists in your head.

'It's a very dirty, practical job. It's not like the fantasy that people – including the likes of me at one stage – might have, that you meet the producer at Pinewood in your best frock and then you go home and you do all sorts of nice drawings and then you go back for the cocktail party after the première. Actually, it's cold and dirty and a lot of the time (as it is for everybody working on a film) you're exposed to all the elements of hot and cold and temperament and the physical thing of building the thing from the ground up. If you don't know (about construction techniques) it is almost impossible to convey to those who are constructing what you want. Very often, drawings are made after consultation with construction people and not before, so that you know the practicalities of what you are doing. It's practicality *versus* cost in the end. It (the set) does have to be safe, it does have to withstand the weather, it does have to withstand funny kinds of use because in films we make buildings that come apart. They don't have plumbing, but they do come to bits. The requirements are different from those in real life, but it's almost like working in the building trade, only a bit more imaginative. I would consider production designing as a hard hat area.

'Films are still very much run by men. It's an area in which the men who run it still think it's a man's world and there are some, in particular, who don't welcome women competitors or equals. An awful lot of people who are the very powerful ones in the film industry have wives that don't work at all which I think gives them their particular colour on where women should be. Those of us who do work are therefore less feminine or a bit odd or something. A few years ago, my agent was approached by a company about my doing a job in India. They arranged a breakfast meeting at the Dorchester and I thought the meeting had gone rather oddly and went back and called my agent. She said, "Well, they didn't realise that you were a woman and they said they thought that probably you would not withstand the climate, your health would break down, you would be a lot of trouble and you wouldn't like getting dirty." What happened was, we went on a recce (a reconnaissance of possible locations) and took a whole month around India. There were two producers and a money man. One of them had Gucci shoes which kept falling apart and another one got every psychosomatic disease under the sun. Sadly, we didn't make the movie because we couldn't find the right locations but it wasn't me who fell to bits, it was them. You sort of laugh it off.

'I worked on a pilot for a big series and there was

myself and a lady buyer (who buys props etc.) and I was looking around for an assistant and a draftsman. There was a very, very good draftswoman, as it happens, and the producer said, "We can't have three women in the Art Department. You'll be crying and tearing each other's hair out." You just have to treat that as the nonsense it is. In the end she did join us and she was extremely good.

'The craft workers (carpenters, painters and so on) are the men who will never tell their wives what they earn for instance, but once they feel that you know what you are doing, as long as you're quite clear and positive about what you want and they understand that you know that it is achievable by them in the time, there are no problems. You become – not one of the fellows because I'm not one of the lads – but one of the group, one of the team and at that point I don't think they treat me any differently than if I were a man.

'When you're working, there isn't time to do anything else as far as I can see. You work and eat and sleep and hope you can find something clean to wear in the morning. But I suppose I do it because I like it and because every new thing that comes along is interesting. I don't think anyone chooses to work on bad films or to do bad work, but even those have some chestnut you can pull out of the fire, whether because of the technical exercise or whether it's because of just trying to get through that particular thing. It really is very different and it does give you the opportunity to use a variety of skills which you've accumulated over a period of time. You become full of a little knowledge about a lot of things.

'If you really want to do it (become a production designer) then you just work on whatever you can. I think it's a good thing to work in as many different capacities as possible, not just so you understand what other people are doing, but to be able to bring out other people's skills as well as you can. Go and have a look at art galleries is what I'd say to most of them and go and have a look at lots of films. Too many people in the film industry are proud to say they never look at paintings and they never go to movies and this I find deeply depressing. If you want to learn, there is now such a catalogue of people in the past whose work is so brilliant you have to go and see it. One needs to fill one's head with all those images that are there just for the looking.'

Julie Sheppard

□ Assistant art director
□ Freelance

Julie Sheppard is a freelance assistant art director/design assistant. She is single, aged twenty-nine and lives in London.

» 'I got 8 O-levels and 2 A-levels and then I worked in a library for a year when I left school. I had been involved in an amateur theatre group in Leicester [where she lived] and basically wanted to be a theatre designer. Everybody talked me out of it, so that's why I started working in the library. Then I decided to go to art college and I went to Leicester Polytechnic where I did a Fine Art course. I wanted to be a painter and, of course, you learn very quickly that you can't earn a living doing that, so my interest in theatre design developed into an interest in film design. I started making films there – just little animation films. Then I didn't know which way to go after that so I applied to the Royal College of Art because they had a film school and I applied to the National Film and Television School. I didn't expect to get in at all but I got a place at both. So I thought that an ACTT ticket was more important than another degree. [Graduates of the NFTS are eligible for ACTT membership. See p.31 for details.] Because we couldn't afford to make full length films at art college, I had made these animated commercials which were sort of criticising the whole thing of advertising for women. One of the commercials was called "Join the Professionals" with army music and was based on the campaign to join the Territorial Army. But this was a big send-up of all that. It was all about being a housewife and cleaning floors. I did lots of little commercials like that. Looking back, I think they're actually dreadful, but they seemed to like them and I believe that's why I got a place at both schools.

'The first year (at the NFTS) is very good if you don't know much about the actual techniques of film-making. It was very different from the way you do it at art college with just one small video camera or one small 16 mm camera. They teach you the set-up of a proper film crew so you have the sound recordist and the boom operator and the clapper loader and everybody. You're taught all the basics and you have to take it in turns to do everything which I now find is very valuable, because I can sympathise with everybody else's problems on the film crew. So the first year at the film school is great. After that, you're all right if you want to be a director, but it's not a terribly good place if you want to be an art director. I didn't particularly have a very enjoyable time there. They weren't terribly interested in production design – basically because they didn't have the facilities to teach it or to let people expand. Big film sets are very, very expensive and they only had one shooting stage and one carpenter, who also had to mend office stools at the same time. They did advertise the fact that they taught art direction, but, in practice, they couldn't actually do anything about it. I believe they're doing something about it now, but while I was there, there were all these debates going on about how they should do it and meanwhile I was not getting any tuition. I spent most of my time using the Film School's name and working on as many feature films as I could, just phoning people up and saying, "I'm a student at the Film School and you don't have to pay me anything and the ACTT approve of what I'm doing. Can I come and work on your film?" I spent most of my time doing that. They'd pay my train fare and things like that.

'I didn't do a lot when I worked on these films. People don't actually like the Film School much. It's not got a terribly good reputation in the industry. I think people resent the fact that people go to the Film School for three years and then leave and expect to be movie directors. There's a lot of resentment among normal film crew people. So you've got all that lot to go through first of all and you're not usually allowed to do much except make the tea. If you find somebody who's sympathetic, you're usually all right and you just keep trying and being a bit thick-skinned. But the most important thing is that, even if you're not actually allowed to work, you're building up a network of contacts for future use. That's quite important when you're starting out on a freelance basis. If you don't know anybody, then where the hell do you start? I found that going out and working on feature films while still based at the Film School was a very good thing and I would recommend that all film school students do it. It's all right making one film at a film school, but then go out and spend the rest of your time working on feature films so you can see what you're going to be up against.

'I didn't actually graduate. You're supposed to make a graduation film. But there were all these rows going on about whether or not they should teach Art Direction and meanwhile I was getting nowhere. So I went along to David Puttnam and ended up getting a job on *The Killing Fields*. So I went off and worked on that and when I came back to England, I thought, "Well I'm not going to bother making a graduation film. I'm going to try and get another job now. If I don't do it now, I never will." And I got another job in two weeks. It was only as an art department assistant, but it was on a feature film and it meant that that was it. I was on my way. [Since then, Julie has worked on numerous television and film productions.]

'I work as an assistant art director or as a design assistant. It means exactly the same thing, but "design assistant" is a television term and "assistant art director" is a film term. The kind of thing I do is I get involved in all the research at the beginning of a film. I don't know why *I* have to do it, but I always get lumbered with it. It's quite interesting, actually. For example, on the film I'm working on just now, I have to find out what a 1967 bus stop in Leicester looked like – all kinds of bizarre things like that. You'd probably go on recce's (reconnaissances) to the location as well and do some measuring up because there might be some construction involved. On films you have a large art department and you have draftsmen and you have art department juniors so you don't necessarily do all that yourself. And then there's the dreadful "standing by on location", which I always get lumbered with. Sometimes it's interesting and sometimes it's terribly boring. It means you're the representative from the art department and you stand by with the film crew all the time in case anything has to be changed. You have two prop men who work for you and who have to do all the lifting and carrying. They have to move the furniture around because you're constantly dressing sets to camera all the time (i.e. moving props and furniture around so that the composition of the scene viewed through the lens is exactly what the production designer and director of photography want). Everything's very flexible. It depends on the camera angle. You might want to lift a desk up six inches, for example. Or you might be doing one scene which takes place in 1967 and then, after lunch, the scene that they're doing is set in 1980 and you've got to go and change all the light switches and all that kind of thing to get the style of that period right. Then what happens is that the director decides to change his mind and you have to improvise and jiggle things around a bit. So either "standing by" can be a complete bore because there's nothing to do or it can be a complete nightmare.

'To do this job, you have to be able to draw. You don't actually have to be a qualified architect, although some art directors will insist that that is a pre-requisite. You do have to have some basic knowledge of interior design, though, and you have to be able to do a plan and elevations (i.e. a three-dimensional drawing of the set), which you wouldn't learn on a Fine Arts course. If you're doing a film set, you do a basic drawing of the plan and elevations and from that you can make a model and the director can look at the model and work out his shots. If he approves, then you can go ahead and get the set built. Then you would do all the drawings of the window sills and door returns and all that sort of boring nonsense for the construction people.

'There are different types of art directors. It depends on where your interests lie. Some people are very, very technical and really are just glorified brilliant draftsmen, but when you get them on the set and try to get them to dress to camera (arrange the set to compose a shot), they can't do it.

'You have to have some kind of basic idea of the history of interior design and the history of art. The Victoria and Albert Museum in London do some really good lectures. When I'm not working, I go round there every day because they do lectures at lunchtimes and things. You also need a good colour sense, really. Everything else – what the latest fabrics are and so on – you can pick up by reading interior design magazines all the time.

'You have to be very tough – especially if you're a female. It's getting better, but men still don't like being told what to do by a woman. You have to earn your respect, which really gets on my nerves. We've got an art department junior just now and she's having terrible problems. She's being harassed all the time. I realise now that I don't get harassed any more, maybe because I've been around for about three years now and they know who I am and I must be doing my job well because I'm freelance and otherwise I would never have come back. I find it quite difficult to deal with harassment. I try not to be intimidated or upset, but it's hard sometimes. You have to develop quite a thick skin.

'My advice to someone who wanted to work in design is, "Don't sleep with the producer and don't sleep with the art director." That still goes on. Nobody would take you seriously and people are terrible gossips. The film industry is a very small world. An interior design course at art college would be a good thing to do. That's the sort of thing I'd recommend.'

19 The researcher

1 Job description

Researchers are the backbone of many television productions. They may work on all types of programmes, including sport, light entertainment, current affairs, documentaries and educational programmes. They are less likely to be employed on dramas or feature films, however, because the research for those is usually carried out by the writer and the various production departments, such as costume design and make-up.

In television, researchers will probably be assigned to a department or a series and will be expected to come up with ideas for programmes. If those are accepted, they will read and investigate all the background material, contact appropriate people to supply information or to be featured on the programme, track down relevant film or video tape material from archives and libraries or private collections, and write a briefing or perhaps even a full script for the presenter or interviewer. It is an extremely challenging job requiring a great deal of initiative.

2 Hours and working conditions

The hours vary enormously from job to job. It may be possible to find a position in which you would work regular hours, or at least have enough flexibility to allow for domestic commitments. Other researcher's jobs could involve, for example, being sent to China at short notice to set up a programme and would necessitate working long and unpredictable hours.

It is a job that can be very rewarding because the researcher can give considerable input to a programme. It is also a job that can be very frustrating, however, because you may not be given full credit for your work and ideas. It is an area in which many women are employed, but some feel that one reason female researchers were often chosen in preference to male ones is because producers think women are more likely to accept a supporting role within the production team. In theory, the natural progression from a researcher's job is to become a producer or programme director. In practice, many women have found it difficult to gain promotion and find themselves stuck as researchers. So, it can be a dead end for women, even though it is an ideal job in which to learn all about programme-making.

3 Qualifications and characteristics required

Although there is a wide difference between the research done for a programme and that carried out for academic study, companies often hire graduates for researcher posts. The rationale behind this is that it helps if you can find your way around a library and already know how to follow a line of inquiry methodically, as well as how to organise material logically and write coherently. Sometimes companies will employ a researcher because she has specialist knowledge. For example, they might hire somebody who had lived in the US to work on a series about modern American culture, or choose a woman who had a degree in Physics to work on a science programme.

Many researchers have a journalistic background and

training. Often a programme is built up from only the germ of an idea, and it is helpful if the researcher has an inquisitive, investigative mind and can then explore the topic fully.

Researchers can be drawn from almost any profession, however. Some of those I contacted were a former film editor, a cinema manager, a teacher and a local radio producer.

The researcher is often the first point of contact with those people who will eventually appear on the programme or contribute information, so it is important that she is able to deal with the general public and has the gift of developing a rapport quickly. Sometimes, researchers work on very sensitive issues, dealing with people who are afraid of the consequences if they talk to the media. A good researcher must be able to reassure them and protect their interests in such a way that they are willing to cooperate. Several women felt that they were possibly more suited to the job than a man might be, because of the stress placed on 'people' skills. They felt that women were generally more sympathetic and sensitive and more likely to draw out controversial information from people by gaining their trust. Aside from the traditional female virtues, however, you also need a certain amount of confidence, self-motivation and assertiveness to follow up programme ideas.

4 How to become a researcher

You should get the best general education that you can, preferably to degree level. It may then be helpful to get some journalistic training and experience. Learn as much as you can about television production. A general textbook such as Gerald Millerson's *The Technique of Television Production* (1985), or Harrison Watts's *On Camera; How to Produce Film and Video* (1984) might be useful reading. It would also be helpful to contact your local television station and ask if you could observe a programme being made. Researchers' jobs will probably be advertised in the local and national press (such as the *Guardian*'s Media and Creative section published on Mondays) and also through ACTT. It is advisable, however, not to wait for jobs to become available, but to write, or preferably visit, television companies to express your interest and leave your CV. If you have any specialist knowledge, for example, in education, then you should emphasise that. If you are lucky, you may be hired on a short-term contract at first, for the duration of one programme or series. If you are asked to come for an interview, try to have several programme ideas ready. It is also worth contacting producers directly, since it is often they who hire the researcher for a programme. You can watch the credits at the end of a production and note the names of the producer and/or executive producer, as well as the company which made the programme. Then you can write to them, expressing your interest and outlining the special abilities and qualifications that you could contribute to the making of that programme. You can also obtain the names and addresses of production companies and individual producers in trade directories such as *Kemps Film and Television Yearbook*, *Film Bang* (applies to Scotland only) or the *BFI Film and Television Yearbook*. ACTT also publishes a directory of members which includes a list of producers.

Anita Oxburgh

☐ Researcher/producer
☐ Freelance

Anita Oxburgh is Swedish by birth, but is now married to an Englishman and has one teenage son. She is forty-two and lives in Edinburgh.

» 'I started as a secretary in Sweden. I met an Englishman, married and stayed in Britain, working as a secretary for a number of years. We went back to Sweden and I got a more prestigious job as a secretary and eventually turned that into a job as a personal assistant and translator. Then I had a baby and started working as a freelance translator. After five years, we moved back to Britain where I continued freelance work and eventually started as a secretary in arts administration. Later I became an arts administrator. After that, I became the managing director of the place I worked at, which was Carlton Studios, a privately owned cinema, restaurant, function and conference centre in Edinburgh.

'The producer who actually set up Carlton Studios, Steve Clarke-Hall, got a commission from Channel Four, which was just starting up. He was looking for people for a weekly series so he asked me to come along and work as a researcher. The reason why he thought of bringing me into it was because I had thought up a project to try and sell to Channel Four which was rejected. I gained quite a lot of experience working as a researcher for two or three years before moving on to become an associate producer and then a producer. I'm just progressing from doing sponsored documentaries and short things for magazine programmes into pursuing projects on my own in the documentary area.

'When I was a researcher, I was working for a magazine programme, so I was required to think up little entertaining eight-to-twelve minute films. They could be on any topic – I know we did something on disco-dancing pensioners. I would look in the papers for anything that was funny or interesting, contact the people and see if I thought that they would work for television – if they were clear enough to talk to. It took me a while to start recognising the things that might be difficult for the potential viewer. When I had actually thought out an idea, it was up to the director to pick from, say, three items, which one he wanted to do. I would then do the detailed research and actually find the place where we would film. I would find out all sorts of details and I would just be there all the time. Eventually, after a year or two, I suppose I started doing all the interviews and more and more of the things myself. It was a very short step then into producing.

'That was the way I happened to get in. I would have been just as happy to work for one of the television companies. I don't think I had a burning desire to be freelance. I still think that there are terrific advantages to working in television companies – there's more security. You tend to get the argument from freelancers that you always have a lot more freedom as a freelance, but because you're so worried about security you actually don't use that freedom. You become as much of a slave, or even more so, than within a company. When you have time off, you think that you'll work up all the ideas that you have lying about, but you get so busy keeping in touch, putting your face forward, that you spend all your energy on getting the next job and the next job may not be a furthering of your interests or career. I do think that my particular personality suited the kind of circumstances I got into. I've grown in confidence very quickly and I do think the disadvantage for me of the bigger organisations is that you have to serve your time and, because I started when I was thirty-seven, I couldn't really afford to sit and wait. I realised that working at the BBC as a researcher in general features was a much more junior job than working as a researcher in an independent company. At the BBC, you have a whole support team that takes care of all sorts of details, like music rights, that you would have to deal with if you were working for a smaller company.

'I do find it very easy to get on with people. I'm not bashful and I suppose I'm quite strong on self-motivation. I think it's quite important that you see for yourself the next step to take, because there's never anybody there to guide you and you have to search out the people that you need to ask for advice. I started off as a researcher really not having the faintest idea what a director needed in terms of information. I was very word-based and going out and assessing what was going to make good television is not as easy as you might think at first. I suppose that's the sort of situation where you need initiative. You also need to be able to stick to things. I put in every waking hour to my job till I felt confident enough to relax.

'I think there's no doubt about it, this kind of job makes terrific inroads on your private life, but then again, that depends on how you organise yourself and what you enjoy. I know people who do this kind of job who have young kids and they find it possible to combine everything. It usually requires a bit of goodwill from people around you to do that, however, and an ability to switch off so you can spend time with your family. At the moment my son is just starting his sixth year and we have to think about university and that's taking up quite a lot of the family's time. That has to be a priority. It's unfortunate if you happen to be in the middle of something that's very urgent but it's always possible to kind of balance things. I need to work. Working is my hobby as well as a job. It would be different if it was just a chore.

'I think sexual discrimination is very difficult to define because I think men and women do operate on some kind of sexual code with each other. In some instances, being a woman gives you advantages and that works particularly well when you're not in a threatening position – say if you're a researcher. But once you get in a position where you have some degree of control over other people, you might even find that you have to be that much tougher than a man to have some kind of credibility. Discrimination can also happen over a period of time in that certain obstacles are put in your way and you have to deliver so many proofs of your ability. Unless you really fight for it, your pay doesn't go up and you get used. I suppose I wait until I feel confident enough in being right. Often you want to deal with a situation when you're angry and you very soon learn that that's the wrong time to do anything about it. Usually when you've built up enough arguments, people find it hard to deny that you're right. You're so afraid of being put down that you never put your case very well, but I think that once you make the effort of gathering your wits and putting your case forward, the battle is half won.'

Jenny Rathbone

☐ Researcher
☐ ITV

Jenny Rathbone is a senior researcher on Granada Television's current affairs programme, *World in Action*. She is thirty-five, is unmarried, has no children and lives in London.

» 'I did a degree at Essex University in Government/Latin America and I then went to Mexico to do research on the position of women in Mexico. When I came back, I got a job with a Third World news agency specialising in Latin America and the Middle East. I was hired because I spoke Spanish and knew about Latin America. So I didn't come into journalism through the front door by working on a provincial newspaper. I worked there for three and a half years. It started off with me and another bloke on half time each and we expanded and I became head of an office of eight or nine people. Then I had a disagreement with the head office in Rome and left. I did a bit of work at the *Financial Times* and then a job was advertised at Granada to work on a programme about Europe. I had an informal interview, then a very heavy board with about six men. I remember going into the interview and gulping. I'd never heard of such a thing as boards and I really wasn't expecting it. I had rather an aggressive interview. They asked me what my hobbies were and I said, "Karate". I didn't get the job, but they recommended me for another one on a local programme. I went through another, less aggressive board, then started on the news desk in local programmes. It would have been really hard if I hadn't already done quite a lot of journalism. I saw one or two guys broken under the strain because they'd come straight from university.

'The idea was that you were just thrown in at the deep end. There was no training. I decided I didn't want to go on screen. Anybody who goes on screen, male or female, gets judged by their appearance. They're commodities. They sell the programme to the viewer and if you are a woman trying to establish yourself as a serious journalist, you don't need that as well. I remember there was one woman who suddenly appeared out of nowhere and all the women in the newsroom felt their hearts sink, because she was really playing the card of the good-looking woman who was going to get on because she was good-looking. I was very lucky because after six months on local news where I learnt a hell of a lot, I then went on to the regional political programme. It was run by a man who actually preferred working with women – for positive reasons. He was important to me because he pushed me and recommended that I was ready for *World in Action*, whereas other men might not have done that.

'It's still a mystery to me how I got on to *World in Action* because both editors were ambivalent in their attitudes to women, though in quite different ways. Both appeared to have difficulty in accepting the idea of women as fully-fledged members of the team. That was six years ago. Since then, there's never been more than three women out of twenty-four people on the production team and none of them have been producers.

'There are precious few women in current affairs, full stop. But *World in Action* seems to have an in-built hostility to women, I suppose because in the 1960s and 1970s it built its reputation on an aggressive, campaigning, dare one say it, macho style of programme making. In the 1980s, the formula has been in crisis, but the programme continues to attract the sort of foot-in-the-door journalists and old patterns of behaviour persist in the absence of any new direction for the programme. There's a lot of talk amongst my colleagues about "my wife" – that person who provides ironed shirts, pays the bills and looks after the children. Under the circumstances, it's not surprising that there's never been a female voice to do the commentary. Being in such a minority means you have to have quite a hard skin and not mind what other people are thinking and saying about you. I had to fight not to get slotted into social services, education and human interest stories and to be allowed to work on the military, nuclear weapons and foreign stories.

'Apart from the sexual politics, however, the job requires being able to get on with all sorts of people, from politicians to pensioners. You work on your own a lot also, so you need to be self-disciplined and self-motivating and have an immense amount of energy.

'The hours are pretty erratic. Sometimes you're not very busy. You can go from being un-busy to being incredibly busy without warning though, and then you have to start cancelling the rest of your life. That's hard on the people you live with. When you're involved in a production, you can be away from home working all hours week after week. It's not the sort of schedule that's easy to combine with children, another reason why there aren't too many women around.

'Of all the researchers' jobs going, this is the most demanding. That also makes it potentially more rewarding. Everyone on the programme is expected to generate ideas. Having fought to get your own idea accepted by the editor or having been assigned somebody else's idea, you then have to go out and make it into a programme. Until you have been assigned a producer then you're the person responsible. You consult with the editor, but you're taking decisions as you go. Your package of information has to be turned into a script, you have to decide on who to interview, what to ask them, in what order, what pictures you need to tie everything together. Then you go out and do it.

'You discuss everything *ad nauseum* with the producer. It depends on the individuals involved how the work is split up between you. You work closely together as a team right through the filming, final scripting and dubbing. The producer gets to do all the fun bits, like directing and editing and he carries the can at the end of the day and is answerable to the editor and the management.

'I can't say I've actually been discriminated against. Although I've failed to get through the producer/director boards for *World in Action*, nobody has yet been appointed above my head. Other female researchers have left in exasperation. New token women have replaced them. I wonder how long I'll stick it out. Two or three years ago, droves of women were leaving ITV to start up Channel Four companies. I made a conscious decision then to stay and fight a rearguard action in the mainstream. Now I wonder if I made the right choice.'

Annie Woods

- ☐ Researcher
- ☐ ITV

Annie Woods is a staff researcher at Tyne Tees Television. She is thirty-seven and is married with a two-year-old child.

» 'I left school with O-levels. I went to a secondary modern so I wasn't able to do A-levels there and anyway I didn't want to. I went to art school at Newport Gwent College and started with painting and then took up a film course. I and several others were disenchanted with the course and left before it ended so I didn't have any qualifications. But it gave me enough incentive to go off and look for a job in the film industry in London. That was in 1969. I walked around Soho, knocking on doors and finally got a job with a commercials production company as a messenger. It was unusual having a girl doing that. I think it was just that I had gone out and knocked on people's doors. That was enough of a surprise for them to keep passing me on to the next person if they didn't have a job, which is how I finally found somebody who did have one. When the production company split into two parts, I went into their cutting rooms as a trainee film editor and finally became a second and then a first assistant editor, mostly dealing with commercials. Later, I got pretty fed up with commercials but there was nowhere for me to move to because there was a slump in the feature film industry. So I applied to the BBC for a post as a trainee in the editing side of the newsroom, where it was all men and you worked twelve-hour shifts. I think that was my most overt example of sexism, because they said that they didn't think that a girl was capable of working twelve-hour shifts and a girl shouldn't be working alongside men. I think they were interviewing me out of curiosity and perhaps, if nothing else, just to put me off. That was in 1973. They wouldn't say that now. I don't think it's because their deep-rooted conservatism has changed, but that they daren't be so open about it now.

'I decided to take a break from the whole thing and went off and did a bit of travelling. When I returned, I went to work in a careers office for a while and did A-levels. As a consequence of that, I went to university as a mature student. I was still in touch with people in the film industry and a friend of mine had moved into television and suggested that I work freelance during my summer holidays. That's how I got back into cutting rooms and into television. I moved up to Newcastle when my husband got a job up here, so I went to Tyne Tees Television and got a job as a freelance editor which soon turned into a staff job. I found the work interesting because there was far more variety than working on commercials. Also, I could see that there were many more career opportunities in television companies than there are in small production houses. It's an advantage to work in a television company that isn't particularly large. Everyone knows each other and the company management already knew me when it came to changing jobs. I moved over from editing to research because I didn't want to remain an editor and I think the management anticipated that one day I would do that.

'As a researcher, you have to admit that you're going to be working in subject areas that perhaps you know nothing about. You can't become an expert, but when you do approach experts, you at least have to have done your groundwork. You have to be open to new areas that you never thought yourself particularly interested in and I think that demands a certain tolerance. Although you work on a team, you're the one who starts the whole ball rolling and you're going to have to work on your own for quite a length of time, probably. So when you do work with other people, you tend to be rather protective about what you've produced as research and then you have to stand around and watch people demolish it. You've got to be able to let go enough to be able to work with a team and yet be able to hold on to the original idea and plan that you had. It's a delicate operation. You also have to be sycophantic, I think, towards members of the public or celebrities or whatever. You may also, depending on the nature of the director or producer, have to be sycophantic with them. Researchers are not highly regarded by some producers and directors. If the only way to make a programme is to do a certain amount of crawling, then that's what you have to do. I've encountered barriers when people don't take me seriously or when they find my reputation as a feminist scary. That can have a negative effect and usually if I suspect that somebody is thinking that, I lay very low. I do tend to try to suppress my own views until I've established myself professionally. That's a bit of a yawn, to have to do that. But it helps that working in a small company like this you do get to know people pretty well and they get to know you well.

'Television research doesn't require technical skills, but it is important to know about the technicalities of other people's jobs. This is because a researcher must set up a shoot or studio programme so that it runs smoothly on the day. That won't happen if you didn't know the film crew would need a power source, or if you didn't realise the sound recordist would need the quietest place to record an interview. Also, the camera operator and director will expect you to know how little (rather than how much) can be achieved in a certain amount of time so that they can schedule appropriately. If you don't know these things, you will alienate the people who have the skills to translate your work into a television programme.

'Mostly what you need are communication skills. You may have to encourage someone to talk about a very painful experience or to admit incompetence or failure or fraud in front of the camera. There are rarely second chances to get this information, so you have to make calculated guesses about when the crew should be there to record such revelations.

'As with other industries, television regards a degree as an indication of a certain level of intelligence and the ability to apply oneself to a task without supervision. A degree is not necessary in terms of its content. History graduates work on science programmes, philosophy students make children's programmes etc. There is not much notice given to other life experience, like raising a family and there is rampant ageism. This operates once you're in, as well, and if you haven't sought promotion to become a producer by your mid-thirties, you're forgotten.

'I think one dilemma in this job that is shared by most working parents is whether you're doing the right thing by your child. I don't think that can ever be resolved conclusively. I think that being a researcher suits a working mother better than other jobs. As a researcher, you spend a certain amount of time doing office hours and then when it comes to filming or shooting in the studio, you know in advance when you're going to be working late and when you're going to be away overnight. My son goes to a registered child-minder. My husband also has a job that takes him away so that causes interesting conundrums when it looks like we're both going to be away at the same time. Then I have to ask my child-minder if she's willing to take Joe overnight. I don't like asking her to do it. It's not ideal by any means. You just go from day to day hoping that things aren't going to rock the boat.'

20 The script supervisor

1 Job description

Script supervisors were previously known as 'continuity girls' and may still be referred to in this way, particularly in television companies, where the job is often combined with that of the production assistant. The title of script supervisor more accurately reflects the responsibilities of this very important job. It is she who tries to ensure that there is continuity in every aspect of a production, even though many scenes may be shot out of sequence – often days or weeks or months apart.

She begins by studying the script thoroughly and breaking it down so she knows what scenes are shot where, at what time of day, with whom etc. During this period, she will probably order her own supplies, including film to take instant photographs, if she intends using that, and perhaps continuity sheets which help her to record relevant information in some sort of order. During this pre-production phase, she will also try to establish a rapport with the director, sometimes sitting in on rehearsals, as they will work very closely together during filming. She may be asked to time the script, using her experience to judge how long the film would last if it was shot according to the screenplay. This helps the producer and director to work out how much time and money will be spent during the production.

Once filming begins, the script supervisor is responsible for keeping track of a great deal of information. She will take note of technical data, such as which camera lens, which filters and even which kind of film were used for a particular shot. She might also record the circumstances of that scene, such as where it was shot, what time of day it was, what the weather was like and who was involved, as well as more subtle variables such as the emotional level of the scene, the movements of the actors and also their eyelines, i.e. whether a character was gazing heavenward, looking at the horizon or focussing on something he was holding in his hand. Thus, the script supervisor becomes a source of information for cast and crew alike, able to tell an actor whether or not he finished the last shot still wearing his hat, reminding camera operators which lenses they used and providing all kinds of detailed information to technical and production staff. Depending on the relationship she has developed with the director, she may also be asked to be a sounding board and provide a second opinion on the effectiveness of performances.

In order to keep track of all this information, the script supervisor will take notes while the production is going on. When everyone else has gone home for the night, she will work on, typing up these notes in a clear format which can be referred to by other members of the crew at any time. A copy of these notes will be given to the editor to help with assembling the various shots into some coherent order.

2 Hours and working conditions

It is obvious from the job description above that a script supervisor can work very long hours while a production is being shot. If a film or drama series is being shot on location, that could mean that she will be away from home in some remote corner of the world for extended periods of time – several months, at least. It is an extremely demanding job, partly because of the stamina required, and also because great concentration is needed. It can be stressful, because so much depends on the script supervisor getting it right. She could have to cope with demands for information from a bewildering number of people and deal with a wide range of personalities. It can also be a fascinating job because the script supervisor is at the hub of the production.

3 Qualifications and characteristics required

Many script supervisors combine the job with being a production assistant, or have previous experience in that capacity. It is advisable, therefore, that anyone wishing to become a script supervisor first obtains secretarial qualifications and then gains some experience as a production assistant. In this way, they would learn a great deal about how films and television programmes are made, which would stand them in good stead when they begin to do continuity. Many television companies will offer training as script supervisors to their production assistants. Alternatively, the National Film and Television School runs courses in continuity for PAs.

Obviously, one of the most important attributes of a good script supervisor is to be organised. Complex and detailed information must be recorded in such a way that it can be easily referred to by almost anyone on the crew. You must be observant and able to concentrate intensely, in order to note down all the relevant points. If the script supervisor makes an error, or allows someone else's mistake to go unnoticed, then it could mean that hours of work will be wasted and various shots will be unusable. It is essential, therefore, that you be meticulous about accuracy. Since you will be one of the pivotal members of the crew, you must be able to work under pressure and cope with all kinds of personalities. You will need lots of stamina and patience because you will probably be expected to work long days, with extended periods when nothing very much seems to happen as shots are set up. Last but not least, you should be someone with a feel for drama, who is sensitive to the emotional nuances of a shot while recording the technical data.

4   How to become a script supervisor

You should get a good general education before taking secretarial qualifications. During this period, you should also learn as much as you can about film and television production. Write to film and television companies asking if you can visit and talk to their script supervisor and watch her at work. Books such as Gerald Millerson's *The Technique of Television Production* (1985), or Ken Daley's *Basic Film Technique* (1980) should provide useful general information. More specifically, Avril Rowland's book, *Script Continuity and the Production Secretary* (1977) and Pat P. Miller's *Script Supervising and Film Continuity* (1986) tell how to do the job.

Once you have obtained secretarial qualifications, you may be able to persuade a freelance script supervisor to take you on as an assistant, to type up her notes, etc. It is quite difficult to get in touch with anyone in the freelance market, however, although some of them are listed in publications like *Film Bang* in Scotland, while others may be contacted through ACTT. (ACTT is planning to publish detailed directories of its members according to profession.)

Alternatively, you can apply for jobs with television or film companies as a production secretary or a production assistant. Some employers are willing to train their PAs to do continuity and the National Film and Television School runs a short course on continuity for production staff. A list of companies can be found in directories such as the *BFI Film and Television Yearbook*, *Film Bang* (Scotland only) or *Kemps Film and Television Yearbook*.

Pat Rambaut

☐ Script supervisor
☐ Freelance

Pat Rambaut is one of the most experienced and respected script supervisors around and works almost exclusively on feature films. Among those she has worked on are *Local Hero*, *The Mission*, *Secret Places* and *The Emerald Forest*. She is forty years old, and lives in Edinburgh with her two teenage sons.

» 'I was brought up in Dublin and I went through school and got my leaving certificate, which is A-level standard. I wasn't particularly bright and clever at school. I then did a year's secretarial training at a polytechnic and got a very good grounding in shorthand and typing. I worked for a few years as a secretary and really enjoyed it. During that time, I went over to London and worked there for a little bit, but then my brother died and I went home again. I didn't mind what I did. I was wandering aimlessly a bit because I was pretty upset. I went for a job as a studio manager's secretary at the film studios in Bray, which is just outside Dublin and which at that time was in full swing. I did that for a year. There was a film being made where they desperately needed a second unit continuity girl which sometimes can be a very simple job. They couldn't find anyone to do it so I got offered the job. I did that for about eight weeks and I learned the basic routine of continuity and how to do the paperwork. It was great fun and it set me off thinking that I'd finally found what I wanted to do. I then went over to London to work for a writer/producer who dictated his scripts to me to type out in rough. After that I worked for a series of different people. I did assistant continuity on a film for six weeks, but after that I just worked as a secretary in films for another six months and couldn't get any more work in continuity. Then I got offered a job as a production assistant – again because there was nobody else free. That was the beginning of my career. I stayed doing that for about six years. Then I stopped working and had my two sons. About four years later, my husband died and about a year after that, I decided to go back to work. I found that everyone I'd known had gone on to do other things and so I had to start all over again because I had no contacts. If you leave the film industry for any length of time, you can be forgotten so quickly. By a fluke, I heard of a job going on the *New Avengers* – this was in 1976. They were doing an eight-month series and they wanted somebody for the second unit. It was three days' work as continuity girl and two days' work as general dogsbody. None of the other continuity girls wanted to do it because it sounded too boring, so I got the job. Then the two units, the main unit and the second unit, became two main units and so I was right slap into it. How I managed to do this with hardly any experience of continuity, I don't know. But the main unit continuity girl taught me how to set about breaking down a script. That is basically how most people start and if you're actually put into that situation, you can't avoid making mistakes like I did. I can remember telling the director to cut a shot because the actor hadn't done his coat up and to my great mortification, I was wrong. But it taught me something which I've never forgotten, which is never cut a shot because there's something wrong with it because all these sort of things can be got round in the editing. In the middle of that eight-month stint, I did an ACTT camera course for non-camera people. I learned a huge amount. I also paid for a week-long 16mm film production course which ranged from writing the script to the final editing stage of a film, and that again was a milestone in learning about the technical side of a film.

'In continuity, the first thing you start off with is the script and the most important thing is that you learn and absorb that script, till you know the story inside out, so that you can take scenes totally out of context and remember where they come in the story. For example, the props department might ask what time of day a particular scene is and it is only by knowing the script thoroughly that you can know the answer. Then you have to set out the script so that you can see how it works – break it down into sets and scenes and do a synopsis and that sort of thing. You also time the script which is of great importance because if the script is over long, it creates havoc with the budget. Nowadays, the script supervisor is often asked to give a second opinion on the timing of the script. I was actually brought out to British Columbia for *The Mission* for a week during the pre-production phase to see locations and talk to the director about how he intended to shoot certain scenes so that I could come back home and re-time the script. You also keep an eye on the time a scene takes as you're shooting it. Another side of the job is the coordination of different departments and also being a final check for those departments, even though they keep copious notes of their own on what the actors are wearing and the make-up etc. I have to have a fairly accurate impression of what was happening in a scene. I usually use Polaroids for that, not only to get a record of wardrobe and props etc., but also to get the feel of scenes in case there are re-takes. Like in *The Mission*, there was a big canoe battle which was shot by the main unit. We then moved on to another scene while the second unit finished off the details of the battle such as exploding bodies, arrows firing etc. I did lots of Polaroids of the battle scenes and when the second unit went off to do their shots they took them all with them. Then they could see things like the position of the canoes which no one could have written down.

'The last bit of my job is the most difficult to describe. That is the very close contact and relationship I have with the director. If I don't establish that, I might as well go home. Often you work with a director you don't know so I try to meet him before, perhaps sitting in on rehearsals. That sets up a relationship before we start shooting, because directors have an enormous pressure on them and it's quite common for them to change and become very tense and difficult, whereas prior to shooting, they were relaxed and easy going. So in my mind, if you don't set up the relationship before you start shooting, then it can be really hard going. I work as his assistant. I watch how the actors play the scenes because that helps the editing department. It's mostly to do with helping the flow of continuity of acting. If you think that a scene will be shot with a master shot then re-shot from different angles, then an actor will possibly need help remembering how he moved and how he spoke and all of that, and that really helps the director to use as much of the film as he wants.

'My two sons go to boarding school and I try hard to work mostly in the school term. I rarely work the two months of the summer. But I don't think I could do this job and come home every night to a family and children and all of that. It's absorbing. I get up about 6 a.m., leave the house at 7 a.m. and, quite often, after I return at 7.30 p.m. or 8 p.m., I have to type out notes for the editor. So at the end of the day, it's not unusual to have two hours work typing and preparing the next day's shooting. I can work sixteen hours a day quite normally. The man I live with is a very understanding person and considers my work as important as his, so he helps enormously by taking a lot of the burdens off me and running the household while I'm working, particularly while I'm abroad. We have managed not to let it affect our personal lives too much. The thing I've found most disrupting over the last two years is when I go away for six months at a time, to places a long way away that one can't come home from during that period. I feel very disoriented. Sometimes I don't actually know where I belong. It takes a long time when one gets back to get one's energies going again so that one can even consider a new film.'

Jill Rodger

☐ Script supervisor
☐ Freelance

Jill Rodger entered the BBC some twenty years ago, having obtained A-levels and secretarial qualifications. She then became a script supervisor, working in drama with Tony Garnett and Ken Loach. Now forty-three, she is married with one child and lives in the North of Scotland. She works freelance on, among other things, feature films for Channel Four.

» 'When I was at the BBC, I went through a training course that was a general thing for production assistants but included some drama stuff as well. They do a lot more drama now, so they do actually have a continuity course now.

'During the pre-production stage, I'll check all my equipment, such as my typewriter, stopwatches, instant film cameras etc. and order all the stationery that I'll need. I take my own seat which is a fishing box cum stool so I can carry all my gear in it. I'd also try and time the script (although this is very difficult to do unless you have a storyboard) and I'd attend any rehearsals. I'd also make contact with various members of the crew to establish a rapport and also to find out things like what sort of information the editor wants me to include in the shot lists and editing scripts. Most importantly, I'd try and get to know the director if I hadn't worked with him/her before.

'Once shooting starts, I try to establish a vantage point as near to the camera as possible and note down things like how each shot is framed, what the shot is, what lens was used etc. I'd also take instant photos if necessary to record where the actors are standing in relation to each other and so on. It's also my job to check that each shot will cut together with the ones before and after it. That is particularly important when things are filmed out of sequence, and means I have to know where each scene comes in the script. I'd try and note details and check things like eyelines – are the actors looking in the same direction and at the same level from one shot to the next. Sometimes an actor can be standing in exactly the same spot but she may be looking at the horizon when she should be looking down if the shots are to match. The importance of timing each shot varies with each film. Obviously, producers don't like to shoot unnecessary sequences, but the director will want to shoot as much as possible and decide what to drop at the editing stage so she may deliberately film each shot longer than planned.

'I'm one of the people who has to give information for the Daily Progress Report to the production secretary who completes it and sends it to the relevant people, such as the financiers etc. I have to let her know the slate numbers, which set-ups we did and also give an estimate of the screen time shot. I'd also need to give details of the still photographer's work, such as the number of hours on the set, how many rolls of film were shot and whether they were black and white or colour etc. If I get time during the day, I might type up my continuity sheets compiling all the information I'd noted down, but otherwise I might have to wait till shooting has finished for the day (or night) and do it then.

'It really depends on the production how much cooperation you get from the other departments. The bigger the production, the better the people tend to be and the more help you get. But you sometimes get costume people saying, "Oh, it's your job to note down what the actors are wearing" and that's really obstructive. Some cameramen won't let me look through the lens which I find most difficult because then I can't see exactly what they're shooting and get all the information I need. The best professionals are the most helpful I suppose because they recognise that it's in their interests to get things right. One thing I would find very helpful (which you don't often get the opportunity to do) is to watch the editing being done. Then you would see for yourself why things don't cut together. Even going to the rushes is helpful, but some people won't even let you do that.

'I certainly think you need a lot of stamina for this job because you have to be able to concentrate for long hours in not always ideal conditions. You always seem to do a lot of standing about too, as well as having loads to carry so you need physical as well as mental stamina. It's important to have the ability to get along with a lot of different people who may become temperamental when under pressure. It isn't desirable to be too opinionated or aggressive, but at the same time, you must be able to stand up for yourself and not be shouted down when you are sure something is wrong. But, equally, it's important to know when to keep your mouth shut. For example, you might throw a nervous actor completely off by pointing out some small detail that's wrong when he might get it right the next time anyway. It helps, also, to be fairly self-sufficient – and not just on the job. You could be away for a long time on a production with a group of people you don't have anything in common with, or be in a place you don't find very interesting, or, worse still, both.

'The advantages of the job, however, are that the work is interesting and varied and you meet all sorts of people, and there's the possibility of travelling extensively. But I suppose the disadvantage is that a lot of people in this business don't have a private life. Their whole life is their job, so it has to be rewarding. That's the danger really. That's where people become disillusioned. Their job is their life and suddenly they're not getting enough out of it anymore. But the compensation is that, certainly in the freelance market, you're very well paid. There's the problem, however, of working long periods away from home for very long hours so that's not good for family life or any regular commitments.

'The increasing use of video instead of film for productions may be a sign of things to come. I hope not. For anyone established in film, the prospect of going into television PA work would seem like a backward step. In the film industry, the script supervisor is very much an integral part of the crew, whereas in television, the PA is often unfairly regarded as just a glorified secretary.'

21 The sound technician

1 Job description

There are a number of jobs involved with the preparation of the sound track for a film or television programme and a sound technician may do any or all of them. For example, she may work as a boom operator. Often the microphones (or 'mikes' as they're usually called) are mounted on portable stands or else are attached to the artistes' clothing. Sometimes, however, the mike must be mobile and capable of being directed towards more than one speaker. In that situation, it will often be attached to a 'fishpole' (which is a long pole rather like a fishing rod), or to a boom (which is a metal arm that pivots on a mobile stand). Both of these contraptions would be controlled by a boom operator so that the microphone could be raised or lowered or turned around very quickly when the sound source changes because someone else speaks or there is a noise from another direction.

In a studio, the microphone and any other sound sources, such as a tape recorder or turntable, would be fed into a sound desk or console, from where the volume and the pitch of the sound can be controlled. It is important to set the volume correctly so that it doesn't exceed the capability of the equipment and result in distortion, and so that it falls within the limits allowed for broadcasting. It can become quite hectic during a production, because the sound technician must not only monitor the levels, but she must 'open' and shut off the microphones as required. You may have seen instances on television when attention turns to a new speaker and, if the sound crew haven't been at the ready, it has taken several seconds before a microphone is turned on for that person, so that her first words are completely lost. If the audio track for the programme is complicated, then there will usually be one or more assistants working with the senior sound technician. It would be their job to cue up records, start and stop turntables and tape machines and perform any other tasks of that nature. Sometimes the sound technician will have to do some equalisation, i.e. she can isolate certain frequencies using the console and then either accentuate or decrease them. In this way, she might, for example, make a very gruff, gutteral voice that was difficult to understand seem clearer by increasing the higher frequencies so that it sounded as if the voice was higher. Some sound technicians specialise in mixing. It is they who would put together all the tracks, such as the music, voices, special effects (like thunder), and background noise (like the wind howling) so that they are all mixed together on one sound track in the right proportion. If you have ever watched a film or television play which was shot outdoors and could hardly hear what the actors were saying because the wind noise was too loud, then you know that that may have been an error in the recording, but could also have been the result of a bad mix which allowed the wind track to overwhelm the voice track.

When film is used, and sometimes also when video tape is used on locations, the sound is usually recorded on to a portable tape recorder. Some technicians specialise in this type of production and become sound recordists. Where there are several microphones in use, they may also be responsible for mixing the different sounds on the spot,

286 / The sound technician

using portable equipment. This can be a nerve-wracking operation, because once recorded, the mix cannot be changed. Often, however, the sound sources are recorded separately on to different tracks, and the mixing is done later in a studio, where the technician can have second chances, because she can always go back to her original separate tracks and start again to record another mix.

Most portable sound recorders use $\frac{1}{4}$ inch audio tape. If the original sound was recorded on this format, it must be transferred on to a broader magnetic tape which can then be synchronised with the film so that sound and images match exactly. Clapper boards, which are like small blackboards with a clapper attached, are used to help with this process. The editor synchronises the loud bang on the sound track with the exact frame of film showing the clapper making contact and is thus able to line up the picture with the sound (see p.95).

2 Hours and working conditions

The hours worked by sound technicians vary with each job. You may work for a television station which makes most of its programmes during the day and has very few live shows going out at night. In that situation, you might work fairly regular hours and few evenings. On the other hand, you may end up in a situation which is very demanding and you will be expected to work at night and put in a lot of overtime. The amount of travelling involved varies enormously also. You might always work in the same studio complex and never go outside, or you might be assigned to a news crew and be chasing around the countryside all day. If you work on outside broadcasts, or on location, then you could spend days, weeks or even months away from home – particularly if you are working on a major drama series or a feature film.

It can be a very stressful job, because everyone else's work depends on the success of yours. It doesn't matter how brilliant a performance an actor gives, nor how beautiful the pictures are if there is no sound or the recording is bad. In broadcasting there is always the urgency of live programmes to deal with also, which can be nerve-wracking when things start to go wrong and you must put them right immediately. You might also find yourself juggling lots of different things during a broadcast, because you might have 'lines' (audio link-ups) coming from other television stations which can some- times cause difficulties.

This is also an area which is dominated by men and there is often some resistance to employing women as sound technicians. In 1985, there were only ten female sound recordists in the film industry out of a total of some 600 working in that section which, Melanie Chait points out, is 'completely unacceptable'. Even when women do get jobs, they have found that it is difficult to be promoted to a senior level, or that it takes longer than it would for a male colleague. This should not deter women from trying to enter this profession, however. As more and more female sound technicians prove that they can do the job as well as, if not better than, many men, then that situation must improve and both BETA and ACTT actively pursue an equal opportunities policy.

3 Qualifications and characteristics required

Many television companies ask that applicants have at least O-level Physics and Mathematics. In addition, it may be helpful if you have studied music or played a musical instrument because this not only implies a sensitivity to sound, but indicates a sense of timing and rhythm. Employers also look for some indication that applicants are interested in sound recording. It may be that they have set up the microphones and speakers for school drama productions, or that they have operated a simple sound console for a local rock group. Such a background would make you eligible to apply for a position as a trainee with a television company. Alternatively, there are a number of courses available leading to appropriate qualifications, such as TEC/City and Guilds or Higher National Diploma or a degree in Electronics, Computer Science or Communications. If you wished to specialise in music recording, you might study to become a music Tonmeister, or there are some film and television courses at colleges of further education which are also appropriate.

If you wish to work in the freelance or independent sectors, or in the film industry, then you may be able to persuade a company or a sound recordist to take you on as an assistant without having any formal qualifications. Since it is a fairly technical profession, however, it is probably best to get some training first.

To be a good sound technician, you must be both resourceful and able to work on your own as well as fit in with a team. Even in times of stress, you must deal with problems calmly and methodically. Often, the sound crew have to work closely with performers and presenters, so you should be able to get along with all kinds of people. Since so much depends on your work you must be reliable and thorough, also.

4 How to become a sound technician

It is important to get at least O-level passes in Physics and Mathematics and it is helpful if you also study music or play a musical instrument. Get as much experience of working with microphones and sound equipment as you can. Volunteer to help with your school or college concerts or drama performances. There may also be an audio-visual department which has equipment you can practise with. Read as much as you can about sound recording. You should find Glyn Alkin's book, *Sound Recording and Reproduction* (1981), or his *T.V. Sound*

Operations (1975) useful as well as Alec Nisbett's *The Technique of the Sound Studio* (1979). If you would like to work for a television company, write to the head of the sound department of each station expressing your interest. If you can, arrange to go along for a visit to observe the sound crew at work. By doing so, you can let them know you are seriously interested and give them the opportunity to assess your potential as a crew member. If you wish to work in the film industry, it may be advisable to get your training and some experience in television first. You can then try approaching established recordists and asking to be taken on as an assistant. A list of names should be available through ACTT or in directories such as *Kemps Film and Television Yearbook* or *Film Bang* (applies to Scotland only).

Melanie Chait

☐ Sound recordist
☐ Freelance

Melanie Chait is originally from South Africa but has lived in this country for eleven years. She campaigns actively for women's rights through her involvement with ACTT. She is now thirty-one and is based in London.

» 'When I came to England eleven years ago, I knew I wanted to make films, but I didn't know how to begin, especially as film schools were predominantly interested in Fine Arts students and my background was in Political Science. While I did a master's degree, I worked part-time at a cinema and someone there knew I was playing around with Super 8 cameras and tape recorders. He told me that there was a shortage of sound recordists and that I should think about taking up sound as a way of having access to film-making. Shortly afterwards he offered me a job on the film he was making. I think that, at that time, most women were getting in through the back door as the sort of training schemes we have now didn't exist and film schools were accepting very few women.

'When I took the equipment home with me, I'd never seen a Nagra [the tape recording machine] before. I spent a whole weekend sitting in my room reading through the manuals trying to work out how it all fitted together. Then I worked on more and more student films, not getting paid, but just getting experience. I'm not convinced that the qualifications often asked for to become a sound recordist, like Maths and Physics, are actually necessary. It is probably useful if you want to do music mixing, sound engineering or maintenance. One's hearing becomes trained with experience and the skills required for location recording, apart from knowing the equipment, are being very professional, organised and quick-thinking and also liking to work with a team. The role of the sound recordist is contradictory because many crews consider the sound element as secondary to the picture and you have to be low-key while the camera department gets on with their thing, but also be good at PR work in order to get your mike where you need it.

'I don't think I experience discrimination in the same blatant way as I would if I were working in a studio. I consciously chose to work in a more independent area of film-making, rather than in the commercial field. So, although I've done some feature films, I work mostly in political documentaries and the people who employ me often have some tenuous understanding of women's issues. This doesn't mean that there isn't the initial scepticism about my abilities and the feeling that you have to prove yourself in a way that men don't, but I haven't felt discriminated against in getting the work, although that is probably more to do with the length of time I have been working as a sound recordist and because I work in the independent sector. I did work for a while in educational television where I was the only female technician and I found the constant direct and indirect sexism exhausting. There's also another level of discrimination that I've encountered when I've produced and directed films for TV which is to do with entrusting large sums of money to women.

'I think one point to bear in mind is that there are still very few women technicians and therefore, right now, I don't believe that we pose a real threat. But, as more women are coming into the film industry, it will be interesting to see if a backlash occurs as men's assumptions of women are being forced to change. In 1985, there were only ten women sound recordists in the film industry out of a sound section of 600. Admittedly, this is an enormous improvement on having only two women sound recordists in 1981, but I still find it completely unacceptable. In all areas of film-making there are now, over the past four years, more women. This increase is due mostly to a conscious policy of the ACTT and to the enormous efforts of the Equality Officer and is not to do with men opening the doors and welcoming us in. It's to do with women fighting for women.

'One thing I always find interesting about technicians is how the men always blame the equipment if something goes wrong, whereas women so often blame themselves – but I don't think this is restricted to the film industry. Women technicians are still far more qualified academically on the whole than men, but hopefully this will change with the recent appointment of a training officer for ACTT, making access easier for working class women, black people and other ethnic minorities.

'The most on-the-job harassment I have had is when I go away abroad with a crew. Often I'm the only woman and there's going to be a bloke who propositions you in some way and you've got to deal with that. You try and get out of it in as delicate a way as you can, because you have got to live with these people for three weeks and you don't want the whole crew dynamics to go sour. If I decide to tell them that I'm a lesbian, the remaining time is often spent by someone wanting to know why.

'My advice to anyone trying to become a sound recordist would be to pester all the women sound recordists because the more you pester them, the more determined they realise that you are. I would also advise doing the National Film School Short Courses and finding out about the union's training courses – it's also a way of letting the union know about you. I think you have to be very patient and determined and it does take a long time. It's also very important to go along on a shoot and watch how the sound department operates, because I've found that a lot of people who may have worked with the equipment, don't actually know how a film crew work.

'I think that socially this job is difficult because work does come first and so your friends get messed around because you can't make it at the last minute. Your relationships break because you go away a lot and when you come back, you're absolutely exhausted. I'd very much like to have a child, but I just can't negotiate how to incorporate that into my life at the moment. If it were possible, I'd have had one by now.'

Sue Cleaver

☐ Boom operator
☐ Freelance

Sue Cleaver is a boom operator based in the Tyne and Wear area. She is twenty-six and is unmarried.

» 'Being a boom operator requires a certain amount of strength but nothing excessive. Mostly you just need willpower to hold a microphone in place for anything up to twenty minutes. You might then have a couple of seconds break before having to hold the mike for a further ten minutes or something like that. I don't think it could be done by anyone who's particularly weak, however.

'When I was at college, I met quite a few people who were in the film industry in the independent sector. The best way of getting into the industry is to know the right people and to get the appropriate union ticket.

'It's essential for anyone who is using equipment (whether at assistant level or whatever) to understand the technology that they're using. So that means, in my case, understanding what sound is, understanding the microphones that I use and understanding the medium, whether it's $\frac{1}{4}$ inch audio tape or video tape.

'On occasion I've been turned down for work, but whether it's because I'm a woman I wouldn't like to say. That sort of thing is very difficult to prove, but I do think the fact that I'm a woman influences people's decisions. In the sector I work in (the independent sector), however, there is very often a willingness and a desire to use women on crews.

'I remember working down in London once in Hampstead and this guy drove up in a silver Porsche and he walked up to the sound recordist and said "My boom operator never used to look like that. They used to be decrepit old men. I wish I could work now." That sort of thing happens quite often. Occasionally it's phrased as "Why's this woman doing a man's job? Why isn't she at home looking after the kids?" I've never actually had a confrontation about sexism on the job, perhaps because I've never pushed it. Actually to confront someone on a job is not a good thing. When you're working, you're getting paid to do the job, and if it doesn't get done it costs a lot of money. So you have to put up with a lot of hassle. That doesn't just mean sexist comments. It includes directors getting extremely irate with you for absolutely no reason. You have to keep totally calm and basically get the job done. To confront people about sexism would interrupt the job. I make the odd sarcastic comment, if I feel it's necessary, but very often I just ignore it. I think I'm fortunate in that a lot of the people I work with, although they're men, don't appreciate those kind of comments either and in a sense they're in a much stronger position to fight against it. I don't think these things can be stopped by my response or lack of it, and I've got a job to do. Perhaps later, when there's the opportunity, I can come back on that kind of sexism.

'I actually live with a sound recordist whom I work with quite often, so our house is full of sound equipment. It's like any business that anybody runs that doesn't involve a nine-to-five day. It affects your private life. If I had children, that would mean I would have to stop work outside on film jobs for a while, which would mean a drop in income and also a loss in career terms. That's a personal choice, however.

'My advice to anyone wanting to get into the film industry would be to get to know the right people who can give you the chance to work, and also the people who can give you the information about the technology etc. that you need to know in order to work. I would say that I think the independent sector is far easier for a woman to approach than the commercial sector would be.'

Clare McAnulty

☐ Senior engineer (sound)
☐ ITV

Clare McAnulty has spent her whole career working in sound, firstly in radio and television with the BBC and later with Scottish Television. She is twenty-five, single and lives in Glasgow.

» 'I went to university when I was seventeen and did Pharmacology for one year but I wasn't enjoying it much and I came across an advert for the BBC. They wanted trainee audio assistants and the qualifications needed were things I had – Physics, a good education and music – so I just applied for it. I'd never heard of such a job before and it sounded interesting. Physics was not my favourite subject at school, but I'm glad I persevered with it. If I hadn't done it, I don't think I would have got the job. It's an advantage to be able to read music, because if you're balancing the sound for a band or orchestra, you can then read the musical score.

'What you need most of all is confidence. That only comes with experience. When you join the BBC as a trainee audio assistant, they immediately send you on a three-month course. It's a good way to start because, after the course is finished, you know exactly what is expected of you. Once your training period in radio is over, you're given a fair amount of responsibility. Your job includes tape editing, cueing-up records and tapes, mixing and transmitting programmes.

'My mother always worked so I never felt I had to choose to either work or be a mother. But I've been doing outside broadcasts recently and the hours are wild. I don't think I could look after a family if I was doing that constantly. You could choose not to do OBs, but you'd be missing out on quite a lot. Sometimes it's a bit of a strain to do the job and keep

my flat going when my hours become very irregular.
TV studio hours tend to be more normal. Mostly, you
start at 9 a.m. and finish after the news programme at
6.30 p.m., the exceptions being Drama or Light
Entertainment, when you tend to work some nights.
With radio, the station opens at 6 a.m., so you had to
be there from 5.30 a.m. By the afternoon, you were
ready to fall asleep and then the next day, you might
have to get up at a more ordinary time so your body
clock is never quite adjusted. I like having days off
during the week though, because that's very useful.

'There is some resistance to women, but I think you
just persist, though not in an aggressive way. At the
BBC, there were fifty in the department where I was
and only five of them were girls. On one occasion in
my career, there was a crew of about five of us and the
supervisor did not look at me and say, "Do such and
such". He said what had to be done, but he wasn't
giving me eye contact although he was giving eye
contact to other people and that's a very subtle thing.
So what I did was ask a question and then he had to
look at me and, once I'd done that, then it was more
difficult for him to turn away.

'Sometimes it's hard to strike a balance between
being feminine and being assertive enough. Being too
earnest can sometimes be translated as aggression.
After seven years working in sound, I still find the work
varied and interesting. One week you could be covering
a large concert, the next week horse racing and the
following week a simple interview for a news item.
The job also involves a fair amount of travelling. It's
never dull.'

22 The vision mixer

1 Job description

A vision mixer operates a console which changes one shot to another on our television screens. It is a television, rather than a film production job. For example, if you were watching a music programme, you might have a shot of a pop group from far away, as if you were in the audience. That might be followed by a close-up of the drummer. Then the title of the song and its place in the charts might be superimposed over that shot so that you can still see the musician. The person who makes all these visual changes is the vision mixer. Usually, she sits at the vision mixing console next to the director. Various visual sources are fed into the console – all the cameras, the telecine (which can show films and slides on a television screen), a captions generator (which can produce titles and printed captions on the screen) and video tape machines (which will play back recorded material). The console is capable of changing from one image to another in a variety of ways. For example, the picture to be used next may be allowed to overlap briefly with the old picture as it leaves the screen. This is known as a dissolve. Alternatively, a simple wipe may be used so that the previous image slides off the screen in one direction as the new image follows along behind until it occupies the full screen. If you watch television programmes carefully, you will be able to observe many different ways of changing images which can be done by the vision mixer. Some consoles also have the capacity for special effects, so that, for example, images tumble or spin on the screen. This technology is often used on the breakfast television programmes or on pop videos.

Usually, during rehearsals, the director will decide what kinds of shots she wants, the order in which they should appear and how she wants the changes from one image to another to happen. The vision mixer will have a record of all this information and will also receive any additional instructions that are necessary during the production, as she will usually be seated next to the director. Nevertheless, the vision mixer still has a great deal of responsibility. The precise instant at which one shot changes to another can make a critical difference and there is often no time for the director to communicate with the vision mixer. It is often she, therefore, who makes the ultimate decision. She has even greater responsibility during live broadcasts, when events may be completely unpredictable and the director must rely on the vision mixer's quick reactions.

2 Hours and working conditions

This is a job which will probably involve shift work and occasional overtime. You may be required to be away from home overnight if you are working on an outside broadcast, but for most vision mixers there is very little travel involved.

It can be a stressful job, particularly during live broadcasts, because so much depends on the vision mixer getting it right. There are other physical strains, also, which affect some people more than others. Most of your work will be done in a gallery, which is dimly lit, looking at rows of television screens. This can cause fatigue, restlessness and eye strain in some people.

This would appear to be a predominantly female

occupation. According to the figures for independent television companies, there are more than twice as many women working as vision mixers than there are men.

3 Qualifications and characteristics required

There appears to be no formal educational requirements for this job, although it would be advisable to get a good general education. Many ITV companies say that vision mixers are often recruited from within the organisation and may previously have worked as production assistants or secretaries. It is necessary, however, to have good vision and colour perception, as well as a degree of manual dexterity. You must be able to sit still for long periods of time and concentrate intensely. Since the programme will be literally in your hands, you must be unflappable. There can be a great deal of commotion in the gallery sometimes, but no matter what happens you must be able to distance yourself from the confusion and work calmly. You also need to have hair-trigger reactions at times, however, to respond to any sudden changes in plan. It helps if you are a a relatively intuitive person, able to anticipate what will happen next and what the director will want. To be a good, creative vision mixer, you also need a sense of rhythm and a feeling for drama so that you are sensitive to the exact moment that the image should be changed to get the maximum impact or to build up the right tempo. Last, but not least, you should have a reasonably logical mind, able to cope with equipment and technology, so that you can translate the director's vision into a series of technical strategies.

4 How to become a vision mixer.

If you meet the basic physical requirements for the job and think that it is one you would enjoy, then you should get a good basic education before applying to television companies. You may be able to enter directly as a trainee vision mixer, but, more likely, you should aim for any job that will get you into the company. Once there, you can make your interest in vision mixing known and observe and learn as much as you can about the job. You may find it helpful to read a general production textbook, such as Gerald Millerson's *The Technique of Television Production*.

Kathleen Ward

□ Vision mixer
□ ITV

Kathleen Ward has worked for Granada Television for most of her career. She is now fifty and is single and lives in Manchester.

» 'When ITV was starting, I wrote a letter to Granada Television and got a job as a secretary. That was when I was about twenty. My career hasn't progressed really, apart from becoming a vision mixer, partly because I never really applied for anything else except for one job about seven years ago as an associate producer and I didn't get it. That was the only one I ever applied for, probably because I had certain responsibilities towards my family. I'm quite confident now that I would have been equally as competent as some of the people that are doing directing or producing, but I never had a great deal of confidence when I was younger. I think it would have been very difficult, though. I think that to be a director or producer or whatever, you have to devote a lot of time to it. You have to be very committed to the job. I've been a vision mixer for twenty-five years. The technology has changed in that time, but the changes happen over a long period and you don't notice them because I suppose you change along with them. But vision mixing has changed as a job since I started. We used to do more live programmes. It was nerve-wracking and quite exciting and challenging really. We still do live programmes, but not as many.

'I suppose it's a fairly technical job. You've got to be quick. You need to be clear-thinking and organised. You can train yourself to do things in sequence, really. You train yourself to watch the monitors and you train yourself to follow your script and if you make a mistake, you train yourself not to think about it. If it's a live programme, you would make another six mistakes if you allowed yourself to dwell on it. I think it's essential to get on with people because you work so closely with them – especially directors, because they've got to have a bit of confidence in you. You've got to be fairly calm with people around you because a lot of them are going to be shouting and bawling and there's a lot of noise. You need a lot of concentration and the ability to switch off if it is all frantic around you. Once you know the board (the mixing console) it's like using a typewriter in that, eventually, you don't even look at it. You have to get familiar with the board to be able to just do it without thinking. Of course, you've got to watch the monitors as well. It's no good punching up a shot if the camera's not focussed. You're watching that and listening to the director and listening to roll cues for the VTR and then you would monitor that the picture was actually there before you took it, and listen so that you know the production assistant has rolled the right video. I mean, it's no use taking VTR "A" if VTR "A" is not there on the monitor.

'It's on the job training. The majority of vision mixers I've trained have come from within the company. They've done something else within Granada. I suppose it is an opportunity for women who are in a secretarial job to do something different.

'If you're doing a drama, it's a lot to do with timing. The director will plan it. When I say timing, it might be just a split second which makes all the difference. The whole point in drama is that the viewer doesn't notice the cut from one shot to another, but that he or she does see the little nod of the head or the look in the eye which gives meaning to the scene before you cut. Some directors will give you every cut, which is quite legitimate, whereas another director will be very grateful for any help you give them.

'I can't honestly say I've been discriminated against. It's my own fault if I've not pushed forward.

[At this point, Pat Baker, a director who had worked closely with Kathleen in the past and who had been listening, added these comments about her experience with vision mixers.]

Pat Baker: 'It is an art. It is rhythm, a feeling. There's a world of time between cutting at the end of one word and at the beginning of the next and a good vision mixer knows that instinctively and you can't tell them when to do it because by the time you've told them, it's too late. It has traditionally been a woman's job. It is also an artistic job. If you have a vision mixer who decides to cut every time the speaker changes, the whole thing is solid. It has no fluidity.'

Kathleen: 'Some people never get the rhythm, do they, Pat? And they never will get it. One thing I always tell trainees is, it's a very good thing when you know you're cutting wrong, because then you know what's right.'

Pat: 'A good vision mixer can get people out of trouble and you can carry directors.'

Kathleen: 'Oh, you can. Sometimes the director will tell you to do something wrong and if you know he's wrong, you will do what you think is right and he would be very grateful to you. It's good to work as a team in a Control Room, that's a good feeling. It's the end result that matters, that you all do a good professional show.'

23 The workshop worker

1 Job description

People who work in the workshop sector are permitted by the unions to function in more than one grade. For example, they can produce or direct, operate cameras, edit film or video tape, create artwork or be responsible for production design or do almost any of the other jobs mentioned in the various chapters of this book. But in practice, workers may often decide to specialise in one or two areas. Many workshops are run as cooperatives and have a particular political or social approach. Some workshops are all black, some are all female, some take a Marxist or left-wing viewpoint, others are strictly feminist. Thus the kind of productions undertaken by those in the workshop sector tend to reflect the political or social aims of that group. The organisation of the group may also be affected by their views and, as a result, the hierarchical structure and the process of decision-making may be more democratic than in mainstream organisations.

2 Hours and conditions of work

Since many workshops rely on grants to keep them going, this could be a very precarious area in which to make your living. Those employed in franchised workshops (see p.28 for an exlanation of this term) earn a rate of pay agreed with ACTT, currently about £10,000 per annum. Everyone in the workshop will earn the same amount regardless of what jobs they actually do. For many people, this is the only sector of the industry that allows them the political freedom with which they wish to operate. This can also be an area of work which is less pressured, allows greater aesthetic freedom and is more tolerant of individuality. The hours which workshop workers would be expected to put in obviously vary enormously from one situation to the next. In many instances, however, there is great flexibility and a willingness to accommodate domestic commitments. Since workshops were set up to give media access to groups which are discriminated against or ignored by the commercial sector, there should, in theory, be no racial or sexual discrimination within the workshops. In practice, this may not always be the case.

3 Qualifications and characteristics required

These vary widely from one workshop to the next. In some, quite a high degree of professional competence is required; others are willing to take on novices and train them in media skills as necessary. It may be more important that you fit in with the group's political and social aims than that you have particular technical skills. If the workshop does have a particular social or political orientation, then they will probably recruit workers who endorse these policies. You should be able to work as part of a team and, since many productions are community based, it helps if you are able to get along with a wide variety of people. Since the workshops have been set up, in general, to run counter to the mainstream and the Establishment, you ought to be someone who is broad-minded, tolerant of unconventional ideas and fairly flexible in your approach to people and work.

4 How to become a workshop worker

You could begin by contacting your nearest workshop and becoming involved in their productions in whatever way you can. That way, you can make yourself known and also gain some experience of working with their equipment. Many workshops take their name from the town or city in which they are located (i.e. Edinburgh Film Trust) and you could start by looking in the phone book to see if there is one in the town or city near you. They may also be listed in the Yellow Pages under television or film production companies, or audio visual services. You can also write to the workshops' organiser at ACTT to locate your nearest franchised workshop. There may be other groups, however, which are not franchised and you may be able to find these locally by checking with nearby film and video suppliers, who often have a good idea of potential customers in the area. Workshop jobs may be advertised in the local and national newspapers, such as the *Guardian*'s Creative and Media section published on Mondays. Openings with franchised workshops will also be advertised through ACTT. In the meantime, the more production experience you can get, the better, perhaps by borrowing portable equipment from your school or community centre. If there are any particular areas that interest you, then read the relevant chapters in this book and learn as much as you can about those particular jobs and skills. You may also find it useful to read some general textbooks, such as Gerald Millerson's *The Technique of Television Production* (1985), or W. Hugh Baddeley's *The Technique of Documentary Film Production* (1975).

Nadine Marsh Edwards

☐ Workshop worker

Nadine Marsh Edwards was one of the founders of
Sankofa Film and Video Workshop which specialises in
media projects relating to black people. She is twenty-
four and lives in the London area.

» 'I did my A-levels then took a year off and worked in
the Social Security Office. Then I went to Goldsmith's
College at London University and took a course in
Mass Communications and Sociology, specialising in
film. I got an upper second degree in 1983, then got a
job as a trainee assistant editor from June till
December. After that, I freelanced till about June.
During that time, I and other people set up Sankofa,
which is a black film and video workshop. We're one
of the franchised workshops under ACTT. We applied
for money from the GLC and Channel Four but we
didn't actually get the funds till June 1984. Since then,
we've done screenings and discussions and 16mm
workshops and VHS workshops mainly for black
people.
  'We set up this workshop firstly because we wanted
to work with other black people. We looked around at
who was in our sort of age group and who had the
same sort of background as us and came up with five
people. We weren't satisfied with the way black people
were represented in the media. The film we're working
on at the moment was going to be a ninety minute
documentary, but from all the discussions and contacts
with community groups that we've had, we learned
that black people didn't want to see themselves in
documentaries any more. So now it's going to be a
documentary drama. We want to show black people in
lots of different ways, not just in the ways you're used
to seeing them on television. We're trying to do quite

political films in a way that isn't boring and is aesthetically pleasing. The next film is intended mainly for cinema exhibition but it should also get a television showing, because we're programming a series for Channel Four and the new film will be part of that. Most of our films are shown in cinemas, community centres and educational centres, as well as at film festivals.

'Sankofa is a cooperative. We all do whatever needs to be done. Obviously, we delegate, but that's not according to any hierarchy, but depends on who's available at the time. The advantages are that you get to try everything. We all came with certain skills and it's like building from those skills by going into different areas. If you didn't have that previous experience and training, then it might be a problem if you weren't really sure what your skills were. You might get a bit uptight because you didn't think you were doing what you wanted to do. Everybody's got different skills in the group. I did editing, so I'm taking responsibility for that area even though other people also work on it. I haven't encountered much discrimination because we've decided to work as a collective and we cushion ourselves against a lot of that. That's one of the main advantages of working here. You don't have to put up with all that stuff because you've chosen to work with those people and if anybody does say anything you disagree with, you're quite at liberty to have a go at them. If you were working for somebody else in a subordinate position, it would be much more difficult to do that. In this business, at the level we're working at, discrimination isn't that blatant. It's definitely there, but in a way, you don't know it's happening half the time. We tend to get called up only if it's a project about women or a project about black people they want done. You get the work, but only in the area they think you're known for.

'I'm really happy doing what I'm doing now. I'm involved in making programmes about the things that I think are interesting and important, so I don't see any reason for going into the mainstream.'

Sarah Noble

☐ Workshop worker

Sarah Noble was one of two women amongst a staff of four at the Edinburgh Film Workshop Trust which has recently become ACTT franchised. Despite the name, the workshop also does video tape productions. At the time of interview, Sarah was twenty-six, single and lived in Edinburgh; at the beginning of 1987 she was tragically killed in a climbing accident.

» 'Photography was my hobby. While I was at university in Edinburgh, I had to do a placement for an honours course in Sociology and Social Administration to get some practical experience. I took that place at Film Workshop to do administration. I actually stayed there for ten months and then went on to work at a commercial printer's for eleven months. I then went back and finished my degree before working on a semi-freelance basis doing slide-tape and grant-aided video production work, until I became employed again at Film Workshop in 1984.

'As far as sex discrimination goes, it's a lot better than the freelance industry but I wouldn't say workshops are free from criticism. It's a very subtle form of discrimination. Workshops are set up specifically to counteract discrimination so they're 500 per cent better than working in the mainstream. But as far as I'm aware, you'd find more men working in the grant-aided sector than women.

'Each year we decide on the programme of work

which is based on our local commitments and issues arising from those. A lot of it is carry-on work from the previous year. Some of the work we will know about well in advance, but you're constantly getting letters from people so you have to have a basis on which you say "Yes" or "No" to certain projects. It's basically projects that fall in with our broad programme of work that we take on. We do a lot of work on environmental or peace issues. We can divide the work into three main areas: making the equipment available to local groups at subsidised rates; training local groups or voluntary organisations to use video or film; and then co-productions when we're producing a programme with a group like the Easterhouse Festival Society or the Association for Single Parents. Under the Workshop Declaration, Channel Four can take up to sixty minutes of that kind of work per year from us for broadcast. We're not really there to encourage people to go into the mainstream industry; we're really there for work locally or in the grant-aided sector. Our aim is to encourage local groups to have the skills to produce their own programmes. The Workshop Declaration allows me to work in any grade. What I tend to do is specialise in one or two grades such as sound recording and editing, although I have the ability to cover other grades. All I can say is I really enjoy what I'm doing and I've got no immediate plans for doing anything else. But the whole situation in workshops is very fragile because you're only financially stable for one year at a time at the very most.'

24 Final words of advice

By now you should have a good idea of which career interests you and may already have begun to follow the advice given for that specific job. There are, however, some general guidelines which are applicable to everyone who reads this book, no matter which career they have chosen.

1 Training options

The chapters you have already covered will have stressed the need to get the best general education that you can, not forgetting the sciences and mathematics if you think you might want to work in certain technical areas. For many of the jobs discussed in this book, however, it would be wise to go on for more specific training at an appropriate trade school, college or university. As you consult the list of courses included in Appendix A, bear in mind that there are six colleges which are recognised by ACTT. These are The National Film and Television School, The Polytechnic of Central London, The West Surrey College of Art and Design, Bristol University, The London International Film School and The London College of Printing. Graduates of these colleges are eligible to apply for jobs in grades covered by ACTT and, if they are successful, will be given union membership with no restrictions. (See p.31 for further information about ACTT membership.)

In addition to the colleges mentioned in Appendix A, however, there are a number of training schemes which are well worth considering.

The Scottish Film Training Trust This group runs a technicians' training scheme, which admits two or three young people every year, gives them a moderate income and assigns them to work on various productions to gain experience. Students who complete the course are eligible for unrestricted ACTT membership as soon as they are accepted for an ACTT graded job. Further information can be obtained by writing to The Scottish Film Training Trust, 70 Victoria Park Crescent, Dowanhill, Glasgow.

JOBFIT A number of organisations associated with the film industry have launched a training scheme known as JOBFIT (The Joint Board for Film Industry Training). Its aim is to train people of eighteen years and over in those technical and production grades covered by ACTT. The course lasts for two years and combines short courses with attachments to various productions in order to gain experience. Those who successfully complete the training are eligible to apply for ACTT graded jobs and when they get one, will be given unrestricted union membership. No specific criteria has been set out for the selection of candidates, but all round competency is important (i.e. that you can read, write and count and have good communication skills) and a strong visual sense. A broad agreement has been reached with the Board that about 50 per cent of the entrants will be female and approximately 33 per cent from ethnic minorities. Further information can be obtained from JOBFIT, 4th Floor, 5 Dean Street, London W1V 5RN.

CYFLE This aims to train Welsh-speaking technicians for the independent television industry in Wales. It is a two-year course which gives training in various grades during the first year, before concentrating on one area of work in the second year. The course provides practical experience working on different productions, plus off-the-job training. The only entry requirements are the ability to speak Welsh and a demonstrated interest in and enthusiasm for the film and television industry. All applications are welcome, irrespective of background, sex or race. Further information can be obtained from CYFLE, Maesincla, Caernarfon, Gwynedd, Wales LL55 1BY.

NEMDC The North East Media Development Board actively assists in the establishment of production units committed to long-term, full-time employment producing a socially useful product. It offers a two-year basic training course for new entrants to the industry as well as short courses for re-training working professionals. For further information contact NEMDC, Norden House, 39-41 Stowell Street, Newcastle on Tyne.

NSCTP The National Short Course Training Programme functions under the umbrella of the National Film and Television School. It offers a variety of courses, of between one and ten days duration, for re-training and up-grading the skills of technicians, writers and performers already working in the industry. The emphasis is on intensive hands-on experience, offering casualised workers the chance to update skills during their career. Further information can be obtained from The National Short Course Programme, Beaconsfield Studios, Station Road, Beaconsfield, Bucks. HP9 1LC.

Since new training schemes are constantly being set up and old ones revised, it is always worth checking on a regular basis to find out what's new. The various unions often have current information about the opportunities available for training in their line of work. Some, like

ACTT, have a member of staff who is specifically responsible for training. You can also write to the Training Advisor for the ITCA (address given in Appendix B, p.334), who will give general advice about careers, although not about specific job openings. The ITCA also organises a variety of training sessions and workshops – mostly for those already employed in the industry, however. A number of ITV companies have their own training schemes in various technical and production areas and you should check to find out what opportunities might be available. It is also worth contacting BBC Appointments or BBC Engineering Recruitment (addresses in Appendix B, p.333) because, apart from various apprenticeships, they also occasionally have holiday relief work available which provides an opportunity to learn about their operations first hand.

There is also a good chance that there is a film and video workshop in your area (see p.28 for an explanation of workshops). Some of these will be staffed exclusively by women and most of them are politically committed to serving the community. You should contact any in your locality to find out if they can provide training, work experience or access to equipment – not to mention a job!

2 Funding for training

There is no one simple source of funds to support you while you undertake media training. You may, of course, be eligible for a government student grant, provided that the course you choose is at a recognised college or university. Some local educational authorities will sponsor trainees who would not otherwise receive funding, but policies vary from one region to the next and you must check on the rules for your area. There are also a variety of government training schemes available for young people, the unemployed and women returning to the workforce after raising their children. Up-to-date information on these should be available at your local Job

Centre or Manpower Services Commission office.

Thereafter, it is a case of putting together your own funding package. Your local library should have reference books giving details of various trusts and foundations to which you can apply for money. It is also worth checking with the relevant trade unions and sources of training information mentioned above, because they may know of funds which are available, or sponsored training schemes which may be set up for a limited period of time. But there is no doubt about it – finding money to pay for media training can be a real test of initiative.

3 Making contacts

Apart from obtaining the best qualifications and relevant work experience that you can, one of the best ways of finding a job in the media is through personal contacts. This means getting to know, and becoming known by those who might be prospective employers and who would be able to give you advice and information about film and television work. The Women's Film, Television and Video Network (WFTVN) offers invaluable help by publishing a directory of female workers in the industry, producing information sheets about different jobs, providing some counselling and training as well as establishing a network of contacts in film and television. They have now expanded their operations into the regions and may have an organiser near you. They can be contacted at 79, Wardour Street, London W1V 3PN. Likewise, Women in Media, an association of women working in the industry, can be a valuable source of contacts. They can be reached by writing to Women in Media, Box BMWIM, London, WC1N 3XX.

In addition, each shop (branch) of ACTT should have an equality representative and several of the other media-related trade unions are in the process of establishing a similar network of representatives. If there is one near where you live, that person can probably put you in touch with women already working in the career that interests you, and may also be able to pass on information about job vacancies.

Getting in the doors of a television or film company can be more difficult. One thing which is worth a try is to write to the Public Affairs department of individual television stations, asking for tickets for any programmes which require a live audience. Then you can observe what happens behind the scenes and watch the various professionals at work. You can also write to the head of the department in which you would like to work, asking if you can visit that station or company to observe what goes on there. Most people remember what it was like starting out as a young hopeful and are often very willing to show an interested visitor around and give advice. If you are able to arrange such a visit, make sure that the staff and the personnel department know that you are keen to work in that area and ask them to notify you of any vacancies which come up.

Freelance workers in the industry can often be too busy and elusive to be very helpful to beginners. It is still worth finding their names and addresses through the relevant union or in trade directories, however. Then you can contact them directly and ask if you can observe them at work or assist them in any way.

4 Applying for jobs

Advertisements for television or film jobs in your area are likely to appear in the local press. Otherwise, they can be found in the *Guardian*'s Creative and Media section which is published on Mondays, or in publications like the *Listener* (BBC only), *Broadcast*, *Television Weekly*, *Stage and Television Today* (for theatre, floor manager and design jobs in particular) *Audio Visual* (for technical jobs), *The UK Press Gazette* (for journalists' jobs), and *Sight and Sound* (for film work). Very often jobs are advertised internally through the relevant union also and you may be able to obtain a copy of the vacancies list from one of their members.

If you do get an interview, but are unsuccessful in getting the job, don't stop there. Telephone or write to the personnel department and ask them what let you down and how you should improve before the next interview, so that you become a stronger candidate. Make it clear that you're not complaining because you didn't get the job, only wanting to do better next time.

5 Coping with discrimination

As you have read this book, it will have become clear to you that one of the obstacles to employment in the film and television industry which women may encounter is sex discrimination in all its many forms. It is important to stress, however, that many women do not experience any difficulty and find their colleagues and employers helpful and supportive. This is also a problem which can and will be overcome, as more and more women enter the industry and acquire the clout to prevent it occurring.

Often, it is not the most glaring instances of discrimination that are the most difficult to deal with. Those can be identified with relative ease and often the victim can find support from family, friends and colleagues and take action through the courts or their trade union. It is the more subtle, on-going forms of discrimination that are the hardest to pinpoint and document and therefore the most difficult to bear because they cannot be tackled directly and stopped. It is cases such as these which result in women giving up their jobs, being miserable, resorting to tranquillisers and even, in extreme cases, having nervous breakdowns. Much discriminatory behaviour works to set the victim apart so that she is even more likely to become a scapegoat for anything that goes wrong. Women in this situation may find themselves alienated, trying to cope alone, ridiculed when it's only their word against someone else's and left wondering if perhaps they really are neurotic, or difficult or at fault. Other women find themselves in circumstances where they feel too vulnerable to take overt action, or else they may not have the kind of personality to cope with confrontations. One of the best ways of coping with discrimination, therefore, is to anticipate the situations you may encounter and to develop strategies for dealing with them while you're calm and collected, instead of struggling with your own emotional upheaval on the spur of the moment. The following are some examples of situations encountered by the women who contributed to this book and the ways they found of dealing with them.

a At the interview There are still some employers who, despite all the disclaimers and laws to the contrary, ask women questions at interviews which discriminate on the basis of sex. If you want the job, that is probably not the time to object. That can come later when you are firmly entrenched and have got the trade union and your female colleagues behind you – although it may be wise to consider that if your would-be employers are like that at the interview, they are hardly likely to have changed by the time you go to work for them, and are you ready for more of the same on the job? If you don't get the job, then you should still report any behaviour which you considered discriminatory to the equality representative of the appropriate trade union or to the Equal Opportunities Commission. The best defence, however, is to anticipate the worst and be prepared for questions like these:

'*Won't the equipment be too heavy for you?*' Some employers seem to think that *manly* heavy work, like carrying cameras, is somehow different and more taxing than women's heavy work, like carrying a two-year-old and a bag of groceries. So it's a good idea to get a tour of the area you would like to work in beforehand and talk to some of the crew to find out just how much heavy work really is involved. Some macho myths are just a hangover from the past, since equipment has become much more compact and lighter over the years and no longer requires brute strength to operate. Even if there is heavy work involved, find out if *anyone*, male or female, would be expected to do it alone. Very often, the whole crew helps to carry equipment and it is usually common practice for more than one person to lift something especially heavy. There may also be people on the crew whose specific job is to carry equipment or props around. Perhaps, too, there are alternatives open to you which a Real Man wouldn't use – such as moving equipment around on trolleys, or using slings or braces to help support heavy weights. At any rate, if you're asked this question, don't hesitate to tell them firmly that you're just as capable as anyone else of lifting things and let them know that you've checked out exactly what is involved before they start exaggerating the pitfalls.

'What will your husband say when you're not home to make the tea, dear?' Working in film and television often means working unsocial hours – whether shift work or just very long days. For some reason, there are employers who consider this aspect of the job to be worse for women than for men. Perhaps what they're really concerned about is that you will be depriving some man of your services by working late. You should say that you don't mind the unsocial hours because you enjoy the break in routine or it allows you to take care of personal business during normal working hours when you're off duty. If it's a question of very long days, then you can say that you're so dedicated that you don't mind, or that you want a job which will be challenging and demanding, or that you need the money. If they ask how such a work

schedule will affect your social life, say simply that you have given that careful consideration and, having discussed it fully with your partner, you're quite prepared to accept that part of the job.

'*What about your children?*' Somehow, if men who are fathers work, this is considered beneficial to their children's welfare. Yet obviously, people who ask women questions like that at interviews have visions of your kids doped up to the eyeballs, starving, sniffing glue or robbing old ladies while you have the time of your life as a production assistant on *Game for a Laugh*. If you are asked this question, don't bridle at the implied insult – simply say that you have made excellent provisions for childcare.

'*Won't you just get married/pregnant in a year's time and leave?*' The fact that employers shouldn't ask questions like these doesn't stop some of them from doing it, unfortunately. You should always say that you plan to continue working after marriage and that, if you have children, you would want to return to your job after maternity leave. You should give these answers even if there is some doubt in your mind at the time, because you don't know what the future will hold and you have every right to keep your options open. An engagement could be broken off, you may never have children or you may find yourself forced to continue working for financial reasons you hadn't anticipated.

'*But sometimes we use bad language, dear.*' One woman I spoke to was refused a job by the head of the production company because 'we only have one toilet and we sometimes use bad language'. One can only hope she swore at him. It's hard to imagine that very many women would be shocked by the use of bad language in this day and age (whether or not they might approve of it, is another matter), when we are subjected to so many four letter words in the media. If the use of bad language does upset you, however, then think carefully about any job you may be offered. I have found it to be a myth that a crew will stop swearing just because there is a woman around.

b On the job Discriminatory attitudes at an interview only have to be tolerated for half an hour or so; but discriminatory attitudes on the job may have to be borne indefinitely. Often, it is subtle and quite minor transgressions which add up to making the work environment uncomfortable, at best, and intolerable, at worst, for women. It is essential, therefore, to discover ways of stopping or defusing such behaviour.

Discrimination, as the word implies, is a setting apart and the more alienated you become, the more effective the discrimination and the more momentum it will gather. If you become the odd one out, it increases the likelihood of your becoming the scapegoat for anything that goes wrong and the butt of other people's personal problems. So one of the most effective ways of combatting such behaviour is to prevent yourself from becoming cut off. Can you find a mentor within the company – another woman or a man who has more experience and can give you advice as well as moral support? Can you develop your own support groups amongst other women and sympathetic men? You may find it useful to talk to people outside the industry, but the film and television business is so unique, that behaviour which even you find acceptable may shock outsiders. Women or men who are aware of the background circumstances are more likely to provide a realistic sounding board and help you achieve a balanced perspective on your circumstances.

Even discrimination which is well-intentioned can be bad simply because it singles you out. One woman found that, unlike her male colleagues, she was never asked to do any heavy lifting. Mindful of the resentment that that could provoke, she began stepping forward and doing the work without being asked. A similar situation occurred when two operators, one male and one female, made a mess of an assignment. The woman found out later that her male colleague got a bawling out, while she was left in blissful ignorance. When she confronted her supervisor, he looked sheepish and said that he would have felt like a bully if he had yelled at her. But that might have been preferable, she felt, to the resentment of the other crew members.

Those who have studied patterns of discrimination and harassment say that one of its main aims is to lessen women's power and prevent them from functioning effectively. This can be achieved by making a woman self-conscious, which in turn makes her inhibited and causes her to lose confidence. Once that happens, it doesn't take long before the woman's job performance is affected. Thus, however difficult it may be, your first priority, if you are being harassed, must be to continue doing your work to the best of your ability.

One of the most common ways of making a woman feel self-conscious is for male colleagues continually to comment on her appearance. I've found that men will quickly tire of making such comments if you turn round and say something, without rancour, about their appearance — especially if you can do it with humour. In general, men are far more easily embarrassed by personal comments than women are. If, however, a male colleague makes remarks which are suggestive or obscene, then that should be reported to a union representative or to the management.

Perhaps one of the most distressing and wearing kinds of discrimination occurs when women find that sexist rumours and reports are being spread about them. These are distressing because often they can neither be confronted nor clarified, so that the victim may be left feeling powerless. This is psychological warfare. Your best defence is to perform your work to the best of your ability, ignore the rumours and make no comment. That is often the best way to bore your malicious colleagues into silence. But don't withdraw into a protective shell. Be polite and friendly and you may shame some of those slandering you into keeping quiet. Of course, where you have proof of what is being said about you by whom and can prove that it is slanderous, then you should go to the management, or to the union, or take legal action. If you feel strong enough, you could decide to confront those involved directly.

Often women find that they are denied opportunities given to men. These can include not being given overtime and not being given more advanced work. One woman reported that all female employees in her department had to complete the full probationary period, whereas men were often allowed to do only a few months or to skip the training altogether. Several journalists mentioned that there were the inevitable attempts to limit them to the 'Mums and babies' stories, while female producers complained that they were often shunted on to women's programmes and denied the breadth of experience that they needed to advance their careers. If you can document that sort of discrimination – particularly if it has happened to more than one woman – then you should approach your union representative and ask that the matter be taken up with management. Keep asking for challenging assignments, using what one woman called the 'water dripping on a stone' technique. Another woman recommended disguising ambition as youthful enthusiasm and keenness. (If you're past the first flush of youth, perhaps you could disguise it as senile dementia.) That way, you may appear less threatening.

Black women and women from ethnic minorities have a particular problem, in that they must deal with discrimination based on race as well as sex. Virtually all of those who responded to my questionnaire or whom I interviewed, reported that there were no black or ethnic workers in their area. Several of the trade unions are beginning to compile data on members belonging to minority racial groups, however, and ACTT, for example, has a black members sub-committee. It may be possible, therefore, for a black or Asian woman who would like to work in the media to get in touch with others of her own race already working in the industry by contacting the relevant trade union. In addition, each union has an official with specific responsibility for equality issues and in almost every case, that includes a mandate to challenge discrimination based on race. Many women in the industry, having experienced discrimination in their own lives, are also sensitive to the predicament of black and minority workers and are willing to offer moral support and practical help whenever possible. Some workshops are staffed exclusively by women from racial minorities. Thus, although a black or Asian woman is likely to encounter greater discrimination than would a white woman, there are groups and individuals who are willing to help, as well as several outstanding examples of women from racial minorities who have broken through the barriers.

Whatever your racial origins, however, the golden rule with sexual harassment or discrimination is 'Don't let it get to you'. Any outburst, whether from anger or distress, can encourage worse behaviour, make you even more vulnerable, or be used against you as proof of your unsuitability to do the job/be promoted and so on. You don't actually have to deny to yourself that you're furious or hurt, but it's wise to work out these feelings in private, by sticking pins in dolls or talking to friends. You will be better able to negotiate an improvement in the situation if you are thinking and alert, not sobbing and overwhelmed with self pity or so angry you can't speak. Whenever possible, avoid being singled out as a troublemaker, because several women complained that the hostility towards them increased after they complained about discriminatory behaviour. Gather as much documentation in support of your case as you can, persuade others in the same situation to join you and then, if possible, get union backing and let your shop steward or union organiser represent you. If you are being sexually harassed, then Women Against Sexual Harassment (WASH) offers confidential advice and counselling to any woman, anywhere in the country. They can be contacted at Sophia House, 32-5 Featherstone Street, London (Tel. 01-250-0340).

Whatever happens, do not allow yourself to be cut off, because that will only make you a more likely scapegoat and allow the situation to escalate in your head because you have no outlet for discussion. Keep communication lines with colleagues open, talk to your friends and make contact with support groups.

Discrimination is something that can and will be overcome. Many of those to whom I spoke testified that, with experience and increased self-confidence, they learned how to cope with and successfully challenge harassment and discrimination. As the novelty of women working in all areas of the industry wears off, as there are more and more female workers to band together and make their needs known, and as more women reach positions of power and can help others, the situation can only improve. In the 1970s, women were told they lacked the authority to become newsreaders. Now an all-male newscasting team seems odd and boring. Things do change.

5 Conclusions

Simply reading this book will not guarantee you a job in film and television but, if you follow the advice given, it can point you in the right direction, armed with the information you need to become a viable candidate for a career in the media. The preceding chapters have given you an overview of the job possibilities as well as some idea of what the work entails and how it may affect your private life. They have also demonstrated how women from a variety of backgrounds and with a range of abilities and personalities have been able to find jobs and working conditions that suit them and their lifestyles. Perhaps, unusually for a career guide, the less glamorous side and the problems you may encounter have also been presented. This has not been done to put you off, but to prepare you for coping with such circumstances and to ensure that, should they arise, you are not so shocked or disillusioned that you give up.

For those who do persevere, the reward is a job that can be challenging, creative and totally fascinating. In spite of the difficulties, most of the women to whom I spoke love their work and would never give it up. There are few industries in which you can find the *camaradarie* of working on a crew, or the adrenalin flow of live television, or the immense satisfaction of seeing the outcome of your efforts on the screen. It is also work which can be very lucrative – a fact not to be forgotten.

Those of us already working in film and television want more women to join us. Never before has there been such widespread recognition of equal opportunities policies. Never before has there been such organised support within the industry on behalf of women. If so many could succeed against all the odds in the past, you can succeed now.

If you do not grab these opportunities, they may disappear forever. Given the influence which television and film have in shaping society's attitudes, that would be a loss not only for those women concerned with careers in the media, but to all of us. We are poised on the edge of a breakthrough for women. With hard work and perseverance, you could be part of making that happen.

Appendix A A survey of some relevant courses

1 Courses offering entry at O-level or equivalent

Address	Course title	Subject area	Notes
Sandwell College of Further Education, Woden Road South, Wednesbury, WS10 0PE	Cert. in TV and Audio Production.	TV production, sound production for radio and TV, technical operations and television design.	1 year. O-level English, Maths, and two other subjects requ'd for entry.
As above	(Proposed BTEC Diploma in Sound Engineering.)	Radio production, or multi-track recording or radio drama.	2 years. O-level English and three other subjects at C+. Prefer O-level Physics.
London College of Printing, Elephant and Castle, London SE1 6SB	Foundation Course in Media Studies.	Broad-based foundation course for studies in communications and the media.	1 year. Must be age 17+ with 5 O-levels.
Ravensbourne College of Art and Design, Wharton Road, Bromley, Kent BR1 3LE	BTEC HND in Design (TV Programme Operations).	Sound working knowledge of prog. operations, incl. lighting, sound, vision mixing, camera, telecine, tape and audio recording.	2 years. 6 O-levels incl. English Language, Maths and Physics. *or* 3 BTEC/ONC/OND.

Note: All courses full-time unless otherwise stated.

2 Courses offering entry at A-level or equivalent.

Address	Course title	Subject area	Notes
Bournemouth and Poole College of Art and Design, Royal London House, Lansdowne, Bournemouth, BH1 3JL	Professional Course in Photographic Media Studies.	Practical course on photography with specialisation in film/TV production.	3 years. 2 A-level and 3 O-levels or Foundation Course and 5 O-levels plus portfolio.
Harrow College of Higher Education, Northwick Park, Harrow, Middlesex	BA Hons in Applied Photography, Film and Television.	70% practical work; 2nd and 3rd year options of studying cultural, commercial, industrial or scientific applications of film and TV.	3 years 2 A-levels and 3 Os or 5 O-levels and Art and Design Foundation Course.
London College of Fashion, 20 John Princes Street, London W1	DATEC Higher Diploma in Theatrical Studies with specialised Make-up options.	The specialised skills of the TV make-up artist.	2 years. A-levels in Art subjects and O-level English and a science or appropriate TEC/DATEC qualifications or previous experience.
London College of Printing, Elephant and Castle, London SE1 6SB	BA Hons in Film and Video.	Theory and practice of film and video plus cultural studies.	3 years. 2 As and 3 O-levels or 5 O-levels and Art and Design Foundation Course.

Institution	Course	Description	Entry requirements
Manchester Polytechnic Capital Building, School Lane, Didsbury, Manchester M20 10HT	BA Hons in Design for Communications Media/ Film and TV Studies.	Film and TV production design; 80% practical work.	3 years. 3 As and 1 O-level *or* 2 As and 3 O-levels *or* 5 Os and Foundation Course in Art and Design *or* ONC/OND *or* equivalent TEC.
NE London Polytechnic, Greengate House, Greengate Street, London E13 0BG.	BA Hons in Fine Art.	Photography, film and audio are included in a wide range of Fine Art activities.	3 years. Normal minimum requ'mts for entry to CNAA degree course.
Polytechnic of Central London 18-22 Riding House Street, London W1P 7PT	BA Hons in Film, Video and Photographic Arts.	Equal emphasis on theory and practice of film, video and photography.	3 years. 2 A-levels and 3 Os *or* 3 A-levels and 1 O-level.
As above	BA Hons in Media Studies.	Theory and practice of mass communication in journalism and television as a prelude to professional work in the media.	3 years. 2 A-levels and 3 Os *or* 3 A-levels and 1 O-level.
Ravensbourne College of Art and Design, Wharton Road, Bromley, Kent BR1 3LE	BTEC HND in Communications Engineering.	Operation and control of professional TV and audio equipment and study of technology and aesthetics relevant to TV.	2 years. A-level Maths and Physics and O-level English *or* City and Guilds or TEC.

Address	Course title	Subject area	Notes
Sheffield Polytechnic, Psalter Lane, Sheffield S11 8UZ	BA Hons in Communication Studies	Academic grounding in communication studies plus development of practical skills	3 years. 2 A-levels and 3 Os *or* 3 A-levels and 1 O-level.
University of London, Goldsmiths College, Lewisham Way, London SE14 6NW	BA in Communication Studies and Sociology.	Theoretical basis of communication plus practical skills in film and TV production, graphic design and photography.	3 years. 2 A-levels and 3 Os *or* 3 A-levels and 1 O-level.
University of Strathclyde Glasgow G1 1XH	BA Hons Joint degree in Film and TV Studies with another subject.	Theoretical and practical skills relevant to a career in the media.	4 years. SCE: 4 Highers at AAAB *or* 5 Highers at AAACC GCE: 3 A-levels at BBB
University of Surrey, Guildford, Surrey.	B. Music & Sound Recording.	Music, physics of sound, recording techniques, electronics, electro-acoustics.	4 years. A-level Music, Physics & Maths + 1 O-level.
West Surrey College of Art and Design, Falkner Road, The Hart, Farnham, Surrey	BA Hons in Photography, Film and Video Animation.	Practical course in photography, film and video animation. Emphasis on experimentation and development of creative and conceptual understanding.	3 years. 5 O-levels and Art Foundation course *or* 2-year BTEC Diploma course.

Courses offering entry at 1st degree level or equivalent

Address	Course title	Subject area	Notes
London International Film School, 24 Shelton Street, London WC2H 9HP	Diploma Course	Technical, creative and aesthetic aspects of drama. All round understanding of processes involved.	2 years. No absolute educational requirements but majority of students have university entrance qualifications.
Middlesex Polytechnic, Cat Hill, Barnet, Hertfordshire, EN4 8HT	Postgrad: Diploma in Film and TV Studies.	Detailed media analysis plus workshops and projects	1 year. 1st degree from university or equivalent.
National Film and Television School, Station Road, Beaconsfield, HP9 1LG	Associateship.	All aspects of film production, including writing, directing, producing, editing, lighting, sound and camera work.	Postgrad. course but degree not essential. Ability and experience considered.

Address	Course title	Subject area	Notes
Polytechnic of Central London, 18-22 Riding House St, London W1P 7PT	Postgrad. Diploma in Film Studies.	Theory and criticism of film and television.	7 terms, part-time. 1st degree or equiv. prefer Humanities or Social Sciences.
As above	MA in Film Studies.	Theory and criticism of film and television.	3 terms, part-time, following Dip. course.
Royal College of Art, Queen's Gate, London SW7	Course will be offered by Film Dept. in 1987/8 onwards.		Contact college for further information.
Univ. of Bristol, 9 Park Row, Bristol BS1 5LT	Postgrad. Certificate in Radio, Film and TV.	Intensive course in radio, TV and film production.	1 year. Good 1st degree.

Appendix B Useful addresses

Anglia Television Ltd,
Anglia House,
Norwich NR1 3JG

BBC Appointments,
Broadcasting House,
London W1A 1AA

BBC Engineering Recruitment,
Broadcasting House,
London W1A 1AA

Border Television plc,
Television Centre,
Carlisle CA1 3NT

The British Film Institute,
127 Charing Cross Road,
London WC2

The British Kinematography,
   Sound and Television Society,
110-12 Victoria House,
Vernon Place,
London WC1B 4DJ

Central Independent Television
   plc,
Central House,
Broad Street,
Birmingham B1 2JP

Channel Four Television Co. Ltd,
60 Charlotte Street,
London W1P 2AX

Channel Television,
The Television Centre,
St Helier,
Jersey,
Channel Islands

Grampian Television plc,
Queen's Cross,
Aberdeen AB9 2XL

Granada Television Ltd,
Granada T.V. Centre,
Manchester M60 9EA

HTV Ltd,
The Television Centre,
Culverhouse Cross,
Cardiff CF5 6XJ

The Independent Broadcasting
   Authority,
70 Brompton Road,
London SW3 1EY

The Independent Television
   Companies Association Ltd,
Knighton House,
56 Mortimer Street,
London W1N 8AN

Independent Television News
   (ITN),
ITN House,
48 Wells Street,
London W1P 3FE

London Weekend Television Ltd,
South Bank Television Centre,
Kent House,
Upper Ground,
London SE1 9LT

The Scottish Film Council,
74 Victoria Crescent Road,
Glasgow G12 9JN

Scottish Television plc,
Cowcaddens,
Glasgow G2 3PR

Sianel 4 Cymru,
Sophia Close,
Cardiff CF1 9XY

The Society for Education in Film
   and TV,
29 Old Compton Street,
London W1V 5PL

Television South plc,
Television Centre,
Northam,
Southamptom SO9 5HZ

Television South West Ltd,
Derry's Cross,
Plymouth PL1 2SP

Thames Television Ltd,
306-16 Euston Road,
London NW1 3BB.

TV-am,
Breakfast Television Centre,
Hawley Crescent,
London NW1 8EF.

Tyne Tees Television Ltd,
The Television Centre,
City Road,
Newcastle upon Tyne NE1 2AL

Ulster Television Ltd,
Havelock House,
Ormeau Road,
Belfast BT7 1EB

Women Against Sexual
   Harassment,
City Centre,
Sophia House,
32-35 Featherstone Street,
London EC1 8RT

The Women's Film, Television
   and Video Network,
79 Wardour Street,
London W1V 3PH

Women in Media,
Box BMWIM,
London WC1N 3XX

Yorkshire Television Ltd,
The Television Centre,
Leeds LS3 1JS

Appendix C Glossary of some terms used in this book

animatic	an animated version of a live commercial which is made as a 'dry run' before thousands of pounds are risked doing the real thing.
assembly editing	when the various scenes of a film are joined up together in the right order but are not yet finely edited.
attachment	a temporary secondment to do a particular job.
boards	job interviews, usually involving a panel of interviewers.
boom	a metal arm which pivots on a portable stand used for positioning microphones.
cell	a sheet of transparent material on to which the drawings for an animated sequence are copied before being photographed.
Chinagraph	a wax pencil used for marking film.
cycle	a repetition of one animated sequence.
dolly	a mobile camera platform.
dope sheet	the instruction sheet which an animator will prepare for the camera operator.
dressing a set	arranging the furniture etc. on a set to achieve the required effect.
elevations	the heights of the areas marked on a floorplan which are drawn in to give a three-dimensional plan.
ENG production	electronic news gathering – denotes the use of portable video cameras, normally used to record news stories.

fishpole	a contraption rather like a broom handle or a fishing rod used to suspend microphones where required.
flat	a piece of scenery which, although it may depict a three-dimensional landscape, for example, is actually painted on a flat sheet of canvas or board.
follow spot	the light that follows the main character as they move about the stage in a theatre.
gallery	the control room for a studio, where the director sits and monitors all the visual and sound elements of a programme and from where she calls the shots.
gantry	a framework rather like the arm of a crane which can be used to support equipment such as lights or cameras.
independent facilities house	a company which provides full studio facilities for hire to independent producers or agencies.
lay track	to synchronise and edit the sound track to match the corresponding pictures.
lighting grid	a criss-cross structure of metal bars overhanging a studio space or stage from which lights can be hung.
magazine	a film container which is loaded with film and then attached to the main body of the camera for use.
mark	as in 'the actress couldn't hit her mark'. Often an unobtrusive mark is made on the studio floor so that an artiste knows where she must stand to be correctly placed from the camera's point of view.
OB	outside broadcast. That's when a a television programme is broadcast from somewhere outside the studio, for example, from a football stadium during a match.
PSC	portable single camera. [see ENG]
recce	reconnaissance of a prospective location for a film or programme.
resolution	image sharpness.
split-level	a technique used in animation whereby

all the different parts of a scene that might move are each drawn on separate sheets which, when placed on top of each other, form a complete drawing.

telecine the equipment which enables ordinary cine slides and film to be shown on a television screen. This term can also be applied to the area in which this equipment is housed.

time code an on-going code measured in hours, minutes, seconds and number of frames which is electronically recorded on to video tape to identify particular shots. This code is only visible when special decoding equipment is used.

VTR can refer to video tape recorders or to the area in a studio complex where the recording of programmes and playback of material is carried out.

workprint a copy of an original film which is used for editing purposes.

wrap a slang term meaning that that's the end of production for the day.

Bibliography

Alkin, Glyn (1975), *T.V. Sound Operations*, London, Focal Press.

Alkin, Glyn (1981), *Sound Recording and Reproduction*, London, Focal Press.

Armes, Roy (1978), *A Critical History of British Cinema*, London, Secker & Warburg.

Baddeley, W. Hugh (1975), *The Technique of Documentary Film Production*, London, Focal Press.

Bernstein, Steven (1987), *The Technique of Film Production*, London, Focal Press.

Box, Muriel (1975), *Odd Woman Out*, London, Frewin.

Brownlow, Kevin (1968), *The Parade's Gone By . . .*, New York, Bonanza Books.

Carlson, Verne and Sylvia (1984), *Professional Lighting Handbook*, Stoneham (USA), Focal Press.

Carrick, Edward (1950), *Designing for Films*, London, Studio. (Out of print; but copies still available for library borrowing.)

Case, Dominic (1985), *Motion Picture Film Processing*, London, Focal Press.

Chamness, Danford (1983), *A Hollywood Guide to Film Budgeting and Script Breakdown*, Stoneham (USA), Focal Press.

Daley, Ken (1980), *Basic Film Technique*, London, Focal Press.

Dmytryk, Edward (1984), *On Film Editing*, Stoneham (USA), Focal Press.

Fogarty, M.P. (ed.) (1968), *Women in Top Jobs*, London, George Allen & Unwin.

Goldman, William (1984), *Adventures in the Screen Trade*, London, Macdonald.

Happe, L. Bernard (1983), *Your Film and the Lab*, London, Focal Press.

Hayward, Stan (1984), *Computers for Animation*, London, Focal Press.

Jones, Peter (1972), *The Technique of the Television Cameraman*, London, Focal Press.

Kaplan, E. Ann (1983), *Women and Film*, London, Methuen.

Kehoe, Vincent J.R. (1986), *The Technique of Professional Make-up for Film, Television and Stage*, London, Focal Press. (Previous edition entitled *The Techniques of Make-up for Film, Television and Stage*.)

Marner, Terence St John (ed.) (1974), *Film Design*, London, Tantivy Press.

Miller, Pat P. (1986), *Script Supervising and Film Continuity*, Stoneham (USA), Focal Press.

Millerson, Gerald (1982a), *Basic T.V. Staging*, London, Focal Press.

Millerson, Gerald (1982b), *The Technique of Lighting for Television and Motion Pictures*, London, Focal Press.

Millerson, Gerald (1982c), *Television Lighting Methods*, London, Focal Press.

Millerson, Gerald (1983), *Video Camera Techniques*, London, Focal Press.

Millerson, Gerald (1985), *The Technique of Television Production*, London, Focal Press.

Nisbett, Alec (1979), *The Technique of the Sound Studio*, London, Focal Press.

Perisic, Zoran (1980), *The Animation Stand*, London, Focal Press.

Pitt, Hugh (1963), *Television*, London, Hale.

Reisz, Karl and Miller, Gavin (1974), *The Technique of Film Editing*, London, Focal Press.

Robinson, J.F. and Beards, P.H. (1981), *Using Videotape*, London, Focal Press.

Robinson, J.F. revised by Lowe, Stephen (1981), *Videotape Recording*, London, Focal Press.

Rowlands, Avril (1977), *Script Continuity and the Production Secretary*, London, Focal Press.

Samuelson David W. (1984), *Motion Picture Camera Techniques*, London, Focal Press.

Souto, H. Mario Raimondo (1982), *The Technique of the Motion Picture Camera*, London, Focal Press.

Tyrell, Robert (1981), *The Work of the Television Journalist*, London, Focal Press.

Watts, Harris (1984), *On Camera; How to Produce Film and Video*, London, BBC. (Previous editions entitled, *The Programme-maker's Handbook*.)

Whitaker, Harold and Halas, John (1981), *Timing for Animation*, London, Focal Press.

White, Tony (1986), *The Animator's Workbook*, London, Phaidon Press.

Wiese, Michael (1984), *The Independent Film and Videomaker's Guide*, Stoneham (USA), Focal Press.

Yorke, Ivor (1987), *The Technique of Television News*, London, Focal Press.

Zinkeison, Doris (1938), *Designing for the Stage*, London, Studio. (Out of print, but copies still available for library borrowing.)

General reference works and directories

The BBC Handbook, available from bookstores.

The BFI Film and Television Yearbook, available from the British Film Institute, 127 Charing Cross Road, London WC2H 0EA.

Careers in Independent Television, available from the ITCA, Knighton House, 56 Mortimer Street, London W1N 8AN.

Careers in Radio and Television by Susan Crimp, published by Kogan Page.

Directions, available from the BFI, 127 Charing Cross Road, London WC2H 0EA.

Education and Training for Films and Television, available from BKSTS, 110-112 Victoria House, Vernon Place, London WC1B 4DJ.

Television and Radio 1987, available from bookstores or from the IBA, 70 Brompton Road, London SW3 1EY.

Working in Television, by Jan Leeming, published by Batsford Academic and Educational Ltd.

Working in Television and Video, available from COIC, Sales Dept, Freepost Sheffield S1 4BR.

Videos

The Amazing Adventures of Tube Woman, produced by The New Girls' Network, available from CFL Vision, Chalfont Grove, Gerrards Cross, Bucks SL9 8TN.

Cue for Change, produced by ACTT, available from Team Video Productions, Canalot, 222 Kensal Road, London W10 5BN.

Index